DISCARD

THE LIMITS OF BLAME

THE LIMITS OF BLAME

Rethinking Punishment and Responsibility

✂

ERIN I. KELLY

Harvard University Press

Cambridge, Massachusetts
London, England
2018

First printing

Library of Congress Cataloging-in-Publication Data

Names: Kelly, Erin, author.
Title: The limits of blame : rethinking punishment and responsibility / Erin I. Kelly.
Description: Cambridge, Massachusetts : Harvard University Press, 2018.
Identifiers: LCCN 2018014686 | ISBN 9780674980778 (cloth : alk. paper)
Subjects: LCSH: Retribution—Philosophy. | Punishment—United States—Philosophy. |
Criminal liability—United States—Philosophy.
Classification: LCC K5103 . K49 2018 | DDC 364.01—dc23
LC record available at https://lccn.loc.gov/2018014686

For Iman and Rayha
with love and admiration

CONTENTS

THE LIMITS OF BLAME

Winfred Rembert, *All Me II*, 2012. Photo courtesy of Adelson Galleries Boston.

INTRODUCTION

Criminalizing People

"MY FREE LIFE—*all* my life—is like I'm locked up in prison and there's a big invisible wall around me."

I mulled this over as I sat in Winfred Rembert's art studio, listening to his story. The small, cluttered room in his house is where he carves and dyes leather canvas stories of his life. Sheets of leather lay on the table, together with carving tools and some finished paintings depicting life in prison, acts of racial violence, and scenes of rural southern life. Tooling leather is a skill Rembert learned in prison.

One of Rembert's series especially caught my eye. It depicts prisoners dressed in the black and white striped uniform of the chain gang. From a distance the compositions seem abstract. Close up you see dozens of individual people, eyes darting right and left, arms swinging axes, bodies twisting, faces grimacing. Several paintings are called "All Me." Rembert explains that he had to be more than just himself to survive the chain gang.

Winfred Rembert was arrested in Cuthbert, Georgia, in 1965 for stealing a car. He took the car while fleeing a civil rights rally that ended in a clash with the police. Arrested the next day, badly beaten in his cell by guards, Rembert managed to break away and flee. People he turned to for help gave him up. A judge sentenced him to twenty-seven years in prison for robbery—a charge he maintains was fabricated—auto theft, escape, and pointing a pistol. In 1960s Georgia these charges meant hard labor. Rembert was forced to work on a chain gang for seven years. He was released from prison in 1974.

I visited Rembert in New Haven, Connecticut, in 2015 as part of an effort to think through some philosophical questions about criminal justice. I asked him to talk with me about his experiences.[1] He looked at me calmly and told me that he didn't see any *justice* in the criminal justice system. Prison, he said, had messed his whole life up. "Once they say the word to me, 'Have you ever committed a crime?' that was it. I've been fighting that battle all my life—ever since 1974. And I've tried to get a good enough job to take care of my family." Winfred has been married to his wife, Patsy, for over forty years. They raised several children. "A prisoner's life is a tough life. Once you get out of jail your life is over, because your jail sentence follows you wherever you go."

Rembert talked about the hardship of life in prison. His art has helped him to deal with the trauma that haunts him. "There's a place in my head that I'm stuck in," he told me. "Every time I try to climb out, I fall back. I fall back and that's what I do my work about. When I fall back, there's a picture waiting on me about trying to beat that struggle." His fingers ran over a piece of leather on the table. I asked him whether his artwork was about his search for freedom. He nodded. "These pictures are about my search for freedom, but they don't give me freedom. I'm free for a minute, and then I'm stuck right again back in the past. You ever seen a bug or something in a cup or a glass, and he's in the bottom going around and around and trying to crawl himself out and he get almost to the top and he fall back? That's me," he said, "Yeah, that's me."

He tilted his head and looked at me. "I think maybe people who make up the rules of how to handle people who commit crimes—I think they have to *rethink* themselves. Because, listen, when you're making up these rules, you've got to realize that making up these rules is going to control someone's life *all* their life. You really have to think big on that. How is this going to affect this person the *rest* of his life?"

Rembert was imprisoned over fifty years ago. If he were convicted today for the same charges, he might have faced "mandatory minimum" sentencing, which could have led to a sentence longer than twenty-seven years. "Truth in sentencing" might have blocked the possibility of early release.[2] If he had been a repeat offender, he might have faced a life sentence without the possibility of parole.[3] While he would not today be placed on a chain gang, he might have been required to work in prison for pennies on the dollar and charged for his own incarceration.[4] He might be sitting in there still, at age seventy-two, instead of tooling and painting leather in a weathered house in New Haven.

This book is a critical study of the sort of philosophical thinking about punishment that might be stretched—and that some people actually do stretch—to rationalize the extreme system of punishment that currently exists in the United States. It is addressed primarily to philosophers and legal theorists, who deal in the language of blame and responsibility. As people who attempt to account for the rules of criminal justice, we should rethink ourselves.

Moral philosophers today accept the use of moral blame in the practice of criminal punishment, echoing the public's attitude toward people who have committed crimes. Criminal conviction, people commonly believe, justifies condemning the convicted morally, stigmatizing and incarcerating them, and denying them important benefits and opportunities upon release—in effect, permanently excluding them from membership in society. This book challenges the prevailing "retributivist" theory of criminal justice, its support in moral philosophy, and its populist counterpart, according to which punishment is intended to impose on morally blameworthy wrongdoers the suffering they deserve. Norms that lead us to mark the convicted as bad people, to applaud long prison sentences, and to create labels like "dangerous offender" and "sexual psychopath" are seriously flawed.[5] It is time to revise those norms and the ordinary thinking about responsibility and blame that they express.

People who think carefully about criminal justice must address the problem that the *legal* criteria of guilt do not match familiar *moral* criteria for blame. Conditions that excuse moral failings—such as ignorance, provocation, and mental illness—have limited application in law. This demonstrates a lack of alignment between law and morality. Considerations that mitigate moral blame are often irrelevant to legal findings of criminal guilt. For example, poverty and other unjust deprivations of

opportunity have no mitigating relevance in the courtroom; nor do serious mental illnesses such as sociopathy and schizophrenia. Some criminal defendants have diminished moral culpability and others should not
be seen as morally blameworthy at all, yet such factors have no bearing on
determinations of legal guilt.

A range of examples underscores this critical misalignment. Some
criminally guilty people are not morally culpable because the acts for
which they have been convicted are not morally wrong. Take a person who
has used illegal drugs recreationally or a person on parole who fails to
perform an administrative task or cannot pay court fees: these failures
constitute violations that may lead to incarceration, but they are not
moral wrongs.[6] In other cases, people commit wrongful acts but under
conditions that mitigate their blameworthiness. Mentally ill individuals are sometimes not rationally or morally competent enough to warrant ordinary moral blame. Other people, while rationally and morally
competent, are burdened by circumstances of social injustice that undermine reasonable opportunities for a satisfactory, law-abiding life. These
circumstances bear on the appropriateness of blame, yet the law is indifferent to them. Though criminal guilt is typically defined by law to require a certain culpable mental state (*mens rea*), criminal law simply does
not take into account an array of mitigating considerations that represent
meaningful and identifiable differences in the moral blameworthiness of
individual defendants. Moreover, the mitigating factors it does admit—for
example, "duress" as an excuse for the commission of a crime—are very
narrowly understood. The law's criteria of criminal guilt, if understood
to indicate a defendant's moral blameworthiness, are highly selective and
often misleading.

Almost without exception, offenses that are not moral wrongs should
not be permissible grounds for incarceration. This means that many
people who are currently incarcerated—for infractions like recreational
drug use, inability to pay fees, and technical parole violations—should
not be locked up. Reasonable proponents of retributive justice would presumably agree. More controversial cases involve people who are plausibly
thought to deserve moral blame. There are people who, on any reasonable account of moral responsibility, deserve blame for wrongful acts
they have committed. They are rational, mentally healthy individuals with

a reasonable set of social opportunities for education, employment, and social recognition, who nonetheless have committed serious and illegal moral wrongs. If moral desert were a plausible basis for punishment, these would be good candidates. But most people in prison don't fit this type, and many of them are suffering punishment they do not morally deserve.

The mismatch between criminal guilt and moral blameworthiness presents a moral problem for a society that takes a punitive, criminal-justice approach to social problems and is eager to condemn criminal lawbreakers. The righteous imposition of a brutal system of punishment on people who don't deserve it is a moral abuse.

An important step toward righting this wrong is to reexamine our moral thinking. This book calls for a transformation in public thinking about criminal justice as well as philosophy's reckoning with it. When it comes to truly objectionable acts, considerations of public safety permit punishment. Still, we should resist the wider and often indiscriminate ap-plication of punishment to morally condemn persons. People who are not blameworthy for their morally objectionable acts do not deserve moral condemnation. In other cases, when moral blame might be warranted, it does not constitute, per se, a justifiable basis for punishment. That is to say, moral blame does not justify criminal punishment.

In making this argument, I understand blame to mean the moral con-demnation of wrongdoers. Blame reaches beyond an assessment of wrong-doing to a personal appraisal of wrongdoers in view of their actions. The most prominent philosophical accounts of responsibility and blame focus on the quality of a wrongdoer's will—largely apart from psycho-logical or social context, and without much attention to a wrongdoer's personal history. Such accounts ask whether an individual's actions demonstrate *ill will*, and they suppose that ill will provides insight into a person's character. The quality of an agent's motives and attitudes, and the sort of person they reveal her to be, are taken to rationalize our moral reactions. We are instructed to focus on whether the wrongdoer acted for bad reasons, reasons we should reject, and whether in so doing, she has expressed disregard for the rights or moral standing of other people. If a person has *bad attitudes,* according to this philosophy, a moralized response is called for, which includes, in the most serious cases, punishment.

When it comes to punishment, blame's defenders typically seek something other than penalties intended to incapacitate, deter, or reform a wrongdoer. They are interested in a condemnatory response, expressing what moral philosophers describe as appraisals of *moral worth*—a kind of moral ranking at the level of personhood. A criminal wrongdoer's ill will is considered blameworthy because it reveals that person's deficient moral worth as, perhaps, a thief, rapist, murderer, cheat, pedophile, gangster, or terrorist. Attaching blame depends on performing this assessment and determining what we should feel, think, and do to express rage, censure, and denunciation and to ensure that the culpable wrongdoer experiences a corresponding loss. Blame, according to this theory, involves enacting the moral responses a wrongdoer deserves.

There are many variations of this sort of philosophy. An approach made popular by the Oxford philosopher P. F. Strawson maintains that ill will understandably provokes sentiments like moralized anger, resentment, and indignation. Strawson connects the moral "reactive attitudes" with a retributive notion of justice, by linking these attitudes with our disposition to inflict harm on wrongdoers. Punitive thoughts and actions, he believes, are fitting responses to ill will. Furthermore, he thinks the value of retribution would ideally be accepted by wrongdoers themselves; judgments of moral desert that support the practice of punishment are properly internalized.[7] He argues that all parties who are sensitive to the demands of morality would naturally affirm the appropriateness of inflicting injury upon wrongdoers.

Strawson stresses a psychological connection between the recognition of wrongdoing and certain emotive and behavioral responses. More rationalistic moral philosophers, like T. M. Scanlon and R. Jay Wallace, stress the *belief* that certain moral judgments, emotive reactions, and sanctioning behavior are warranted by virtue of a wrongdoer's personal qualities. For instance, they emphasize the reasons we have to mistrust, disapprove of, and distance ourselves from someone who has wronged us. Morally minded legal theorists emphasize the value of committing to more punitive behavioral responses, including criminal punishment. According to these thinkers, since criminal wrongs—or at least *mala in se* crimes such as murder, rape, robbery, and kidnapping—include some of the most morally reprehensible acts, which we properly condemn, moral blame appropriately follows as a punitive *public* response, at least when the wrongdoer is not excused, that is, when a person is properly found criminally guilty.[8] In this way criminal punishment is justified as a kind of public blaming—blaming that is deserved by criminal lawbreakers who commit the sort of heinous wrongs that earn broad and severe condemnation. The general point of this family of views is that blame—a condemnation directed at the agent—is called for when a person has acted wrongly and displays bad intentions, motives, and attitudes. Criminal punishment serves as a justified expression of outrage that affirms the moral inferiority of these wrongdoers and inflicts deserved pain on them.

Punishment understood as justified public blame is expressed through the stigma and deprivations that accompany criminal punishment. Through the humiliation and indignity of punishment, a serious social stigma is imposed on people who have been convicted, especially those who are incarcerated. This is generally true of criminal punishment in much of the world. The stigma of criminality, when it is formally imposed through conviction and sentencing in a court of law, is also accompanied by the retraction, often permanent, of important entitlements and rights in addition to basic liberty. In many U.S. states, for example, the right to vote is withdrawn, as is eligibility for public assistance and student loans, even after a convicted person's sentence has been served. Many job applications require disclosure of felony convictions, however minor the crime or however long ago it was committed. It is not illegal to discriminate against felons who apply for housing, employment, mortgages, or admission to college. Many states deny certification to ex-felons in professions like automotive repair, construction, and plumbing. These measures deepen the stigma of criminality by extending its reach in social and political space and over time. As the legal scholar Michelle Alexander has argued, felons become second-class citizens for the rest of their lives.[9]

The stigma of criminality expresses a moral conclusion about the criminally guilty in view of their criminal behavior: they are morally blameworthy because they are legally guilty. Yet, as suggested above, the basis of criminal conviction is often morally inadequate to produce this assessment. The expanding domain of strict liability offenses—including crimes introduced under recent antiterrorism statutes, such as enabling the use of property or funds used in acts of terrorism or possessing information of a kind useful to persons preparing for acts of terrorism—provides a stark illustration of the serious weakening or even absence of any legal requirement to establish the defendant's moral blameworthiness.[10] Strict liability requires no demonstration of *mens rea*, hence it is possible for individuals convicted under these statutes to have had no intention or knowledge that their property or information would or might be used to facilitate acts of terrorism. But even regarding paradigmatic crimes of intent, such as shoplifting or burglary, for which some deliberate and illegal wrongdoing must be demonstrated, social and psychological factors that shape our moral evaluation of people have little or no bearing on criminal liability. The influence of mental illness or racial injustice, for instance, has little to no relevance to findings of criminal guilt. In most cases, mental illness functions as an excuse only when it fits the legal definition of insanity, a highly specialized notion that does not include bipolar disorder, autism, or many other forms of mental illness. And courts have thrown out racial discrimination as a basis for challenging criminal conviction and sentencing—for the perverse reason that such discrimination is too common.[11] A person facing a statistically higher likelihood of a harsher sentence because of his race cannot use that unfairness as a legal basis for objecting to his sentence.[*]

Even though the psychological and social traits of defendants have been declared irrelevant to criminal proceedings, they still bear on the stigma of criminality. And they constitute *aggravating* rather than mitigating factors. For example, in the United States, expectations of criminality are intensified by the stigma of racial subordination—the legacy of two hundred and fifty years of slavery and one hundred years of "Jim Crow" laws.[†] A 2017 study of plea bargaining discovered that among defendants with

---

[*] The world's prison population is overwhelmingly male. For that reason, in this book I will use the male pronoun when referring to a person who is accused or sanctioned by a criminal justice system. Otherwise I will use a generic "she" or "her."

[†] In discussing the racialized population in the United States, I will use "Black" to refer to what is roughly akin to an ethnic group—Africa-identified persons born in the United States—most of whom are (at least partly) descended from slaves. I avoid the more inclusive "black," which I understand to be a racial category historically rooted in a theory that Africa-identified people constitute a natural race. I will use "white" as a generic term referring to people identified as of European descent.

no prior criminal record, whites were 25 percent more likely than Blacks to have charges reduced. It also found that when arrested for misdemeanor charges, whites were 75 percent more likely than Blacks to have charges dropped or reduced to charges that carry no prison time.[12] A plausible interpretation of this finding, suggested by the researcher, is that prosecutors consider race a proxy for a defendant's dangerousness or moral badness. The normalization of aggressive law enforcement tactics that target Black Americans and the explosion of the Black prison population over the last thirty years reinforce racialized expectations about the identity of criminals.[13] The stigmas of color and criminality interact to achieve a powerful form of social alienation and exclusion.

A similar dynamic extends to some groups marginalized by ethnicity or religion. Reactionary policy proposals exploit stereotypes that demonize immigrants and other social outsiders.[14] In the United States, for example, the number of undocumented migrants who are incarcerated is on the rise. It is a felony to enter the United States with false documents or to reenter the country after being denied entry.[15] In the first eight months of 2017, almost 100,000 people who were suspected of being in the country illegally were arrested by federal authorities. This represents a 43 percent increase over the same period in 2016,[16] and the current administration has announced its intention aggressively to increase the number of federal immigration jails.

The Limits of Blame shows how the alleged moral implications of criminal conviction are indefensibly taken to justify the social stigma of criminality and the permanent expulsion of people who have been convicted. Moral blame stakes a certain claim: a person's voluntary and wrongful criminal act reveals more or less permanent aspects of that individual's character or personhood; these undesirable aspects mark that person, by virtue of his or her criminality, as defective, tainted, and morally inferior. Heinous crimes are the paradigm criminal offense for the blaming enterprise. They prompt the logic of this conception of criminal justice. But then we extend this paradigm and logic to the criminally guilty in an all-too generic way. Because we see a person's choice to commit a crime as a sufficient trigger for moral blame, we exaggerate the difference between "offenders" and ordinary people, we gloss over differences in the severity of offenses, and we carelessly aggregate people who have committed crimes into a single, stigmatized social class. Within this class, all are condemned, even though this aggregating tendency is at odds with our professed allegiance to delivering each person's just deserts.

The American criminal justice system multiplies the blaming project exponentially through policies designed to streamline the conviction of vast numbers of people—90–95 percent of those who are prosecuted—without any trial or judgment by a jury.[17] At the same time, and paradoxically, it condemns every convicted person individually as an offender. A maximal emphasis on incarceration, often lengthy and without even minimal rehabilitation or reentry programs, imposes on people who have been convicted an enduring social identity as members of a class of social outcasts. This represents a system run amok, yet the basic logic of a certain morality of criminal justice is stretched to rationalize it. The practice of insisting on an individual's responsibility, while at the same time ignoring the social and psychological context of a person's moral choices, and then aggregating the results by (literally) holding convicted people "accountable" en masse, is the heart of criminal law's popularized conception of justice and the moral philosophy that undergirds it. We are doing a lot with blame—far more than any plausible moral philosophy could support.

Of course, some felons have done horrible things, and as a society we have good reason to vindicate the rights of crime victims and to protect ourselves. Morality permits us to incarcerate people when doing so is necessary to defend our basic rights. We also have reason to deny important opportunities and responsibilities to people who are unreliable and dangerous. Yet the blame industry reaches well beyond a pragmatic need for protection from truly dangerous persons and a moral need to repudiate their harmful acts. It massively overreaches: the stigma of criminality attaches to the convicted as a group and condemns them summarily. The criminal class includes people who have been found guilty of offenses that do not render them unfit for educational opportunities or gainful employment, much less other basic entitlements of citizenship, such as voting. The blame industry demotes people with criminal convictions to enduring unequal membership, whether or not they continue to pose a danger, when and if they are released from prison and given an opportunity to reenter society. The indelible blemish on personhood that attaches to criminality enacts the moral rejection of felons as an undifferentiated social group, a group that includes the mentally ill, the intellectually disabled, and children. Sweeping into its wake anyone who has been convicted, and some who are merely accused, the stigma of criminality helps to maintain a social underclass, ensuring an almost inescapable bottom layer to an unjustly stratified society.

It is my contention that a popular conception of individual moral responsibility masks the systematic nature of social inequality that is solidified by the criminal justice system, especially that found in the United States. A conception of responsibility that connects wrongdoing and moral desert is used to rationalize indefensible criminal-justice practices. We are encouraged to think that criminal conviction metes out verdicts of individual blameworthiness, and this judgment, in turn, functions, by way of its alleged ground in criminal guilt per se, as a basis for thoroughgoing social typecasting. The very point of criminal justice, so understood, is to assign moral responsibility to individual wrongdoers through findings of criminal guilt and the imposition of a stigmatizing punishment they are thought morally to deserve.

We should resist this form of moral identity-making because it normalizes social injustice, narrows our moral perspective, and precludes a morally sensitive appreciation of the psychological and social adversity confronting many people who commit crimes. A blaming perspective focused predominately on manifestations of *ill will* too readily overlooks the social and psychological context in which a person's beliefs and attitudes are formed, and this focus distorts its moral findings. For example, when poverty and racial injustice are ignored, and the significance of mental illness, immaturity, or mental deficiency is disregarded, conclusions about the blameworthiness of many criminally guilty persons are exaggerated. When the relationships between criminal justice and social justice and between individual responsibility and collective responsibility are not thoughtfully calibrated, they become dangerously unbalanced. As a result, criminal justice institutions are permitted—and exploited—to punish without measure or shame. This is what has happened in the United States.

There is a viable alternative. We could reserve incarceration—the extreme punishment that it is—for truly serious crimes and only when it is required to ensure a reasonable measure of public safety. That is, we could lock people up when and because they have violated and continue to threaten other people's basic rights, and only as a last resort. We could address the social causes of crime with comprehensive measures, including socioeconomic justice, and take seriously the values of democracy—its promise to treat all of its members as equal persons with the same basic rights and liberties. We could begin to view criminal punishment as punishment of members of a community who do not lose their membership in it when they break its rules.

The blaming system has wildly overrun its proper limits. It is time to reconsider the point of criminal justice. This book takes up that challenge and argues that when we attend to the justifiable aims of a criminal justice system, we find, perhaps surprisingly, that delivering blame is not among them. It is enough to declare, when it is true, that people who have been convicted of crimes have acted wrongly and that we have reasons to uphold and to protect the rights of people who have been harmed or threatened. We need not go beyond those conclusions to moralize about and to condemn criminal wrongdoers as inferior human beings. We can and should reject the use of criminal punishment as an instrument of public blame. The state does not have, and should not be given, the moral authority to allocate "deserved suffering." If we suppose it does, we misrepresent the proper scope of its legal verdicts. We should stop exaggerating the appropriate role that evaluations of responsibility play within a criminal justice system, and we should reorient our moral thinking about criminal law. We are doing too much with blame. Occupying a less righteous stance would enable us to affirm and protect our basic rights through a more measured and fair criminal justice system. *The Limits of Blame* offers some new ideas to move us forward.

Chapter 1 examines current American criminal-law doctrine and, specifically, its principles of liability to criminal sanctions. It elaborates the law's notion of personal responsibility and examines whether this legal notion justifies the view that criminal sanctions are appropriate expressions of moral blame. I argue that it does not. Legal criteria of guilt do not match moral criteria of blameworthiness. I focus especially on cases showing that some criminally liable persons suffer mental disability that is severe enough to imply that the punishment they get oversteps their moral blameworthiness. *Criminal* culpability does not per se entail *moral* culpability, and thus legal sanctions should not be used to express moral blame.

Chapter 2 anticipates reform proposals designed to rescue retributive justice by individualizing criminal punishment so that it corresponds to what a defendant deserves. These proposals will not work. Importantly, the notion of moral desert depends on an evaluation of a defendant's *moral competence* and, in particular, on whether a criminal wrongdoer was capable of having complied with the law. This dependence opens the door to an epistemic problem about the feasibility of producing evaluations of moral competence, a problem the courts have recognized. Proponents of blame typically maintain that inability excuses, compromised ability is mitigating, and mere unwillingness does not excuse or mitigate. But this view is unworkable if we cannot, in practice, tell the difference between a wrongdoer's *inability, compromised ability,* or *unwillingness* to be guided by right and wrong. Skeptical modesty about our ability to make these judgments calls into question appraisals of blameworthiness and desert closely associated with criminal punishment. The courts have epistemic reasons to fall back on a "reasonable person" standard of criminal liability and to resist individualizing criminal guilt and punishment according to personal blameworthiness.

Chapter 3 introduces an understanding of *moral* excuses that widens our options for thinking about how to respond to wrongdoers. This account does not depend on determining the limits of an agent's moral competence. Instead, excuses address the difficulty of personal hardships a moral agent has faced. Factors like mental illness and social injustice can mitigate blame, whether or not the wrongdoer was capable of doing better. Awareness of the difficulty of morally responsible behavior for some people, and under some circumstances, opens up a range of possibilities for morally engaging—or not engaging—with them. Sensitivity to context allows us to see that it may be psychologically possible and morally reasonable to forego blame in favor of seeking to understand a person's moral troubles. This might lead either to a more dispassionate, clinical perspective or to a different kind of emotional engagement in which we experience empathy toward the wrongdoer. These responses are viable alternatives to blame and social exclusion. The possibility of compassion, in a wide range of cases, casts doubt on whether blame is deserved.

Chapter 4 argues that blame is ill suited to the public nature of criminal justice, which differs from personal morality. When we evaluate a person's *moral* culpability, we typically want to know why a person acted wrongly, and we evaluate the reasons for her action, as well as her culpability for endorsing those reasons. But information about a defendant's reasons for acting is rarely needed to establish criminal guilt; motives are mostly irrelevant to *criminal* culpability. In other words, prosecutors are not required to produce evidence about what motivated a crime in order to establish that it took place. In this way, determinations of *criminal guilt* differ appreciably from assessments of *moral responsibility* for wrongdoing. There is a compelling rationale for this difference. Moral blame is optional, at least in many cases. It contains an element of personal choice about how to relate to a wrongdoer in view of her wrongdoing. By contrast, the rules of criminal justice apply coercively. Justification of these rules must be supported by public reasons that all members of society could accept. As such, the institutions of criminal justice should not be in the business of blame.

Chapter 5 sets forth a nonretributive account of punishment as "just harm reduction." I argue that serious criminal wrongdoing makes a person eligible for criminal punishment even when that person is not morally blameworthy. We can punish without blaming, provided that relevant legal procedures are followed, standards of criminal wrongdoing are satisfied, and fair institutional protections for individual rights are in place. A nonretributive, nonblaming theory of the nature and limits of criminal sanctions would aim to reduce the harm that crime does by, for example, deterring criminal behavior, incapacitating lawbreakers who pose an ongoing danger to other people, redressing harm to crime victims, and seeking alternatives to incarceration that would prepare people who have committed crimes to improve their prospects for law-abiding lives. The just application of criminal sanctions would express moral disapproval of truly objectionable criminal acts, and it would do this without morally condemning the wrongdoer as a person. Revoking personal condemnation as an aspect of our current punishment practices, however, would require a deliberate effort to change public attitudes about criminal punishment.

Chapter 6 takes up the problem of law enforcement under conditions of social injustice and probes the limits of a criminal justice system's legitimacy. Social injustice presents special problems for philosophical theories according to which liability to punishment depends on the state's moral authority to blame criminally guilty individuals for their criminal acts. This provides us with further reasons to reject the idea that punishment should have a blaming purpose. But social injustice also presents a problem for *any* theory of punishment, including an account of punishment as just harm reduction. It may undermine the morally justified authority of the state to enforce legal rules, whether or not punishment expresses blame. People should not be burdened with serious, harmful consequences for breaking the law when they have been deprived of a reasonable opportunity to lead a satisfactory, law-abiding life. Social injustice undermines legitimate law enforcement and dooms prospects for achieving justice through criminal law. If we opt anyway for harm reduction measures that include incarceration, people who are incarcerated are due just compensation for the harms we impose on them.

ONE

ACCOUNTABILITY IN CRIMINAL LAW

Aしmost 2.3 million people currently sit in prison or jail in the United States. This number is equivalent to the size of the combined populations of the cities of Boston, San Francisco, Atlanta, and Miami. The size of the incarcerated population is larger than that of fifteen U.S. states—from New Mexico, with a population of just over 2 million, to Wyoming, population 576,000. It is hard to imagine how many buildings, cells, and employees it would take to incarcerate the entire population of New Mexico, or all the people who live in Boston, San Francisco, Atlanta, and Miami.

By some estimates, over half of the incarcerated population is mentally ill.[1] The prison population also includes intellectually disabled inmates, probably at a higher rate than they are represented in general population.[2] Clearly, the law puts into practice a notion of individual responsibility that permits us to criminalize people who are mentally ill, mentally disturbed, and intellectually disabled. The law maintains that, despite their illnesses or disabilities, people who have been convicted had a reasonable opportunity to refrain from their criminal actions and thus to avoid criminal sanctions.

There are some good reasons for the law to be cautious about excusing less than fully rational people from eligibility for criminal punishment. When such a person commits a serious crime, we have reason to use the criminal justice system to reject his wrongful conduct and to protect ourselves from the threat he poses to our rights. It is morally permissible for us to do this, even when a criminal wrongdoer is not fully rational and lacks a normal measure of control over his own conduct. Though we should be reluctant to impose incarceration on anyone, and we should expand the menu of consequences the state is entitled to impose on people who have committed crimes to include, for example, treatment for mental illness and drug addiction, we are permitted, within reason, to use the criminal justice system to protect our rights from people who have demonstrated a willingness to violate them. Of course, retributivists are not satisfied with a rights-protection rationale for criminal punishment. Instead, they maintain that the state should distribute punishment according to moral desert: The state should ensure that criminals get the punishment they deserve.

Standard criminal-law conceptions of accountability, though, complicate efforts to rely on a retributive theory of punishment to explain or to justify current legal practices. Retributivists aim to ground punishment in blameworthiness and desert, yet in criminal law, the criteria of criminal liability call for the punishment of actors who may be neither blameworthy nor deserving of punishment. This implies that our system is not genuinely retributive. To be so, it must set much higher standards of accountability—standards that would not permit the punishment of individuals whose moral blameworthiness is seriously in doubt. It would need to establish, case by case, that each defendant is blameworthy enough to deserve the punishment he gets, whether it be a monetary fine, community service, or a prison sentence.

In the United States, many crimes, including nonviolent and even trivial offenses, as well as violent crimes, trigger severe punishment. Although the U.S. Constitution prohibits the imposition of "excessive fines" and the infliction of "cruel and unusual punishments," these limitations are almost toothless. As a result, exceedingly harsh sentences are permitted and routinely imposed by the courts. For example, in *Ewing v. California,* the U.S. Supreme Court rejected Ewing's appeal of his twenty-five-years-to-life sentence for stealing three golf clubs, a theft that constituted his "third strike" under the California law that imposes a sentence of twenty-five years to life in prison on repeat offenders whose third conviction is for a "serious or violent" felony. The Court argued that granting Ewing's appeal "would fail to accord proper deference to the policy judgments that find expression in the legislature's choice of sanctions."[3] The Court attested that, short of a sentence such as life imprisonment for a parking violation, legislation mandating extremely severe punishment is permitted within our legal system.[4]

Excessive punishment is unjust. It is a disgrace to the United States, and any reasonable retributive theory would reject it.[5] The problem for the retributive theory does not come down to the practice of over-punishment. Even apart from that serious problem, the criteria of legal guilt and punishment in our system are not well calibrated to judgments of blameworthiness and desert. This does not necessarily mean that less-blameworthy and less-deserving criminal lawbreakers should be excused from punishment. Perhaps many should not be. But the mismatch between punishment and moral blameworthiness should prompt us to understand the basis for punishment, when it can be justified, in nonretributive terms. The retributive theory is out of joint with the law's principles for determining guilt, even when those principles are reasonable. The legal criteria it makes sense to accept, including the law's verdict that a person who commits a crime is normally eligible for punishment, are not best supported by the retributive principle. This is because legal guilt does not imply moral blameworthiness.

Later I will argue that we should take a "just harm reduction" approach to criminal justice. Thinking in terms of harm reduction would lead us to correct the problem of over-punishment, and to ensure that the punishments we impose are both beneficial to society and not unfair to the people who are punished. It would also lead us to acknowledge that a criminal justice system cannot, without the support of a broader set of just institutions, achieve justice. Problems like socioeconomic inequality and racial injustice interfere with the state's capacity to deliver criminal justice. Yet even in an unjust society, a criminal justice system might be used, within reason, to reduce the harms associated with crimes, provided that it treats the convicted fairly. Aiming for just harm reduction would, however, require us to change the way we regard people who have been convicted of crimes as well as how we justify and organize the practice of criminal justice. It would require us to correct our tendency toward maximal punishment, and it would direct us to refrain from using the criminal justice system to morally condemn people, some of whom cannot reasonably be said to deserve punishment.

Retributive Justice

Advocates of retribution hold that wrongdoers merit a punitive response proportional to their blameworthy wrongdoing and that therefore wrong-doers should suffer corresponding harms.[6] Retributivists disagree about whether wrongdoers deserve to suffer "pain and anguish" or that they deserve only that their lives go less well.[7] In cases of serious wrongdoing, however, most retributivists believe that wrongdoers deserve physical or psychological pain; as philosopher Douglas Husak puts it, a culpable wrongdoer "should feel *bad* about what he has done."[8] Papers advocating retribution drive home this point with thought experiments directing us to imagine scenarios in which a person commits a serious crime, yet we lack reasons to punish on grounds of deterrence, incapacitation, reha-bilitation, or other consequence-sensitive considerations. In such cases, retributivists argue, we would still insist that retributive punishment is a requirement of justice.[9] Something is amiss when we fail to make a wrong-doer feel bad.

Philosophical attempts to justify the retributive ideal rely heavily on purportedly intuitive assertions about the foundations of justice, or mo-rality, or the essence of human decency, and they are unsuccessful. One of the most influential defenders of retributive justice is legal scholar Michael S. Moore. The crux of his argument is an introspective appeal to the guilt he would feel if he had committed a horrific act of violence against another person. Moore proclaims, "My own response, I hope, would be that I would feel guilty unto death. I couldn't imagine any suf-fering that could be imposed upon me that would be unfair because it exceeded what I deserved."[10] While one might admire Moore for his stated willingness to own up to any grievous wrongs he might commit, his expression of a hypothetical willingness to endorse whatever form of suffering might be inflicted upon him hardly offers a compelling rationale for a measured and fair criminal justice system. By his own testimony, his retributive sentiments are unbounded.

Of course, intuitions play an important role in justifying conceptions of morality—a role that, generally speaking, is not always suspect. John Rawls described the process of formulating and justifying a theory of justice as a process of reaching "reflective equilibrium."[11] The political philosopher aims to capture common beliefs about justice in a coherent set of moral principles. This involves adjusting familiar moral intuitions so as to formulate them as principles and revising the principles to make them consistent with one another, while taking care that the principles retain the support of an array of important intuitive judgments. Rawls begins with a set of intuitions about justice: a just society is a fair system of social cooperation, all people should have the material means needed to attain acceptable life prospects, all are entitled to due process of law, slavery and other forms of servitude and oppression are wrong, citizens should be treated as free and equal, everyone should be secure in their personal property, have decent health care, opportunities for education, and more. He organizes this collection of beliefs about the requirements of justice into a set of principles that would protect equal basic rights and liberties for all citizens, including rights associated with due process and the rule of law, assure that everyone's political participation has fair value, protect fair opportunities for education and employment, and guarantee a distribution of material goods that is acceptable to even the least well-off members of society. The principles he proposes can, he believes, guide us in establishing and assessing a political state's institutions on the basis of "public reasons," reasons that could be shared by all reasonable members of society, whatever social positions people happen to occupy.[12]

By showing how intuitions yield insight when considered systematically, critically scrutinized, and extended to new questions, Rawls demonstrates that the work of philosophy can produce a theory of our intuitions without resting on any Archimedean point. There is no single grounding value from which the theory begins or on which it ultimately rests. Unlike the approach taken by many retributive theorists, basic notions of criminal justice are considered together with broader questions of social justice.[13] Criminal sanctions are understood as part of a system of law that should "have the consequence, in the long run, of furthering the interests of society."[14] These interests, Rawls argues, should be those that could be endorsed by all reasonable members of society on the basis of shared reasons. It is when and because intuitions about justice plausibly establish a standard of public justification that they are worth taking seriously.

A Rawlsian approach to criminal justice, which is not oriented fundamentally around the value of retribution, seems to retributivists to be missing something crucial. The elusive element, however, proves to be impossible to justify with "public reasons." In a compelling survey of philosophical attempts to justify retribution, philosopher John Mackie has formulated what he refers to as "the paradox of retribution." The paradox, he says, is that "on the one hand, a retributive principle of punishment cannot be explained or developed within a reasonable system of moral thought, while, on the other hand, such a principle cannot be eliminated from our moral thinking."[15] The paradox of retribution follows from granting a foundational status to the retributive principle, for if a fundamental commitment to retribution were revoked, the value of retribution could be eliminated from our principles of justice, and the paradox would dissolve. Though retributive theorists do not see how, I believe it is both possible and urgent to retract commitment to retribution from a theory of criminal justice.

Mackie shows that popular attempts to justify retribution rationally are not convincing. Criminal wrongdoing does not imply the necessity of punishment (or, as Mackie puts it, the relation between crime and punishment is not analytic). Consequences, including the satisfaction retribution offers to some crime victims and the educative effects of bringing criminals to justice, are not relevant to justifying an entirely backward-looking principle. (According to retributivists, punishment is justified according to what wrongdoers deserve, not by the consequences of punishing them.) The idea promoted by some professed retributivists, that through punishment a criminal discharges a debt to society, also has a consequentialist ring, and seems closer to the notion of reparation than retribution.[16] The Hegelian idea that punishment somehow annuls the crime is not promising, Mackie argues: "The punishment may trample on the criminal, but it does not do away with the crime."[17] And the related idea that punishment "absorbs and wipes out guilt" presupposes rather than explains the retributive thesis.

Mackie considers the proposal that what is negated by punishment is the unfair advantage a criminal gains by committing a crime.[18] He finds this formulation of the value of retribution equally implausible. The proposal focuses on the wrong thing—advantage rather than wrongness or guilt—and it supposes something that is not always true: that the criminal gains something through criminal wrongdoing. Wrongful benefits are most plausible in the case of property crimes, but do not characterize relationship-destroying actions, like domestic violence, or inchoate crimes, like attempted murder. Furthermore, the notion that people who do not commit crimes suffer the burden of restraining themselves seems wildly off. Surely, for most people, refraining from murder or kidnapping does not demand genuine self-restraint.[19]

Still, as Mackie correctly notes, retributive justice holds great attraction for many people. He explains this by reference to natural selection and sociological theory. He stresses the role retributive conventions play in stabilizing social cooperation, and he hypothesizes that our moral sentiments have evolved as responses to a collective recognition that certain types of behavior trigger resentment and opposition. Specifically, he connects our attachment to the notion of just deserts with the emergence of the concept of moral wrongness, a concept he dissects into three components: the notion of an action's being harmful, its being forbidden, and its calling for a hostile response.[20] According to Mackie, the harmful and forbidden nature of wrongful acts is *conceptually connected* with the judgment that generally harmful and intrinsically forbidden conduct calls for a hostile response.

Mackie's thesis that retributive justice is a necessary component of a practical, familiar, and attractive system of moral thinking is mistaken, and a central task of this book is to challenge it. Though attachment to the value of retribution is popular, and Mackie is right about the vulnerability of the retributive principle to rational challenges, he is wrong to think that the principle cannot and should not be eliminated from our moral thinking. The puzzle about retribution is not a genuine paradox. Even if we accept Mackie's hypothesis that hostile responses are genetically and sociologically prior to our moral concepts and gave them life, we can and should discard the retributive principle of punishment. We should do this because retribution is at odds with important requirements of justice.

British legal theorist and moral philosopher Victor Tadros identifies the essence of the retributive principle that can and should be rejected.[21] We can, he says, distinguish between what is appealing in the retributive philosophy and what is not. He urges us to agree with the retributivist that it is morally good for people to acknowledge their wrongdoing. Admission of wrongdoing involves personal reflection that enables positive personal change. A person who recognizes her wrongdoing can understand the relational damage her wrongdoing has done, redress those harms, when possible, and provide reassurance that the wrong will not be repeated. It is also natural for a person who has wrongfully harmed another to feel bad about it—to experience guilt, to concern herself with what her wrongdoing says about herself, and to feel moved to apologize and to make amends. We have reason to suspect that something is wrong with a person who does not feel remorse about wronging others; her judgment is off or her heart is unresponsive, and we have good reasons to try to get her to change. But, argues Tadros, this does not imply that by lacking a bad feeling, she is missing something that is morally required or intrinsically valuable. We can reject the value of suffering, apart from the changes that it enables, or the sensitivity to other people it reflects. He writes, "Pain will go with recognition of wrongdoing. But we should see pain as an inevitable but negative side effect of the good of recognition rather than as good in itself."[22] Retributivists insist on the positive value of the pain and deprivations culpable wrongdoers are made to suffer, yet the burden is on the retributivist to convince us that this is what justice requires. It is not enough to argue that a wrongdoer's pain enables a wrongdoer to recognize that she has done wrong. If true, this would show that a wrongdoer's suffering has instrumental value, not that it is morally necessary.

Astute challenges by Mackie, Tadros, and others have not deterred retributivists from formulating highly refined retributive justifications of criminal sanctions.[23] In relation to the grounding intuition that a culpable wrongdoer deserves proportionate harms, which essentially involves a commitment to that belief, retributivists debate whether it is the

wrongdoer's choices or character traits that provide the basis for retribution. Theoretical differences on this point are overstated. Choice theorists
insist that even a person who acts out of character can be blameworthy,
yet they must offer a plausible basis for distinguishing between choices
that are relevantly free and those that indicate diminished responsibility.
In order to explain what makes a person's choice an adequate basis for
the attribution of responsibility and desert, choice theorists rely on the
notion that free agents have responsibility-bearing capacities to make
choices. Yet it is a short step to the conclusion that when "capacity-
responsibility" is displayed and a person chooses badly, vicious character can be inferred.[24] Character theorists, by contrast, begin from intuitions about the presence of culpable character traits and use these
impressions to guide our judgments about when capacity-responsibility
is on display. They argue that observable character-revealing patterns of
behavior enable us to determine when a choice is sufficiently under an
agent's control.[25] But they must also grant that uncharacteristic actions
might be illuminating, prompting us to revise our grasp of an individual's character and to admit that a character profile is hard to establish
conclusively.

Some retributive theories respond to what they view as the expressive
meaning of crime. According to philosopher Jean Hampton, perpetrators
should be made to suffer, psychologically if not physically, the anguish
they have caused their victims. Though we are not required by justice to
rape rapists, we might achieve justice by incarcerating them and forcing
them in therapy sessions to assume the role of the person they raped, while
offering them no sympathy and no respite from the insistence that they
confront what they did.[26] Punishments like this are intended to negate
what Hampton sees as crime's expressive message: namely, that the
victim was worthy of mistreatment and violation.[27] That message is re-
futed, she believes, by forcing the perpetrator to experience a harm that
is proportionate to the harm the victim suffered. Leveling down reestab-
lishes the victim's equality and affirms her dignity.

Others retributivists assign a communicative role to punishment. Antony
Duff emphasizes the importance of expressions of public censure. He is
less attentive than Hampton is to the suffering that punishment is intended to cause the convicted. Instead, he emphasizes the value of

censure for communicating a community's values. Duff characterizes punishment as a form of secular penance that aims morally to persuade a criminal wrongdoer to recognize and repent his wrongdoing.[28] Though Duff's attention to consequences stands in tension with the essentially retrospective core of the retributive thesis, his insistence that the convicted *deserve* to suffer public censure affirms a connection to the retributive theory, as does his belief that hard treatment is necessary adequately to communicate deserved censure.[29] Andrew von Hirsch also stresses the idea that punishment has communicative aims. He argues, however, that retributive penalty is symbolic, and should be minimal.[30] Although both Duff and von Hirsch's theories are less punitive than some other retributive theories, and although they place value on results such as inducing wrongdoers to experience remorse and achieving reconciliation between perpetrators and victims, their commitment to a version of the retributive ideal makes them susceptible to some of the objections surveyed above.

The common thread in various articulations of the retributive theory is that a person who engages in culpable wrongdoing deserves to suffer. Moreover, for retribution to serve as the basis for a theory of criminal punishment, retributivists must explain why the state, in particular, is morally authorized to inflict that suffering. I will address the state's authority in Chapters 5 and 6. This chapter is devoted to showing that existing legal criteria of criminal liability do not fit any reasonable version of the retributive thesis. They are not even close. Both character- and capacity-based judgments required by retributive theories depend on evaluations of individual dispositions and circumstances that are largely irrelevant to legal determinations of criminal guilt.

Liability to Criminal Punishment

Liability to criminal sanctions almost always requires a voluntary act (*actus reus*) and a culpable state of mind (*mens rea*). A voluntary act involves a *doing* by an agent. The Model Penal Code (MPC)—a highly influential effort by academics and judges working under the auspices of the American Law Institute to provide a systematic criminal code—characterizes a voluntary act by reference to bodily movements that are "the product of the effort or determination of the actor, either conscious or habitual."[31] Voluntary acts contrast with involuntary acts such as convulsions, movements during sleep, and conduct resulting from hypnotic suggestion. A famous teaching example is provided by *Martin v. State,* in which the court found that an intoxicated man who had been carried to a highway by police was not guilty of "being drunk on a public highway," since he did not voluntarily appear there.[32] Of course, an act can be voluntary without being intended to produce a harmful outcome, as is the case in reckless and negligent behavior that results in injury. Acts are voluntary if they require some determination on the part of the agent, even if the agent lacks knowledge of the moral quality of the act because he is (legally) insane, lacks control over the impulse that prompted the act, or lacks awareness of its possible consequences (as in negligent behavior). Such excuses, from a simple mistake to extreme duress, apply inside the broad domain of voluntary action. They do not negate the *actus reus* of a criminal offense.

Voluntary acts of commission or omission are treated as "objective" or observable matters of fact. Though voluntariness speaks to mental state, it is understood as something that can be inferred from the observable qualities of action. A person who is not in the grip of a seizure, engaged in sleepwalking, hypnotized, or physically forced by another person to behave as she does, is acting voluntarily, so far as the criminal law is concerned.

In contrast with the "objective" elements of an offense, *mens rea* must be proved on the basis of evidence that the defendant "subjectively" possessed a certain mental state at the time the crime was committed. *Mens rea* typically refers to an agent's level of awareness in acting. In most cases, evidence must be presented to show that the defendant had a certain intention, some particular knowledge about what she was doing, or that she consciously disregarded an unreasonable risk of harm to others. When it comes to mistakes of fact, many states have adopted the Model Penal Code's proposal that if the defendant labors under a mistaken factual belief that negates the required mental state element, she cannot be found guilty of that offense, even when the mistake is not reasonable.[33] This suggests that a person's unreasonableness, perhaps due to mental illness or intellectual disability, restricts her liability to criminal sanctions. Liability is in principle limited in this way, though acquittal on this basis is uncommon.

Because different crimes are defined by reference to different mental states, among other factors, a defendant's incapacity to form a certain kind of intention might establish his innocence of the particular offense charged. For example, assault with intent to commit murder requires that the defendant act with an intention to cause the victim's death. It thus presupposes that the defendant had the capacity to foresee and intend that consequence. The mere ability to form an intention to attack another is insufficient. In *People v. Ireland,*[34] a California appeals court reversed a felony-murder conviction on the ground that the jury should have been instructed to consider whether the defendant, who had been suffering under emotional pressure and had consumed prescribed medications and alcohol, was capable of "malice aforethought" at the time he shot and killed his wife. The lower court had instructed the jury to find the defendant guilty of second-degree felony-murder if it determined that the homicide was the direct causal result of an assault with a dangerous weapon. The court of appeals ruled that this was a mistake and that the jury should have been instructed to consider the defendant's ability, at the time, not just to commit the act but to form the intent to kill.

The possibility that a defendant is incapable of forming an intention stands in some tension with the permissible role of *presumptions* in the prosecution's case. The law often allows *mens rea* to be established on the basis of a presumption. This means that the *mens rea* element of the crime can be inferred on the basis of some other facts. For example, if some item is found together with the defendant in his car, the defendant can be presumed to possess the item—that is, to have knowledge of its possession. The U.S. Supreme Court has held that a presumption is constitutionally acceptable when its truth is "more likely than not" and provided that the jury is instructed that it may choose to accept or reject it.[35] The role of presumptions means that *mens rea* might be established on the basis of circumstantial evidence. Sometimes the *mens rea* for a specific intent crime is proved by reliance on the general presumption that a person intends the natural and probable consequences of his acts. For example, a person who points and fires a gun at another person can be presumed to intend to kill the other. The Court holds that presumptions are permissible provided that they are not introduced as mandatory—in other words, a presumption cannot be used to shift the burden of persuasion regarding the intent element of the offense to the defendant.[36] Thus, the prosecution is permitted to argue that a defendant who, at close range, aims and shoots a gun at someone, killing her, intended her death, yet if there is evidence to suggest that the defendant did not believe that the gun was loaded, the burden is on the prosecution to prove beyond a reasonable doubt that the defendant acted with the requisite intent, not on the defendant to prove that he acted without such intent. Presumptions also operate to establish recklessness. According to the Model Penal Code, a reckless person "consciously disregards a substantial and unjustifiable risk."[37] Observed behavior is often the basis for a jury's finding of recklessness. For example, a person who shoots into the air on a crowded street is presumed reckless.

Reliance on presumptions, even if they are rebuttable, to establish *mens rea* threatens to erode the purportedly subjective character of the *mens rea* element of crimes. Why? Because it means that the mental state of *a particular defendant* can be established on the basis of a conclusion about the typical mental state of *most defendants* in circumstances similar to the defendant's circumstances. In this way, the scope of particular person's liability is a function of what it is reasonable to believe about most people.

Moreover, in cases of criminal negligence, no evidence of subjective mental state, whether direct or indirect, is required.[38] Instead, the prosecution is permitted to rely on an "objective" standard to demonstrate *mens rea*. More specifically, the *mens rea* is established by direct appeal to a reasonable person standard. The Model Penal Code defines a negligent actor as someone who "should be aware of a substantial and unjustifiable risk that the material element exists or will result from his conduct."[39] A defendant can be held to have acted with criminal negligence if a reasonable person in the defendant's circumstances would have been aware of the risk involved and refrained from so acting. This criterion leaves open the question of what, exactly, counts as the defendant's circumstances, and whether those circumstances might include psychological abnormalities or diminished mental capacities. On this matter, courts have been reluctant to consider psychological characteristics to belong to the defendant's circumstances. By contrast, physical limitations do count among the circumstances that bear on which expectations count as reasonable. Blindness or serious physical injury might undermine a judgment of criminal negligence when such physical limitations bear on the defendant's ability to perceive and avoid a risk that persons of ordinary physical ability would grasp. Courts have not treated a defendant's psychological limitations in an analogous way. They have resisted individualizing the negligence standard to fit an individual defendant's psychological limitations. Low intelligence, temperament, and mental illness have not been included as factors that can be used to limit a defendant's liability for criminal negligence.[40] In this way, "objective" evidence of an individual's mental state calls into question the relevance of a defendant's psychology altogether.[41]

In *State v. Patterson,* a Connecticut appellate court upheld a conviction of criminally negligent homicide although the defendant had an IQ of 61, which, according to the court, places her within the bottom one-half of 1 percent of the population. The defendant withheld water from a two-year-old boy in order to prevent him from wetting his bed, and after four days the boy died of dehydration.[42] The defense argued that the defendant was not capable of perceiving the risk to the boy, but the court ruled that "even if . . . the defendant was incapable of perceiving the risk of death . . . we cannot consider the defendant's diminished mental capacity in the context of criminally negligent homicide because we employ an objective standard." In other words, the defendant's inability to perceive the risk that her actions would kill the child was irrelevant to her guilt because a reasonable person would have perceived the risk. In judging whether negligent homicide has been committed, the law holds all defendants to the same standard of reasonable conduct.

While in negligence cases *mens rea* is established by direct reference to a reasonable person standard, strict liability crimes require no proof of *mens rea* at all. Statutory rape, at least in some states, as well as some prevalent narcotics and firearms statutes, do not require that the prosecution prove that the defendant acted with negligence, much less recklessness, knowledge, or purpose. For example, under some statutes, a person is guilty of rape by having sexual intercourse with a person under the age specified by statute (for example, sixteen), even if the accused had every reason to believe that the victim was older than that age.

In short, the criminal law maintains that when it can be established that a defendant satisfies the act and mental state requirements of an offense—however removed the mental state requirements are from the defendant's actual psychology—and provided that the defendant has no justification or excuse for the behavior in question, he is liable to criminal sanctions. These criteria set the legal standard of avoidability: they define the sense in which a person could have complied with the law and with morality. Or, otherwise expressed, the law holds that it was possible for that person to have avoided his crime, and reasonable to have required it of him. The law regards his will and action as relevantly free.

As indicated, particularly with respect to crimes that hinge on negligence and strict liability, but even with respect to crimes requiring certain forms of intentionality, the notion of "reasonable opportunity to avoid" that is built into the twin requirements of *mens rea* and *actus reus* is weak. *Some and perhaps many actors who are accurately deemed criminally guilty will not have had a realistic chance to avoid committing the offense under the circumstances in which they committed it.* Some do not understand the danger they pose to others. Some are not able to control their impulses. Some do not understand the nature of the actions they are performing or what the law requires. Some lack basic concern for other people. People are held criminally liable for decisions clouded by mental illness, impulsivity, immaturity, intellectual disability, drugs, and alcohol. In many cases, the opportunities convicted persons had to avoid committing their crimes do not resemble what we ordinarily think of as reasonable prospects to comply with the law.

The law's conception of reasonable opportunity to avoid criminal sanctions is a function of how it treats not only a defendant's subjective limitations and, of course, her liberty interests, but also the rights of other people not to be harmed. The importance of protecting people's equal rights not to be harmed provides some reason to resist making a defendant's liability depend on her psychology, both because it can be so difficult to assess a person's psychological limitations and because a person with psychological problems may pose serious risks to other people. Still, an individual's subjective limitations are crucial to morally reasonable judgments of blameworthiness and desert. The courts' limited sensitivity to these considerations raises doubts about a retributivist theory of criminal punishment, if that theory is meant to rationalize anything like current criminal law doctrine. Even if the law were to pay more attention to an individual's subjective limitations, it would be unlikely to approach anything like evaluations of individual moral desert. Examining how excuses function in criminal law helps to make this point.

Excuses in Criminal Law

The requirements of *mens rea* and *actus reus* set only a weak requirement of reasonable opportunity to avoid. Is that requirement made stronger through the legal recognition of excuses that defeat liability despite proof that the defendant committed the crime charged? Surveying the nature of legal excuses confirms the reluctance of courts to individualize criteria of criminal liability to a defendant's psychological capacities and limitations. In considering how excuses function in criminal law, I will be especially concerned with law's regard for a defendant's moral competence: his capacity to recognize and to be guided by moral reasons. Legally recognized justifications and excuses typically rely on a reasonable person standard in a way that does not permit as relevant a consideration of a defendant's moral incapacity or diminished moral capacity, yet moral competence is relevant to blameworthiness.

The application of an objective standard of reasonable conduct is found in the court's understanding of the scope of the "provocation" defense. This defense reduces a charge of murder to the lesser offense of manslaughter. The Model Penal Code defines two principle components to the defense. First, the defendant must have acted under the influence of extreme emotional disturbance and, second, there must have been a "reasonable explanation or excuse" for the emotional disturbance.

In the murder case *People v. Cassasa,* the defendant tried and failed to use the provocation defense.[43] The defense argued that Cassasa acted under the influence of extreme emotional disturbance because he was obsessed with the victim, in whom he had a romantic interest. After she broke off their relationship, he was "devastated" and began behaving bizarrely. He entered the apartment below hers in order to eavesdrop on her. He also broke into her apartment when she was not there and lay in her bed, armed with a knife. On his final visit to her apartment, he stabbed her to death when she refused his offer of a gift.

The trial court found Cassasa guilty of second-degree murder. The court of appeals affirmed his conviction, finding that the defendant had acted under the influence of extreme emotional disturbance, but that the defendant's emotional reaction at the time of the commission of the crime was "so peculiar to him" that it could not be considered reasonable so as to reduce the conviction to manslaughter. Since a reasonable person would not have been provoked by the circumstances that in fact provoked the defendant, Cassasa's emotional disturbance did not mitigate the charge against him from murder to manslaughter. Interestingly, the court also argued that Cassasa's disturbed state was not the product of external factors but was rather "a stress he created within himself, dealing mostly with a fantasy, a refusal to accept the reality of the situation." In other words, the court suggests that Cassasa at some level "chose" to feel disturbed rather than face reality. In this way, the court emphasized its finding that the cause of the stress was Cassasa's responsibility, rather than a feature of his situation, thus removing the cause from the set of emotional disturbances for which there could be a reasonable explanation or excuse. But the court also seemed to imply that Cassasa's emotional disturbance was under his control and that, in that sense, he could have acted otherwise. Perhaps the court was, in this case, uncomfortable with the legal criteria for responsibility and so searched for a metaphysical rationale, since whether or not the disturbance was under Cassasa's control is irrelevant to the legal notion of provocation. The defense of provocation fails when it is demonstrated that a reasonable person would not have been triggered by the circumstances that disturbed the defendant, even if the defendant could not have avoided the provocation.

Duress as a legal defense resembles the provocation defense. The Model Penal Code defines duress by reference to what "a person of reasonable firmness in [the defendant's] situation would have been unable to resist."[44] The courts have found that a person's size, strength, and physical health can be accounted for as aspects of the actor's situation, but not matters of temperament or mental health, with the possible exception of "battered women's syndrome." Some courts have ruled that battered women's syndrome is irrelevant to the "purely objective" reasonableness standard, while others have found that a history of domestic abuse is relevant to whether the defendant "reasonably believed that her life was in danger" for the purposes of determining whether she acted under duress.[45] In assessing whether the defense of duress applies, courts that understand a history of domestic abuse to be relevant would instruct juries to consider not whether a reasonable person per se would have formed the belief that her life was in danger, but whether a reasonable person who has endured domestic abuse of the sort suffered by the defendant would have done so.

When it comes to duress, courts are divided on age and intellectual disability. In *State v. Heinemann,* the court rejected a sixteen-year-old defendant's duress defense, claiming that although her immaturity made her more vulnerable to duress, her defense was precluded in view of "the legislature's determination to treat sixteen year olds as adults for purposes of [eligibility for trial in juvenile court]."[46] In *Commonwealth v. DeMarco,* the court found that "the fact that a defendant suffers from 'a gross and verifiable' mental disability . . . is a relevant consideration" to the question of whether an objective person of reasonable firmness would have been able to resist the threat.[47] Yet in *United States v. Johnson,* the Court considered the relevance of intellectual disability to a duress defense and claimed that "unlike . . . non-mental physical disabilities, mental deficiency or retardation is difficult to identify, more difficult to quantify, and more easily feigned. For these reasons and others, it was the common law rule going back to at least 1616, and still is, that an adult suffering from a mental deficiency is nevertheless held to a reasonable person standard."[48]

The reasoning I have highlighted in discussing provocation and duress characterizes legal reasoning about excuses more generally. Circumstances that would render expectations of a reasonable person's compliance with law unreasonable form the backbone of legal excuses. And the circumstances that constitute an unreasonable obstacle to law-abidingness for a reasonable person are mostly limited to factors other than temperament, personality, or mental health. Relevant constraints on free will are not individualized vis-à-vis subjective moral capacity. With few exceptions, the criminal law sets and holds everyone to the same set of expectations,

expectations that it deems reasonable despite the fact that it is harder—perhaps *much* harder—for some people to meet those expectations. But since the difficulty some people have complying with the law might well be relevant to whether or how much we should blame them, we should avoid inferring moral blameworthiness from criminal guilt.

The Insanity Defense

The narrow room allotted by law for evaluations of subjective capacity implies that a person has "free will" even though that person may be subjectively incapable of taking moral reasons seriously. The exception to this is "insanity": the utter breakdown of rational thought. The criminal law of almost every state permits insanity as a complete defense against criminal charges. A successful insanity defense thus results in acquittal, though, in practice, such acquittals are rare because the legal definition of insanity is so narrow.

The majority of states follow the so-called *M'Naghten* formulation, which requires the defendant to establish that "at the time of the committing of the act, [he] was laboring under such a defect of reason, from disease of the mind, as not to know the nature and quality of the act he was doing; or, if he did know it, that he did not know he was doing what was wrong."[49] This formulation fixes on a defendant's cognitive impairments, which must be so severe that the defendant either had no idea what he was doing or no understanding that it was wrong. Mentally ill defendants whose impairments are motivational or volitional do not benefit from this definition of insanity and are subject to normal prosecution.

By contrast with the *M'Naghten* formulation, the drafters of the Model Penal Code favored a broader conception of insanity. The MPC maintains that "a person is not responsible for criminal conduct if at the time of such conduct as a result of mental disease or defect he lacks substantial capacity either to appreciate the criminality (wrongfulness) of his conduct or to conform his conduct to the requirements of law."[50] Thus the MPC definition allows, while the *M'Naghten* definition does not, that motivational impairments, potentially encompassing sociopathy, could support an insanity acquittal. The MPC commentaries emphasize this difference:

> One shortcoming of the [*M'Naghten*] criterion is that it authorizes a finding of responsibility in a case in which the actor is not seriously deluded concerning his conduct or its consequences, but in which the actor's appreciation of the wrongfulness of his conduct is a largely detached or abstract awareness that does not penetrate to the affective level. Insofar as a formulation centering on "knowledge" does not readily lend itself to application to emotional abnormalities, the *M'Naghten* test appears less than optimal as a standard of responsibility in cases involving affective disorder.[51]

Thus the MPC rejects *M'Naghten's* exclusive focus on cognitive impairments and opts to recommend including the recognition of emotional impairments. In the 1960s and 1970s, some courts embraced versions of this broader conception, but the trend since the 1980s has been to narrow the definition—a trend fueled in part by the jury's acquittal by reason of insanity of President Ronald Reagan's would-be assassin, John Hinckley, which in turn prompted Congress to legislate a narrow definition of insanity applicable to defendants accused of federal crimes.

In practice, the difference between these formulations may be inconsequential. Researchers estimate that "no more than .25 percent of terminated felony prosecutions" involve insanity acquittals, and both experimental and historical studies indicate very little difference in the willingness of juries to acquit on the basis of insanity on any of the formulations of its criteria.[52] Politics aside, the MPC formulation raises difficult evidentiary issues, as the court emphasized in *United States v. Lyons*, when it rejected the "volitional prong" of the MPC formulation. The court asserted that "a majority of psychiatrists now believe that they do not possess sufficient accurate scientific bases for measuring a person's capacity for self-control or for calibrating the impairment of that capacity."[53] It concludes, "We see no prudent course for the law to follow but to treat all criminal impulses—including those not resisted—as resistible." In other words, prudence in the application of legal rules dictates that impairments of an agent's will are not excusing.

On either formulation, but especially the *M'Naghten* version, the legal category of insanity is much narrower than the medical category of mental illness. Mental illness spans a wide range of abnormalities, including many impairments that are severe yet fall short on either the cognitive or the volitional prong of the MPC definition; these include everything from high anxiety to debilitating depression to psychotic delusions. People who suffer from a diagnosable mental illness might be truly disturbed, confused, or irrational, yet they may retain an understanding of the moral difference between right and wrong as well as some limited capacity to control their behavior. Though they are not legally insane, their responsiveness to moral reasons may be starkly compromised. This is true of many people who commit terrible crimes.

In moral terms, responsibility is typically understood to assure rational and moral competence, in particular, as I have suggested, the capacity to understand and to be guided by—that is, to *care* about—*moral* reasons. These include reasons not to cheat or deceive other people, reasons not to touch people's bodies without their consent, and reasons not to discriminate on the basis of race, gender, or other features of socially disfavored groups.

Sensitivity to moral reasons is critical to at least two primary functions of morality. First of all, it is important to the *action-guiding* aims of morality. Morality is directed to those who can grasp and apply its principles and who are, at least in ordinary circumstances, motivated to do so. This supposes a moral subject's rational capacity for understanding and deliberation as well as her moral concern for the needs and interests of other people. A subject with these competencies can and often does act for moral reasons.

In its action-guiding role, law is both like and unlike morality. Like morality, the law affirms action-guiding rules. Yet the criminal law's reliance on sanctions to secure compliance with its rules permits it to influence people's behavior without presuming that its subjects are *morally* motivated. The law's directives are relevant to people who possess some rational ability to protect their own interest in avoiding criminal sanctions, whether or not they care about the moral interests of other people.[54] Thus, restricting the insanity defense to cases of cognitive (rather than volitional) dysfunction is consistent with understanding the law as a set of action-guiding norms. Volitional impairments, when they concern a person's responsiveness to *moral* reasons, might not inhibit a person from responding to the threat of criminal sanctions for self-interested reasons, and hence they might not impair a person's ability to comply with the law. But a result of a definition of insanity that focuses exclusively on a defendant's cognitive capacity is the possible conviction of individuals whose capacity to be motivated by moral reasons is diminished, even very significantly.

A second function of morality concerns how to *evaluate people* in view of their actions. When is a person a suitable subject for familiar aspects of moral evaluation, including blame? A familiar philosophical position holds that our "reactive attitudes" and other blaming responses, including punishment, are properly directed only at a person who is capable of being guided by moral reasons. This thesis has enjoyed some legal recognition. In *Morissette v. United States,* the Court asserts, "Historically, our substantive criminal law is based on a theory of punishing the vicious will. It postulates a free agent confronted with a choice between doing right and wrong, and choosing freely to do wrong."[55] Indeed, blame typically reflects not only our understanding of a wrongdoer's moral qualities, but also our sense of her capacity to modify her behavior in view of the requirements of morality. A wrongdoer's moral capacity to have made a better choice is important. In particular, we view blame as appropriate when an agent had the ability to be sensitive to the needs and interests of other people, yet failed to act properly toward them. The point of blame is partly to indicate that a person has rejected reasons she had—reasons for her to have acted differently—and that her capacity to have done better justifies our dissatisfaction with her.

Focusing the legal definition of insanity on a person's *cognitive impairments* refuses the insanity defense to people with motivational impairments, even though their emotional problems may compromise their moral blameworthiness. While they may be deemed guilty of their crimes, it might be misguided to blame them morally for their wrongdoing. When a person's capacity to appreciate morality is compromised, perhaps she could not have acted morally. A morally capable wrongdoer is somebody who was capable of acting for moral reasons that she failed to take seriously but could have. When we have good reason to doubt a person's capacity, or full capacity, for moral responsiveness, our moral attitudes and behavior toward her may shift. Although we may be frustrated or disappointed by her behavior, our considered response lacks the moralistic edge characteristic of blame. It seems morally inappropriate to blame

someone for acting badly when that person was not capable of understanding and being moved by the requirements of morality. Because her
action does not represent her rejection of a morally better course of action that was available to her, it seems pointless to condemn *her* in moral
terms for her choice.

Skepticism about moral capacity is especially likely to come up in the
arena of criminal justice. A retributive rationale for criminal punishment
purports to gain its foothold in moral blame. But judging that a person
was capable of having acted better can be hard to do confidently, especially when that person is mentally ill, and we might come to doubt his
blameworthiness. Some advocates of retribution attempt to circumvent
this problem by tailoring the insanity defense narrowly, so that an evaluation of insanity can more easily be made. But when we narrow the insanity defense, we use the criminal justice system to incapacitate some
wrongdoers who are not blameworthy for their wrongdoing, despite the
legal finding that they are not insane. This problem upsets the retributive theory of punishment.

The criminal law is indifferent to individual capacities partly because
it does not want to invite defendants to argue, as some surely would, that
they are morally dense or unmoved by moral reasons, thereby leaving ju-
rors to sort out whether such claims are true, on a case by case basis. In
other words, it is sometimes by design, rather than by accident—or vi-
ciousness or racism on the part of judges and legislatures—that criminal
law's specification of the conditions under which one is subject to legal
punishment departs from morality's specification of when a person can
be blamed. No wonder, then, that criminal law poorly fits the retributivist's
model, which is predicated implicitly on the availability of a complete and
nuanced account of the circumstances of each wrongdoer's wrong in
order to determine guilt and a fitting punishment.[56]

Moral Blame and Criminal Sentencing

In the face of the arguments above, someone faithful to the idea of retributive justice might attempt to rescue it by emphasizing that the phase of
a criminal trial that determines guilt is separate from the phase that
sentences the convicted. She might argue that appraisals of blame-

worthiness are properly made only in the sentencing phase. While it might be true that guilt does not imply blameworthiness, she might say, considerations that may be introduced at sentencing—such as the defendant's character virtues, contributions to society, or difficult circumstances—provide a broader basis upon which to calibrate a judgment of blameworthiness.

This argument is open to several objections. Most significantly, it underestimates the social meaning of conviction.[57] A criminal record is consequential and can be devastating, even apart from the particular sentence a defendant receives. It may severely limit a person's ability to earn a living, to secure housing, to go to college, and to retain custody of children. Some of these consequences are unjust, and should be remedied. But it is bound to remain true under a retributive rationale for criminal punishment that criminal conviction carries with it a life-altering social stigma.

Furthermore, the legal trend has been away from enhancing latitude in sentencing, at least in the United States.[58] For crimes subject to a statutory mandatory minimum sentence, judicial discretion to take morally mitigating factors into account cannot, in many cases, prevent the imposition of a very harsh sentence. For other crimes, judges have more discretion regarding a defendant's sentence, though this discretion does not often lead to a significant reduction. This is because in the sentencing phase the prosecution is allowed to introduce evidence to enhance culpability that was not admissible at the guilt phase, and because victims are often allowed to deliver impact statements regarding how a defendant's crimes have affected them. In short, the consideration of mitigation during sentencing has not produced, and has little promise of producing, a regime of criminal punishment that punishes in accordance with a defendant's alleged moral desert.

It is true that the U.S. Supreme Court has raised some concerns about how the moral competence of defendants bears on their appropriate sentence, yet it has done so in only a limited range of cases involving the harshest sentences, mostly concerning the death penalty. Nevertheless, those cases merit scrutiny: Might they indicate that the Court thinks the severity of punishment should be influenced by an assessment of the defendant's moral competence?

In *Atkins v. Virginia,* the U.S. Supreme Court accepted that intellectually disabled individuals have diminished capacities to process information, to communicate, to learn from experience, to engage in logical reasoning, to control impulses, and to understand reactions to their behavior. The Court found these impairments relevant to the permissibility of the death penalty, on several grounds. First, it held that intellectually disabled individuals who have committed murder are less culpable than the average murderer, and hence do not deserve the death penalty, which is reserved for maximally culpable killings.[59] Second, the Court reasoned that the cognitive impairments from which intellectually disabled people suffer make them less responsive to sanctions and hence undermine attempts to deter them from committing capital offenses by threatening them with the death penalty. Finally, the Court concluded that the impairments render these defendants more apt to be wrongfully convicted: intellectually disabled defendants are susceptible to wrongful conviction through false confessions and a diminished ability to assist their lawyers, and they face diminished prospects for mitigation in sentencing since "their demeanor may create an unwarranted impression of lack of remorse for their crimes."

The Court has also expressed concern about the rational and moral capacity of juveniles and applied to young death-penalty defendants the same concerns voiced about the intellectually disabled. In *Roper v. Simmons,* it held that it is unconstitutional to apply the death penalty to juveniles. The Court argued that immaturity diminishes culpability, as does the susceptibility of juveniles to peer pressure, and that neither retribution nor deterrence provides adequate justification for imposing the death penalty on them.[60]

Furthermore, in *Ford v. Wainwright,* the Court prohibited the execution of the insane, invoking what the Justices took to be a national consensus "that such an execution simply offends humanity."[61] As a matter of federal constitutional law, insanity thus operates as a mitigating factor in punishment when it comes to the death penalty. The Court possesses some basic concerns about inflicting the very harshest of penalties on defendants whose rational and moral competence is seriously impaired.

That the Court raised general concerns about the justifiability of the death penalty for the insane, the young, or the intellectually disabled is notable, but its acknowledgment of these concerns only in relation to the death penalty limits their reach.[62] The Court emphasizes that the death penalty is a unique and rare form of punishment, implying that considerations that limit its application might not apply to other punishments, including many cases of life without parole, the hopeless fate that is gaining a reputation as "the other death penalty." Surely we might wonder why diminished responsibility, unsettling when we consider the harshest penalty, should not also be unsettling when we consider other extremely harsh sentences.[63] Worries about the moral accountability of the mentally ill and juveniles are especially pressing for those who argue that punishment should always be applied in proportion to desert.

Actually, when it comes to juveniles, the Court has extended its reasoning somewhat. In *Miller v. Alabama*, it claimed that adolescence is "marked by rashness, proclivity for risk, and inability to assess consequences," and that these characteristics should be treated as mitigating factors when it comes to sentencing juveniles to life without parole.[64] The Court concluded that mandatory life sentences for juveniles constitute cruel and unusual punishment in violation of the Eighth Amendment. Similar reasoning in *Jackson v. Hobbs* suggests that criminal liability should track both moral culpability and "capacity for change," as well as skills in reasoning about costs and benefits, which give the threat of legal sanctions possible deterrent effect to at-risk youth.[65] But again, the fact that life without parole is rarely imposed on juveniles in the United States (and in other countries) figures centrally in the Court's reasoning and is treated as a basis for limiting the reach of these decisions.

Apart from the Court's reluctance to impose the very harshest punitive measures on the intellectually impaired or juveniles, judging moral capacity on an individual basis remains stubbornly at odds with how the law governs sentencing. While mitigating considerations are permitted in the sentencing phase after guilt has been established, neither mental illness (short of the stringent legal notion of 'insanity') nor youth typically mitigates sentences. The result is a large population of inmates in U.S. jails and prisons who are mentally ill, intellectually disabled, and immature.[66] Furthermore, juvenile cases are commonly referred to adult criminal court, particularly (but not always) for serious crimes. A "direct file" statute passed in the state of Florida, for example, permits prosecutors wide discretion to refer juveniles to adult court, including any sixteen- or seventeen-year-old who is accused of a felony, violent or not.[67] In three states—Pennsylvania, Wisconsin, and Nevada—children as young as ten years old can be tried as adults for murder. Although the Supreme Court has decided that a *mandatory* sentence of life without parole cannot be imposed on juveniles, thirty-seven states still allow it as an optional sentence, leaving room for judges to impose a life sentence at their discretion.[68] Many states have responded to the federal constraints by resentencing juveniles to what are de facto life sentences—fifty, sixty, or seventy years.[69] Studies show that, in general, juveniles in criminal court do not normally receive lighter sentences than their adult counterparts, and some evidence indicates that they are actually treated more punitively.[70]

The criminal law is of two minds about sentencing. As we have seen, when it comes to the harshest penalties, the law is somewhat sensitive to questions of moral competence. It places some limits on the punishment of the intellectually disabled, juveniles, and the insane. On the other hand, expressing concern about public safety, the courts permit juveniles to be tried as adults, and even the severely mentally ill and disabled can be convicted and punished very harshly for criminal behavior. In *United States v. Lyons,* a case mentioned earlier, the court's majority argued explicitly that as a society we cannot afford to consider the potential moral relevance of most mental incapacities. In particular, the court asserted that it is not practical to consider a person's diminished capacity for self-control, because "the line between an irresistible impulse and an impulse not resisted is probably no sharper than between twilight and dusk."[71] This suggests a broad skepticism about the relevance of assessments of moral incapacity to criminal justice. Furthermore, in *Penry v. Lynaugh* the Court noted that introducing a defendant's intellectual disability as a mitigating factor may be a double-edged sword that enhances the likelihood that the jury will treat it instead as an aggravating factor of future dangerousness.[72] Whether or not moral blameworthiness is relevant, in theory, to how we ought to treat criminal wrongdoers, the courts are wary of attempts to bring it to bear on criminal sentencing.

Legal Culpability versus Moral Blameworthiness

The law's resistance to making criminal liability contingent on a defendant's moral competence makes it hard to maintain a popular rationale for criminal sanctions—namely, that people convicted of crimes deserve the punishment they get. A fundamental disconnect between criminal liability and moral competence implies that criminal sanctions cannot be justified as a matter of moral blame. This causes a problem for the retributive ideal as well as, more broadly, for accounts of the expressive and communicative meaning of punishment, if that meaning involves moral blame in the ordinary sense. An intellectually disabled woman found guilty of criminally negligent homicide cannot convincingly be said morally to deserve the legal consequences of her actions. If there are legally liable defendants who are not morally blameworthy enough to deserve punishment, expressive views cannot justify punishing them. Despite the fact that legal culpability is popularly identified as a form of moral blame, legal guilt must be distinguished from moral blameworthiness. If the imposition of criminal sanctions on people with diminished moral competence can be justified, it should be in terms that do not depend on blameworthiness and desert.

Of course it is open to retributivists to accept some version of my criticism, and to argue that they offer a theory that justifies a version of criminal law very different from the one we actually have. In other words, the value of retribution might in principle be invoked as a guide to reforming the criminal law in order to make it more sensitive to considerations of individual blameworthiness.[73] In Chapter 2, however, we will see that this line of thinking is not promising. We will look more closely at the notion of *moral competence* as it relates to practices of moral blame. Our focus will be morality, not law, as our aim is to see whether there are viable moral practices that could be incorporated into the legal system in order to address worries about the possibility of realizing retributive ideals of justice. Retributivists believe that criminal law promises to deliver just deserts. But, as we will see, this promise is empty.

There is no stable conception of individual desert for the law to approximate. Even apart from law, judgments of individual moral accountability, blameworthiness, or deservingness—appraisals of a wrongdoer's moral desert—are based on generalizations that abstract from individual wrong-doers and their circumstances in various ways. These judgments rely on appeals to saner moments, different circumstances, and even different people in appraising the moral competence of a particular individual. But the role of generalization across time and people opens the door to skeptical doubt about a given wrongdoer's moral responsibility. We should worry about the role generalization and abstraction play in judgments of moral desert.

Retribution is especially vulnerable to skeptical challenges. It is not broadly interlaced with other important considerations of justice, despite the fact that it aspires to serve as their foundation or, at least, is commonly understood to be essential to justice. We could jettison a commitment to deserved suffering without giving up moral judgments, moral sentiments, or a commitment to justice, though we must reformulate some popular understandings of these notions.

TWO

SKEPTICISM ABOUT MORAL DESERT

A PERSON MIGHT BE criminally guilty and eligible for punishment without being morally blameworthy for his criminal wrongdoing. This misfit between moral and legal culpability is disturbing, because the public discourse surrounding criminal justice is morally charged. The view that people who have been convicted of crimes morally deserve punishment is commonplace—even celebrated—and it depends on the notion that criminally guilty persons are morally blameworthy for their criminal acts, a conclusion that is not substantiated by criminal conviction, at least in many cases. Still, even officials in charge of the criminal justice system adhere to the belief that criminal lawbreakers deserve moral condemnation.

For example, William Barr, attorney general under the first Bush administration, approvingly quoted Hal Stratton, attorney general of New Mexico, who said, "I don't know anyone that goes to prison on their first crime. By the time you go to prison, you are a pretty bad guy."[1] Statements like this shape public opinion and contribute to the stigma of incarceration. Even being *suspected* of committing a crime can be stigmatizing, as Ronald Reagan's attorney general, Edwin Meese, conveyed in a rather sinister statement. Meese said, "You don't have many suspects who are innocent of a crime. That's contradictory. If a person is innocent of a crime, then he is not a suspect."[2]

It is tempting to think that the law should be reformed to establish a tighter alliance between legal and moral culpability, yet such proposals for reform should be resisted. The concern to render criminal punishment moderate and humane is laudable, and the need for reform is urgent, but the notion of moral blameworthiness will not function well as the basis of legal guilt. We should abandon efforts to justify state-imposed punishment as morally deserved. We should reform the criminal justice system without aiming for moral desert and retribution.

Moral Competence

Blaming behavior, including punishment, depends on the notion that a person who deserves blame is at least minimally competent to understand and respond to the demands of morality. Moral competence has two dimensions: a cognitive dimension of moral understanding, perception, or knowledge, and a volitional dimension that involves caring about morality and being moved by moral reasons in deciding how to act. Morally praiseworthy agents display both dimensions, and people who fail to act rightly might falter along either one. Still, moral blameworthiness presupposes basic moral competence—the capacity most people have to grasp and act from moral reasons, even when, in fact, they fail to do so—and the diminished moral competence of some criminal wrongdoers threatens retributive accounts of criminal justice. Someone who is unfit for normal moral expectations does not deserve criminal sanctions, when desert is understood as a matter of moral blameworthiness.

Some desert-believers deny this. They deny that moral expectations and standards of appropriate response typically do or should be responsive to judgments of moral capacity. They argue that our expectations range over persons generally and that our responses should match the realized quality of a person's will, not how it came about or whether it could have been exercised differently. They hold that the choices people actually make, regardless of their capacity to choose better, seal their moral fates. Or, expressed more subtly, because choice always depends on judgment, we should presume the presence of an agent's reflective ability, and this is adequate to establish moral desert, even when choice is heavily influenced by emotion. According to retributive legal theorist Michael S. Moore, emotions figure into choices we make by reflecting our judgments and motivating us to make certain choices that we use those judgments to justify. Moore writes, "We—the persons or selves who are the subjects of responsibility—are more than the faculty of reason that does battle with the faculty of emotion; we are our emotions as much as we are our reason."[3] He concludes that we are responsible for all the choices we make, even those that are highly emotionally charged and perhaps not within our control, because all the characteristics we possess that influence our choices, together with our actual choices, make us who we are. Since emotions do not "short-circuit" choice but "are both products and cause of the judgments we make as we decide what to do," we can be deserving or undeserving on their basis.[4]

Philosopher David Schmidtz expresses a similar view. He writes, "Desert makers, if there are any, are relations between outcomes and internal features of persons. We need not (and normally do not) assume anything about what caused those features. . . . When a person's internal features support desert claims, the support comes from appreciating what those features are."[5] Schmidtz continues, "Sometimes, we simply give people credit for what they achieve, and for what they are. And sometimes, simply giving people credit is the essence of treating them as persons rather than as mere confluences of historical forces. . . . Jane's character is not something that happened to her. It *is* her."[6] A view of the self as thickly comprising traits that give rise to desert claims is shared by political theorists Michael Sandel and William Galston, among others.[7]

Schmidtz's point that we sometimes give people credit for what they are obscures the difference between various kinds of desert claims. There may be some rewards we deserve simply based on features that we have or have cultivated, for example, awards for beauty, intelligence, speed, agility, or promise. But this understanding of desert is inadequate when it comes to blaming behavior. Deserving punishment, for example, is not like deserving to win a talent competition, a leadership award, or a merit scholarship. Deserved punishment tracks not realized abilities but moral failures. That we can be identified in part through our weaknesses does not seem morally to determine the meaning of our failures for how we should be treated in view of them. Even if our various attributes thickly comprise ourselves, it is hard to accept that a person could deserve blame, much less punishment, for what she happens to be or to have done, whether or not she could have been or done better. Sometimes what people deserve depends simply on what they are like, but we should be wary of assigning blame on that basis alone.[8]

Moral blame does not attach simply to a person's being a certain way. Blame draws substance from a moral "ought," from the idea that a person ought to have done something other than what she did, and hence it depends on the notion that she had moral reasons for acting better. But this moral evaluation of her is a weak basis for determining what she morally deserves unless there is a plausible sense in which she could have acted on those reasons.[9] Moral desert, as I understand it, is the view that culpable wrongdoing morally determines how we should respond. Blameworthiness makes a negative response to wrongdoing appropriate. The difference between desert with regard to punishment and other forms of desert, together with the serious consequences of the stigma of criminality, puts pressure on moral desert-believers to affirm a criminal wrongdoer's moral competence. A person who is blameworthy for criminal wrongdoing must have been capable of bringing his choices in line with his values, and of assessing and endorsing or revising his values.[10] More precisely, he must have been capable of revising his values and commitments to bring them in line with what morality requires.[11] Moral desert requires a person-specific and retrospective notion of moral competence. And this raises the worrisome possibility that sometimes a person could not have done better, even when he recognized in some way that he was behaving badly.

This worry can trouble us, not only when it comes to disturbed criminal defendants, but more generally. Ordinary interpersonal relationships typically involve a mutual commitment to viewing one another as free to do what morality requires. And this commitment involves a person-specific judgment. We presume that an ethical framework is subjectively relevant to the other person. Usually this means that we trust that our value as a person whose interests ought to be respected, who is entitled to concern and consideration, actually informs and guides another person's interactions with us. As a result, when moral reasons fail to motivate a person's behavior, we may find it hard to resist the thought that she could have done better under the circumstances in which she failed. Our moral reactions—expressed, for example, through our resentment or hurt feelings—are premised on the other person's individual moral competence to have acted as she ought to have. We treat her morally faulty choice as something that was up to her, despite flaws in her character or dispositions that she would have had to overcome.

This presumption is familiar within personal relations. We presume another person's competence to do as she ought, and we hold her responsible for her part in the relationship. We typically do this by regarding her as answerable for her moral transgressions and by criticizing or blaming her for disregarding moral reasons. "Why did you do that?" is usually not merely a request for an explanation; it functions as a personal rebuke and points to better alternatives—alternatives that we affirm were available to the person whose behavior we are criticizing. Moral reproach implicitly affirms an agent's moral competence, and this implication is reflected in the negative evaluation we make of her, in view of her morally faulty action. We assert that her faulty behavior reflects badly on her, morally speaking. Admonishing her marks this judgment and our response as interpersonally significant; its sting depends on the thought that in so acting an agent has, without justification, relinquished a better option.

Blame can be expressed in a variety of ways—through displays of anger or resentment, by significantly altering expectations or "writing somebody off," by demanding apologies or contrition, or by engaging in explicitly punitive behavior. We should distinguish between rationales for blaming responses that are entirely retrospective and those that also include forward-looking considerations. This distinction cuts across the range of responses we might inclusively classify as blaming responses. A dedicated backward-looking rationale for blaming responses, I submit, puts more pressure on judgments of moral competence. These accounts invoke what Derk Pereboom calls "basic desert."[12] Basic desert is the notion that an agent deserves blame or praise just because she has culpably performed a wrongful or an admirable action, whether or not blaming or praising does any (further) good. Retributive conceptions of justice are among these essentially backward-looking accounts of blame. As we have seen, the notion at the core of a retributive conception of justice is that wrongdoers are due a punitive response that is proportional to their blameworthy wrongdoing: wrongdoers should suffer harm because and to the extent that they are culpable for having done wrong. Retributive views are most clearly identified as theories of punishment and usually self-identify as such.

There are also desert-based dimensions of moral theories not commonly categorized as retributive. Moral theories that are not explicitly retributive in nature—such as the views held by many contemporary Kantians—may refrain from asserting that wrongdoers deserve to suffer. Nevertheless, they may share with retributive approaches the view that blameworthy wrongdoing morally determines how others should respond and typically renders attitudes of resentment and vengeful anger, as well as punitive behavior that expresses these attitudes, appropriate.[13] So understood, "fitting" responses are gauged not by their likely effects or their aspirations but only by what a wrongdoer deserves for what she has done. Claims about what a person deserves are assessed by reference to her established qualities qua agent, qualities for which she is held to account. According to this way of thinking, a person is accountable because her personal attributes are a matter of her own doing; it is not merely unfortunate that she has them. Her unreliability, dishonesty, cruelty, or self-centeredness is the product of her agency, and this fact bears on what she deserves. Here an agent's moral competence must figure centrally. An agent could deserve negative responses as such to her bad judgment and faulty choices only if she were morally capable of doing better.

Nonretributive moralities incorporate forward-looking considerations into judgments of appropriate response. An appropriate blaming response might be influenced by how blaming an agent would affect her future deliberation by provoking her guilt or sharpening her conscience. Blame might aim to influence the behavior of other people by setting an example. Or it might belong in some other way to a blamer's self-protective strategy of avoiding future injuries or recovering from injuries suffered. Victims might affirm their moral worth through engaging in moral criticism and by blaming those who have caused them harm. A person who stands up for herself by blaming someone who has mistreated her may thereby affirm a sense of esteem in her own eyes as well as in the view of other people. Self-protective strategies might aim to get a wrongdoer to apologize or to make amends, although they need not.

Strategic, nonretributive notions of blame would seem to be less committed than exclusively backward-looking accounts are to a wrongdoer's moral competence to have acted well. Blame might be directed paternalistically toward a wrongdoer as a person in need of moral education, to provide incentives for better behavior, or even to promote a moral transformation, rather than as someone who was capable of doing better (that is, without the moral pressure of blame itself). But insofar as blame is not merely a self-protective withdrawal on the part of the blamer and is addressed in some way to the wrongdoer, it typically carries a presumption of moral competence. Blaming a person makes sense only when we assume that she is capable of choosing to conform to moral imperatives and acting accordingly, even if her ability to do that depends on the incentive that blame provides. Furthermore, we usually assume that a person we criticize could make the choices we demand of her for moral, rather than merely self-interested, reasons. This presumption shapes our response to a person who fails to act well. We treat her as having been morally capable of acting better than she did.

Thus our moral responses to wrongdoing, whether retributive or nonretributive, typically rely on our supposition that a wrongdoer ought to and was capable of treating other people better. As a result, our expectations sit uncomfortably with an understanding of her psychology as deficient in moral responsiveness to the rights and interests of other people. We may be disturbed by the thought that the dynamics of a person's psychology could make it the case that her perception of the relevant courses of action might not and perhaps could not have included an action she ought to have taken. The possibility of explaining a person's morally unjustifiable actions by reference to her impulses, circumstances, prior experiences, or dispositions threatens our investment in viewing her as capable of meeting the demands of morality, however influenced she may be by her past experiences, psychological traits, or other causal features. Because we premise our moral expectations and disappointments on a person's moral competence, they are unsettled by explanations that focus on the causal influence on her behavior of factors other than moral judgment and moral motivation.

The threat here is not causal determinism per se, but only certain sorts of causes—those that produce actions contrary to the demands of morality. We may come to doubt whether *explaining* a person's actions by reference to psychological factors other than those that constitute her moral agency could be compatible with *justifying* our moral responses, even though our moral dismay leads us to seek explanatory causes in order to understand why she acted as she did. This tension between causal explanation and moral justification helps to explain why the violation of our moral expectations can be so unsettling. We are caught between, on the one hand, moral indignation—which supposes a view of someone as accountable for her actions—and, on the other hand, our desire to make sense of her behavior and, perhaps, to soothe our own hurt feelings by recognizing the many factors external to morality that have influenced her choices.

This worry becomes more pressing as a person's moral transgressions become more extreme. The sociopath's insensitivity to another person's pain threatens to be morally disabling.[14] We might wonder whether mental illness or other factors that are causally relevant to explaining aberrant behavior, such as an association with a traumatic experience, or the influence of an authority figure, have affected the scope of an wrongdoer's genuine choices in morally significant ways. For example, a famous experiment at Yale University in 1961 showed that college students were willing to inflict seemingly extreme pain on subjects at the mere request of researchers.[15] While this study does not prove that people who made these choices could not have acted better, it does suggest that a person's social circumstances influence what she views as compelling reasons for action.

Factors like these, that influence which reasons for action count from an agent's perspective and how much each counts, bear on our sense of her freedom to do better. The absence of coercion, duress, insanity, and the other standard legally excusing conditions does not suffice to establish that a course of conduct is freely chosen in the sense required to justify blaming responses. Sadly, persons who would commit serious moral wrongs may be deficient in their moral sensibilities, misguided in their moral judgment, and defective in their mental or psychological development, even though they are not recognizably "insane." Furthermore, incapacities might be hard to detect insofar as they are triggered only by particular circumstances and perhaps rarely. Some people become very anxious crossing bridges or standing in crowds. They have trouble functioning rationally in these situations. Others become aggressive when they feel threatened, or panic when they are alone. Some people dissociate and reenact past traumas. We cannot always identify or anticipate psychological abnormalities or morally disabling social influences, and they raise difficult questions about whether we can reconcile them with familiar notions of individual moral responsibility.

Minimal Rationality

Some philosophers argue that if morality requires a course of action and a person is minimally rational (say, is not eligible for the insanity defense), then we should conclude of that person that she could have done what she was morally required to do, even though she failed to do it. This argument can be presented in a way that draws on a more general framework for thinking about possibility. The idea is that if there is a counterfactual scenario, similar to the actual scenario, in which the person *would* have acted as she ought in fact have acted, then we should say that she *could* have acted that way in the actual scenario. A counterfactual "would" licenses an actual "could."

Daniel Dennett illustrates this sort of counterfactual hypothesis by discussing an example from J. L. Austin that refers to the game of golf. Austin writes:

> Consider the case where I miss a very short putt and kick myself because I could have holed it. It is not that I should have holed it if I had tried: I did try, and missed. It is not that I should have holed it if conditions had been different: that might of course be so, but I am talking about conditions as they precisely were, and asserting that I could have holed it. There is the rub. Nor does "I can hole it this time" mean that I shall hole it this time if I try or if anything else; for I may try and miss, and yet not be convinced that I could not have

done it; indeed, further experiments may confirm my belief that I could have done it that time, although I did not.[16]

Tackling Austin's puzzle, Dennett takes issue with Austin's claim, "I could have holed it," given "conditions as they precisely were." "Conditions as they precisely were" would lead to the same result, according to the thesis of causal determinism, which Dennett characterizes as follows: "There is at any instant exactly one physically possible future, [and] this set of worlds has just one member, the actual world, the world in which Austin misses."[17] But causal determinism, according to Dennett and many other contemporary philosophers, is no threat to moral competence.

According to Dennett "I could have holed it" supposes not that I would have holed it under the very same conditions. Rather, "I could have holed it" supposes that I would have holed it under similar conditions, such as conditions in which I applied a bit more pressure to my putt or in which I was not distracted by a bird. Dennett writes:

> We suggest that Austin would be content to consider "Austin holes the putt" possible if, in situations *very similar* to the actual occasion in question, he holes the putt. We think that this is what he meant, and that he would be right to think about his putt this way. This is the familiar, reasonable, useful way to conduct "further experiments" whenever we are interested in understanding the causation involved in the phenomenon of interest. We vary the initial conditions slightly (and often systematically) to see what changes and what stays the same. This is the way to gather *useful* information from the world to guide our further campaigns of avoidance and enhancement.[18]

Indeed, this is the way experimentation proceeds in science. Initial conditions are systematically varied to test a hypothesis. In this sense, a field of possibilities is explored. Applying this framework for thinking about possibility to human action should lead us to understand that a person's capacity to act in a certain way does not imply that she could have done otherwise under the actual circumstances in the sense of having had the power to produce a different outcome under those exact circumstances. Rather, we evaluate counterfactual claims about a person's capacity for action by reference to how the agent would act under similar, though not identical, circumstances. Sometimes we might vary only certain factors internal to the agent, in order to test a relevant hypothesis. In Austin's case, we might suppose the conditions of the green (putting surface) and weather to have been exactly the same, and we imagine that he aimed ever so slightly more to the right to compensate for the slope of the green, or that he focused his concentration more acutely on the follow-through, or that he bent his knees just a bit more during the swing. If the agent would have holed it in any of those counterfactual scenarios, then he could have holed it under the actual scenario.

To test an agent's moral competence, we consider the factors that led a wrongdoer to act badly—the reasons she took herself to have to act as she did—and ask whether the agent would have acted on those morally faulty reasons under different yet relevantly similar circumstances. A frustrated parent who slaps her child might not do the same thing were other adults present. The agent's motives (that is, her frustration) under the alternative scenario maintains a needed connection to the actual scenario, even though the counterfactual scenario may also provoke other motives, including motives that would override the agent's actual motives—such as a desire to be viewed by other adults as a caring and decent parent. If she would not have acted badly in the alternative scenario—despite the allure the bad reasons have had for her—we say she *could* have acted otherwise under the actual circumstances in which she failed to act well.[19] The challenging question is how different the counterfactual circumstances could be, while still retaining relevant similarity to the actual situation in which the agent behaved as she did.

Some philosophers maintain that continuity in a person's minimally rational evaluation of her options establishes a relevant similarity between the counterfactual and the actual scenario: a person's minimal rationality implies her moral competence to act well.[20] The idea is that an agent's demonstrated ability to recognize reasons implies the possibility of her acting morally. Immanuel Kant (1724–1804) took this view.

Kant explains his thinking in two steps. First he invites us to consider an adulterer who defends his wrongful action on the ground that his lust was irresistible. Kant is unsympathetic. He writes, "Suppose that someone says his lust is irresistible when the desired object and

opportunity are present. Ask him whether he would not control his pas-
sion if, in front of the house where he has this opportunity, a gallows
were erected on which he would be hanged immediately after gratifying
his lust. We do not have to guess very long what his answer would be."[21]
Kant's point is that a rational person with an "irresistible" lust can be
made to see that his lust is not really irresistible. All he needs to do is to
imagine a scenario in which the cost of his decision to act on his lust
makes it rational, from a self-interested perspective, to refrain from
doing so. The value a rational person places on life—the reasons his
love of life gives him—quickly lead him to conclude that he would resist
his lust in the imagined counterfactual situation where he faces death.
The counterfactual circumstance is one in which the personal costs of
engaging in wrongdoing are much higher than they actually are, yet
Kant deems it relevant for appraising the lustful agent's ability to control his lust. This does not establish the agent's *moral* competence,
since his self-control is based on reasons of self-interest rather than
morality, but it does present a paradigm in which the agent's recognition of a prudential reason to control his lust leads him to the judgment
that he could do so.

Kant then shifts to a harder case, in which a person's *moral* competence
is tested by a scenario that challenges his love of life. Kant invites us to
ask a man who understands the requirements of morality "whether he
thinks it would be possible for him to overcome his love of life, however
great it may be, if his sovereign threatened him with sudden death unless
he made a false deposition against an honorable man whom the ruler
wished to destroy under a plausible pretext."[22] Kant reasons that a rational person would readily admit he could overcome his love of life and
refuse his sovereign's immoral demand, even though he is not confident
about the likelihood that he actually would, given the strength of his desire to live. Kant's view is that the moral reasons he has to refuse the immoral request imply that there is a relevant counterfactual scenario in
which he would refuse his sovereign's demand, even if it is not more likely
than alternative scenarios in which he accepts the immoral demand in
order to preserve his life.

Kant's position is that a morally competent agent's motivational dispositions to act well might be very weak but that this weakness would not

undermine his moral competence. As long as a person who acts badly had a reason to act better, there is a possible scenario, albeit different in many respects from the actual, and perhaps less likely than other scenarios, in which he would have controlled his desire to act badly. On that basis, we can hold him to be morally competent and accountable for his wrongdoing. To deny his accountability would be to maintain that there is *no* scenario under which the agent rejects his bad motives for action, which is to say that he is driven entirely by irrational motives.

Kant takes this view because he accepts that morality can be very demanding. He thinks the difficulty of meeting moral demands should not undermine our confidence in a moral agent's competence to satisfy those demands, however unlikely it is that he will actually satisfy them. The wrongdoer who succumbs to immoral motives is responsible— blameworthy, punishable—for his moral failure.[23] He is responsible as long as he recognizes that he has some reason to act morally, in which case there is a possibility that he could do what he ought to do.

When it comes to mentally ill defendants, the law takes roughly this view. The widely influential *M'Naghten* insanity test, formulated by the British House of Lords in 1843, states that a defendant shall not be found guilty if there is evidence that "he was laboring under such a defect of reason as (1) not to know the nature and quality of the act he was doing or (2) not to know that the act was wrong."[24] This standard is operative in most American criminal law jurisdictions. It excuses from criminal liability only defendants who fail to meet minimal requirements of rationality. As we saw in Chapter 1, many forms of mental illness do not qualify as grounds for an insanity defense by this criterion. Kant's adulterer would surely pass the *M'Naghten* test for moral competence, and so would anyone with even the weakest inkling that a course of action he has in mind is morally wrong.

Kant thought that insofar as we take ourselves to act for reasons of any kind, we must understand ourselves as free to act on our best reasons. He argued that without a commitment to our freedom, so understood, we could not activate or make sense of our own agency. Acting for reasons essentially involves a perspective that is both reflective and normative. Thus Kant proposed, in effect, that we reverse-engineer our notion of freedom to fit the demands of rational agency: we should understand ourselves to be as free as we need to be in order to make sense of our-selves as creatures who act for good reasons.[25] Kant also thought that since we share a common rational nature with other people, we must ascribe a similar freedom to them. The framework upon which we rely to act and to make sense of human behavior is a rational one, and failure to ac-knowledge the universality of its application would be inconsistent.

Kant is correct that we understand ourselves and other people as fun-damentally responsive to reasons, and it is true that a rational framework for understanding human behavior is useful and even inevitable.[26] Setting aside cases of clear rational dysfunction, it makes sense to treat one an-other as rational creatures, and implausible to think we could negotiate human relationships without doing so. Nonetheless, skeptical doubts about the scope of a person's moral competence can arise when a person struggles with the demands of morality, and we might begin to wonder whether Kant's notion of moral responsibility is too strict. We might wonder whether the counterfactual scenarios in Kant's thought experi-ments are relevantly similar to actual scenarios we encounter. We may come to doubt a rational person's moral competence.

Kant thought that any rational being must acknowledge the binding nature of morality: moral demands are imperatives of reason. Yet he admitted that however hard we try, we might fail, morally speaking, to demonstrate good will. (According to Kant, a person with a good will is a person who acts out of respect for the moral law.) Kant wrote with convic-tion that "we like to flatter ourselves with the false claim to a more noble motive; but in fact we can never, even by the strictest examination, completely plumb the depths of the secret incentives of our actions."[27] If we cannot ever really know why a person acts, presumably this also means that we cannot judge with confidence that she could have acted better, a judgment that depends on whether she would have acted other-wise in an alternative scenario. In fact, Kant believed that epistemic wor-ries about responsibility cannot be solved. Such worries are serious, given that claims about responsibility are person- and situation-specific. Kant himself took the persistent threat of the possibility of failure very seri-ously, enough so as to require faith in God. He thought that the possibility of morality depends on religious faith.[28] In effect, he conceded that skeptical worries about "moral worth" are impossible to defeat.

Nevertheless, Kant believed that morality requires us to commit ourselves to the possibility of right action. He reasoned that because we can
know what we *ought* to do, we have reason to believe that what we ought
to do is something we *could* do. His view is that judgments about moral
competence make most sense when we view them as judgments about
what it is reasonable to commit ourselves to, morally speaking, rather than
as metaphysical claims that could survive epistemic worries. Yet normative claims about which commitments are reasonable to make have metaphysical implications that are subject to skeptical challenges, at least in
some cases.[29] Rewriting claims about what we *could* do simply as claims
about what we *have reason* to do is implausibly deflationary. Metaphysi-
cally deflationary renderings of moral claims do not adequately reckon
with the moral difficulty of compromised agency. "Ought implies can" is
not equivalent to "ought implies ought" or "ought implies 'has reason to,'"
unless "has reason to" includes claims about a person's psychological dispositions and their reach.

A Kantian commitment to the principle that "ought implies can" is not
plausible. In Chapter 1 we saw that the law does not depend on the idea
that everyone who is bound by legal rules must be morally competent.
Legal norms have a point when most people are able to comply with them
for moral reasons. A legal system does not function well unless its subjects are, generally speaking, morally able and willing to comply with its
demands. Though it is inevitable that some people will conform to the
law for merely prudential reasons, others will flaunt the law, and still
others will simply be unable to meet its demands, as long as most people
can and do respect legal norms, we can rely on them to order our social
relations with one another. We can admit skepticism about the moral
competence and blameworthiness of some individuals, while upholding
legal norms. We can afford to worry about the moral justifiability of
blaming people who, while minimally rational, struggle with personal
problems and challenging circumstances. We might decide on moral
grounds that counterfactual scenarios that vary external circumstances as
radically as Kant's examples do should be counted as too *dissimilar* to
the real world. That is, we might decide that it is not reasonable to expect compliance with morality when the possibility of compliance is re-
mote. A person who satisfies a compulsion to commit a crime like assault

or theft might have refrained had the police been present, but that does not imply that he was capable of controlling himself when they were not there. We might conclude that Kant's sense of when a wrongdoer "could have" acted well is not morally relevant. But if our understanding of moral responsibility is more qualified than what Kant proposes, it fits poorly with the principles of criminal law. A minimally rational person might be liable to criminal punishment though he is not morally blameworthy for his crime.

The *Durham* Experiment

From 1949 to 1979, Judge David Bazelon sat on the United States Court of Appeals for the District of Columbia Circuit. (The "D.C. Circuit" is often described as the second most powerful in the country behind the Supreme Court.) Judge Bazelon was concerned about the bearing of mental illness on criminal responsibility. He believed that the legal basis of the insanity defense had fallen out of step with progress in the "behavioral sciences." Since the nineteenth century, the court adhered to the cognitively oriented *M'Naghten* test for insanity. In *Smith v. United States* (1929), an earlier decision from the D.C. Circuit, the court supplemented *M'Naghten*'s focus on cognitive ability by also recognizing the excusing nature of conduct driven by an "irresistible impulse":

> The modern doctrine is that the degree of insanity which will relieve the accused of the consequences of a criminal act must be such as to create in his mind an uncontrollable impulse to commit the offense charged. This impulse must be such as to override the reason and judgment and obliterate the sense of right and wrong to the extent that the accused is deprived of the power to choose between right and wrong. The mere ability to distinguish right from wrong is no longer the correct test either in civil or criminal cases, where the defense of insanity is interposed. The accepted rule in this day and age, with the great advancement in medical science as an enlightening influence on this subject, is that the accused must be capable, not only of distinguishing between right and wrong, but that he was not impelled to do the act by an irresistible impulse, which means before it will justify a verdict of ac-

quittal that his reasoning powers were so far dethroned by his dis-
eased mental condition as to deprive him of the will power to
resist the insane impulse to perpetrate the deed, though knowing
it to be wrong.[30]

Bazelon applauded the addition of the irresistible impulse test, but he worried that some forms of nonculpable agency were not covered by it. In
the 1954 case *Durham v. United States,* he wrote an opinion for the court
that adopted a broader insanity test. Under the "Durham rule," a defendant would be excused from criminal responsibility if a jury found that
an unlawful act was "the product of mental disease or mental defect."
Bazelon's aim in *Durham* was to make the insanity defense available to
any defendant whose criminal action was "produced," that is, *caused*
by mental illness. The Durham rule would extend the insanity defense
to defendants whose impairments were neither primarily cognitive nor
impulsive. Bazelon wrote, "We find that the 'irresistible impulse' test is
also inadequate in that it gives no recognition to mental illness characterized by brooding and reflection and so relegates acts caused by such
illness to the application of the inadequate right-wrong test. We conclude that a broader test should be adopted."[31]

Bazelon understood the application of the Durham rule to involve a
normative judgment. Production, or causation, by mental illness indicates
an agent's *incapacity* to have conformed to the requirements of law, yet
incapacity is not equivalent to impossibility. Bazelon reasoned that a criminal act is the product of mental disease or defect when it would not be
reasonable to expect the criminal to have complied with the law. Suppose
that we know that a person P with psychiatric diagnosis D has x percent
chance of committing criminal act A. What should the value of x be for
us to draw the conclusion that P's mental disorder D produced act A?
Where do we set the relevant threshold? A legal norm offers an answer to
this question about how serious an impairment must be before it is no
longer reasonable to have expected the defendant to have controlled his
behavior. Only when it is *unreasonable* to expect the defendant to have
controlled his behavior should it be concluded that the criminal act was
the product of disease or defect. The causal judgment depends on a
legal norm.

Bazelon appealed to negligence in tort law as a model for thinking about the normative appraisal required in a determination of criminal guilt. The law's definition of negligence—failure to exercise the degree of care that would be exercised by a reasonable person of ordinary prudence— requires a judge or jury to reach a judgment, in a given case, about how much care a reasonable person would have taken in the defendant's circumstances to avoid causing harm. In addition, negligence law calls for a judgment as to whether a defendant's failure to take adequate care functioned as a "proximate" cause of the plaintiff's injury—that is, whether the defendant's carelessness "directly" caused the injury, or whether, instead, other forces for which the defendant was not responsible had interceded, thus rendering the defendant's carelessness irrelevant (from a legal perspective) to the injury.[32] Both factors—fault and proximate cause—require a decision-maker (typically, a jury) to exercise judgment. Bazelon wrote, "In the same way the jury decided the 'fault' issue in negligence cases, we wanted the jury to decide whether the mental abnormality was too serious and the causal connection [between the abnormality and the wrongdoer's action] too direct to impose guilt in criminal cases. Thus the jury would make factual determinations, but also would fix the legal norm against which the mental condition and its relationship to the behavior must be measured."[33] According to the legal norms that govern liability for negligence, a mere failure to take some precaution, along with a mere causal connection between that failure and an injury to another, does not suffice. The failure must be determined to have amounted to action that a reasonably prudent person would not have taken, and the causal connection must be determined to have been sufficiently direct to count as a proximate cause. Likewise, Bazelon argued, the question of whether a defendant's crime should be excused on the ground of insanity requires a *judgment* under applicable legal norms as to whether his conduct was connected "in the right way" to a psychological incapacity or weakness.

The application of the relevant legal norm depends on psychological facts, specifically, facts about how difficult it would have been for the defendant to resist engaging in the criminal behavior. Bazelon reasoned that expert testimony should be brought to bear on matters of fact concerning this level of difficulty. He instructed juries to decide, in view of those facts, what it was reasonable to have expected of the defendant under the circumstances in which the criminal act was committed. The jury would be informed by facts about the defendant's psychology, and would measure the moral relevance of those psychological facts against other relevant factors, including the importance of protecting the public from the criminal actions of mentally disturbed individuals. A jury's evaluation of a defendant's insanity defense would thus be a function of an understanding of the psychological facts together with the value the jury assigns to the defendant's interests, on the one hand, and considerations of public safety, on the other. Just as the requirements of due care become more stringent when the possibility of injury to another person is greater, the degree of self-control it is reasonable to expect, even of a person with psychological problems, increases with heightened danger to others. A jury would decide that a defendant's behavior was "produced" by a disease only when they found that it would have been *unreasonable* to expect self-control, in view of the agent's psychological problems and his danger to other people. They need not believe it was impossible for the agent to have controlled herself. The court envisioned that, in this way, the relevant legal norm would be specified and applied by a jury.[34]

As noted, Bazelon considered appraisals of psychological difficulty by experts to be crucial to the application of the Durham rule. Yet he discovered over time that it was extremely difficult to get experts to provide such information without themselves rendering a conclusory judgment about whether a defendant's mental disease or defect produced the criminal behavior—the very judgment that was the business of the jury. Experts tended not to be forthcoming about the nature of their examinations of a given defendant, or about what they understood about the origins and dynamics of the defendant's condition. They did not specify the basis of their conclusions or the limits of their knowledge. Instead they tended summarily to affirm or to deny that the Durham rule was satisfied in the case. In an attempt to find a way around this problem, in *Washington v. United States,* Bazelon's court held that experts were actually forbidden from rendering a judgment on whether the criminal act was the product of a mental disorder. Bazelon found that this instruction was ineffective:

the experts ignored it. Eventually he concluded that the Durham experiment was a failure. In 1972 he ruled with the majority in *United States v. Brawner* to overturn the Durham rule. Today most jurisdictions have returned to a version of the *M'Naghten* rule.

Lessons from Durham

Why did experts in Bazelon's court insist on delivering conclusory testimony? In a given case of egregious wrongdoing, an expert might identify a cluster of traits exhibited by a defendant that fits a psychiatric diagnosis. This might provide an explanation, in some sense, for abnormal behavior, but the explanation is limited in scope. This is partly because prevailing classifications of mental illness do not include guidelines for understanding how dysfunctional traits cause particular behavior. According to one way of thinking about mental illness, a mental illness is a set of symptoms correlated with a characteristic pattern of behavior. The *Diagnostic and Statistical Manual for Mental Disorders* (DSM) suggests this view, by offering a kind of checklist of symptoms for diagnosing mental illnesses. So understood, a diagnosis of mental disorder implies nothing about how or why a person has the symptoms, why she engages in the characteristic pattern of behavior, or how likely it is that she will do so.

A psychiatric diagnosis does imply that a mentally ill person has difficulty acting according to certain norms of rationality, sociality, or morality. We should understand a person with a psychiatric condition to have a diminished capacity for acting in accordance with these norms, while persons whose psychology is not dysfunctional might be considered free to act in accordance with norms of rationality, sociality, and morality. But without a grasp of what causes a person to exhibit certain symptoms, it is difficult and perhaps impossible to tell *how* difficult it is for an impaired person to think, feel, and act normally. To calibrate the difficulty of overcoming the challenges posed by a psychiatric problem, we need some grasp of the conditions that trigger a person's behavior abnormalities. We could then anticipate how a person's behavior would or would not change when relevant factors are varied. For example, agoraphobia is mild or severe, depending on the size of the crowd that triggers it, among other factors. Only across a complex field of possibilities could we appraise a person's impairment and grade its severity.

In fact, our scientific understanding of the causes of human behavior is not refined enough to enable us to formulate anything more than a rough approximation of the relative difficulty for a given person of reckoning with a psychological problem. Moreover, such approximations have a significantly impersonal basis. An individual evaluation depends on a generalization over a class of people exhibiting a cluster of symptoms, behavioral patterns, and certain self-reported psychological states, yet there could be significant variation within this class. Self-reports are also strikingly opaque on the matter of how hard the agent *tried* to resist the aberrant course of action. As a result, the predictive power of any psychological assessment is poor.

Rough and impersonal generalizations are not the sort of individualized judgments sought by a court of justice. A loose approximation of how people who display the characteristic symptoms of a psychiatric disorder tend to act, under circumstances that often provoke those symptoms, is an inadequate legal basis for a defense or a conviction. The court seeks proof that an individual has committed a certain criminal act and, in response to an insanity defense, that the defendant was not incapable of having complied with the law. But evidence supporting a more precise appraisal of the likelihood that a person who has displayed characteristic symptoms of psychiatric disorder in the past would act, under the defendant's circumstances, in the way the defendant acted—evidence that the jury could use to determine whether a psychological abnormality *caused* the defendant to commit a crime—was not something experts were able to provide. Psychiatrists in Bazelon's court were willing to offer individualized appraisals of the psychological capacities of defendants, but the nature of those judgments was intuitive and their bases mostly unelaborated. Psychiatrists had trouble explaining the reasons they had for judgments they made about the cause of a particular person's behavior, beyond citing statistical generalities or referring to the psychiatrist's clinical experience interacting with the individual in question. Moving beyond statistical generalizations or a summary judgment about the psychiatrist's overall experience with the patient, in order to provide the jury with concrete evidence that would support an individualized assessment, was not something they were able to do. This presented a problem for the court.

Part of the problem is our limited knowledge of human psychology. Another is that medical classifications were not invented for legal purposes; their primary purpose is not to explain or to predict behavior by reference to psychological causes. Rather, medical classifications are oriented to clinical research questions and treatment protocols. There is also a difficult strand of this problem that relates psychological evaluation to social context. Psychological traits are responses to circumstances and other stimuli as well as being determinants of behavior. Understanding a person's responses in context is important for distinguishing between normal, deviant (willful), and dysfunctional behavior. Symptoms of psychological dysfunction are subject to social and cultural variation, and appraisals of dysfunction depend on social and cultural norms, as well as measures of individual distress. Blood revenge, honor killings, "bride" abduction, and belief in evil spirits are normalized in some groups and are indicators of individual psychological disorder in others.[35] Cultural factors also influence where the severity threshold of pathological distress is located. According to Ruth Benedict, the Zuni of Arizona regard extreme passivity and fatalism as belonging to a philosophically grounded and culturally defined personality style.[36] Characteristics that would be regarded as symptoms of clinical depression in mainstream American society are considered normal and even admirable traits by the Zuni.[37] This does not make the concept of clinical depression a Eurocentric construct, but it does mean that what counts as an example of it must be understood in relation to cultural norms and learned behavior.[38] A person might display the characteristic symptoms of a psychiatric disorder for reasons that do not indicate an underlying pathology or dysfunction.

Furthermore, psychological distress is an understandable and normal response to stressful and traumatic circumstances. For example, a person serving a prison sentence might experience the psychological traits identified with depression. In that circumstance, depressive symptoms might not indicate a psychological pathology. Similarly, experiencing the humiliation of poverty with no realistic prospects for earning a decent living can lead to depressive symptoms; this might not be a sign of compromised mental health. On the other hand, symptoms and behavior that seem normal as responses to difficult circumstances or forms of mistreatment are consistent with underlying damage to a person in ways that are hard to detect. For example, reactions of distress that seem like normal responses to loss or trauma may be identified as pathological when they do not recede with the passage of time.[39] When circumstantial stressors causing distress are ongoing, however, it may not be possible to parse normal and dysfunctional distress.[40]

Sometimes pathological symptoms are revealed only in unpredictable ways. The shock and disbelief of family members when their loved one commits a serious crime are not uncommon. Not all of this is denial. We can be wrong about a person's value commitments and priorities, how successfully a person has survived troubling experiences, or, more generally, how psychologically healthy a person is. Among individuals who might seem untroubled, we might be surprised later at behavior we did not anticipate. For example, unexpected suicides reveal hidden traumas and psychological pain. It is often hard to identify the severity of an individual's suffering. Suicide is the tenth leading cause of death among Americans, claiming over 40,000 lives in 2013, and it is the second leading cause of death for Americans between the ages of fifteen and thirty-four.[41] Not all suicides are unexpected, but many of them are.

It is therefore understandable that the experts in Bazelon's court did not stick to the facts and resorted instead to conclusory normative judgments. They offered opinions on the question of what it is reasonable to expect, given rough behavioral predictions across a relevant classes of cases, in view of the various interests at stake, and given what they perceived to be relevant social norms. But in so doing they usurped the role of the jury.

The court's experiment with the Durham rule does not inspire confidence in the ability of experts to answer difficult questions about the moral capacities of criminal wrongdoers. The possibility of serious though not totalizing psychological impairments—ones that can be difficult to identify and to calibrate—can threaten our confidence in a given person's moral competence at the time of action. When a person fails morally, we might well wonder what underwrites our belief that she was competent enough to have done better. We may come to doubt, in a given case, that a moral "ought" implies "can" or, rather, that a moral "should not have acted badly" implies a "could have acted well."

Although the Durham experiment failed, it carries with it important lessons. Evaluations of moral competence depend on norms. An assessment of moral competence is a function of the *reasonableness* of moral demands. We judge someone to be morally competent only when it is reasonable to expect that person to act well, and we could insist that at some level of difficulty—not impossibility, but difficulty—expectations of moral success would no longer be reasonable. A judgment of moral competence, so understood, would not be a function of the applicability of a moral "ought." Moral oughts and reasonable expectations might diverge. A person might fail to act as she ought to without disappointing expectations that reasonably take her psychological limitations into account: she might be excused from blame and responsibility for her moral failure, although her agency as a wrongdoer remains intact. Thus we might accept Kant's proposal that whether a rational agent "could have" acted better depends on a normative judgment, yet insist that the mere possibility of right action is not a reasonable basis for moral expectations. Instead, we might maintain that a morally competent individual is someone about whom we can say, not only that it is possible but also substantially likely, that she would act well. To do so, however, raises moral questions about how likely is "likely enough" and difficult epistemic questions about whether the relevant standard has been met—questions that, in many cases, should lead us to reject attempts to make criminal liability depend on moral blameworthiness. The supposition of moral competence on which moral blameworthiness depends cannot be established on the basis of evidence available to courts of law. Therefore, criminal liability should not depend on that evidence.

Bazelon's experiment demonstrates that a notion of individual responsibility that is calibrated to the difficulty of complying with the demands of morality and law cannot function well as a legal norm for determining criminal liability. It will not work because it is so hard to provide evidence that enables us to understand how difficult it would have been for a person to have acted better than she did. Psychiatrists cannot produce evidence that would enable a jury to decide whether a defendant who committed a crime was or was not capable of complying with the law. If psychiatrists cannot do it, neither can the courts.

Nevertheless, appreciating the possibility that a wrongdoer's moral competence is limited can guide and temper our personal responses to people who are found criminally guilty. Our moral thinking can be sensitive to the fact that it is more difficult, sometimes much more difficult, for some people to meet the demands of morality. We might temper our blame without relinquishing the moral ought. Chapters 3 and 4 develop and expand this idea. The hardships that mitigate blame include psychological problems, and they also extend to circumstantial difficulties, including social injustice.

Humanizing Morality

Interpersonally, we commit ourselves to an understanding of one another as morally capable of conforming to ethical norms. The moral expectations that guide personal interactions and are a source of the value we place on relationships depend on this commitment. An allegiance to viewing one another as morally capable, however, comes with an ambivalence that emerges when our expectations are disappointed. The source of this tension is the vulnerability of a person's moral competence to skeptical doubt. Skepticism about moral capacity makes the justification of our blaming practices insecure.

Kant and his contemporary followers might object that the ambivalence I have identified in our understanding of each other as capable of acting for moral reasons indicates less than full respect for humanity. I disagree. I think the righteous condemnation we feel toward others can function as a vent for the anxiety we feel about real limits to our own self-understanding and self-control, limits Kant himself recognized. I have argued that our rational agency is bounded by psychological factors we do not control and that sometimes these limitations preclude acting for moral reasons. We could stake the possibility of justice on denying this, as many Kantians would. Or we could accept our limitations and design our institutions accordingly. We could negotiate skepticism about moral competence without relinquishing the importance of a more humanizing morality, provided that we give up on the notion of retributive justice.

We should distinguish between the evaluation of acts and the evaluation of people. Evaluations of people are fluid and contextual, and are not the subject of moral imperatives, or so I will argue. There can be a variety of morally reasonable responses to wrongdoing, including the possibility of compassion for wrongdoers and modesty about our own grasp of human psychology. People who violate the law and transgress the rights of other people sometimes have hard lives. Morality can be sensitive to personal difficulties and appreciate the challenges involved in calibrating their relevance to questions of personal responsibility. In fact, we will see that a morally sensitive theory of excuses will take us beyond assessments of individual moral capacity, even those that are responsive to psychological problems and challenging social circumstances, in order to appraise the difficulty for even morally competent agents of the morally right course of action.

THREE

BLAME AND EXCUSES

A WRONGFUL ACT—whether an insensitive remark, a negligently caused harm, or a heinous crime—invites moral responses ranging from righteous anger, retributive harming, or pained resignation to cool detachment, understanding and acceptance, therapeutic engagement, or empathetic distress. Amidst this array of possible responses to wrongdoing are two kinds of moral judgments: the judgment that an agent's act is wrong, and the judgment that the agent is, or is not, worthy of blame. These kinds of judgments might complement one another, or they might come apart: not every wrong is blameworthy.

Moral philosophers mostly neglect the significance of wrongdoing that is not blameworthy, yet the possibility that some wrongdoers are less culpable is important, for it can help us to think about the range of approaches we might take toward individuals who act wrongly. It can help us to recognize that a blaming response to wrongdoing is not merely the auxiliary of moral standards of right action, made morally necessary by violations of those standards. Moral responses to wrongdoing must be understood in relation to their ambitions, which include shaping future personal or impersonal relationships according to the values, for example, of love or political membership.[1] Various possible and reasonable aspirations for relationships typically permit a variety of responses.

Judgments of wrongness are act-focused: they concern an action's failure to meet criteria of morally permissible behavior—in particular, whether an action can be justified to people who are negatively affected. Philosophers engage in lively debate about how to calibrate negative effects and how exactly harmful consequences bear on standards of morally acceptable behavior. Here I simply take a stand. Moral thinking that takes wrongdoing seriously must be sensitive to what philosophers refer to as "deontological considerations." Such considerations evaluate action with deference to the objections of people who are most harmed by it. A deontological perspective tracks the harms of deception, intimidation, and torture, for example, with particular attention to the people who are deceived, intimidated, and tortured. Harms like these are not justifiable to people who suffer them, even when the harm done is balanced, overall, by good consequences, say, through benefits to third parties. By contrast, consequentialist theories perform moral evaluations solely by reference to the consequences overall, for all people affected, directly or indirectly. If a terrorist is tortured, some might argue, society could be made safer by information the torture yields, and if so, the use of torture would be justified. Deontological objections to torture are not defeated by this sort of argument.

A deontological morality also recognizes that there are forms of behavior—assault, molestation, kidnapping—that are morally wrong, whether or not the wrongdoer's action expresses ill will and apart from evaluations of the wrongdoer's responsibility. Wrongdoing is identified by reference to whether the act in question conformed or did not conform to a relevant moral norm, irrespective of whether the wrongdoer should be blamed or punished for having committed the wrong. Wrongdoing is not best thought of as a matter of the wrongdoer's accountability. A person who lacks moral responsibility for her actions might nonetheless wrongfully violate another person's rights.

Determinations of blame and blameworthiness are person-focused rather than act-focused. They concern how to respond to someone who has acted badly. Moral responses such as anger, punishment, or pity might be considered appropriate, even deserved, in view of considerations that reveal a wrongdoer to be more or less blameworthy. Excuses inhibit blame as a response to wrongdoing and create room for sympathy and other non-punitive responses. Understanding how considerations that diminish a wrongdoer's accountability can support a compassionate response to wrongful conduct opens up a range of reasonable responses to wrongdoing.

Compassion is a response naturally associated with mitigating blame, yet we might think of compassion as belonging to a family of emotions and attitudes, including kindness, sympathy, empathy, pity, understanding, sorrow, mercy, and generosity. Excuses appeal to this pool of attitudes and emotions in various ways.[2] Dispassionate responses to wrongdoing are also morally permissible and not incompatible with acknowledging the moral seriousness of wrongdoing. Appreciating the array of possible responses enables us to see that taking wrongdoing seriously does not demand a blaming response.

The distinction between justification and excuse, as I discuss it in this chapter, is a moral one. It differs from a distinction that has received considerable attention in legal theory. Legal theorists distinguish between *justifications,* such as self-defense, which function to convert prima facie unlawful conduct into lawful conduct, and *excuses,* like insanity, which do not render the excused actor's conduct lawful, but nonetheless mitigate a defendant's responsibility and call for reduced punishment or no punishment at all. In many jurisdictions, insanity excuses a person from punishment even though she committed a criminal act.

Legal theorist Mitchell Berman has pointed out that there is a structural similarity between these moral and legal distinctions.[3] Morally speaking, a person who acts in a justified way has not acted wrongly. Legally speaking, a person with a justification has not committed a crime. Moral considerations relevant to determining whether an action is morally wrong and legally admissible considerations for determining whether a person's act is criminal, both involve evaluating actions with reference to action-guiding norms.

Excuses, whether morally or legally established, indicate diminished responsibility. A person who has a *moral* excuse is not blameworthy, even though he may have done something wrong. For example, a person threatened by another person with violence might comply with the other's demand to assist in robbing a store, and moral blameworthiness for assisting the robbery might be mitigated by the threat. Moral factors that bear on a person's blameworthiness for his wrongdoing are analogous to legally relevant considerations for determining whether a person who has committed a criminal act is punishable. A person who acted under threat might be able to establish the *legally* recognized excuse of duress, and if he does establish it, he is liable to a lesser punishment or escapes punishment entirely. Both moral and legal excuses involve assessing a wrongdoer's personal circumstances and mental state, and both apply within the domain of established wrongdoing. They concern personal responsibility for wrongdoing.

The structural similarity between legal and moral excuses, however, is misleading. Legal excuses commonly signal lack of moral blameworthiness, but the reverse is not true. Many morally relevant excuses lack legal recognition. In other words, the universe of moral excuses is significantly broader than the universe of excuses recognized in criminal law.[4] As we have seen, a person might be legally guilty and eligible for punishment without being morally blameworthy, for instance, because she is mentally ill, immature, or desperately poor, but would not on these grounds be entitled to a lesser criminal punishment.

A system of criminal law should rely on moral reasoning to rationalize its catalogue of criminal offenses. Only serious moral wrongs should be criminalized, and this calls for changes in the criminal law, since most criminal justice systems include some infractions that are not morally wrong.[5] Moral reasoning also supports the legal recognition of excuses, including insanity, duress, and infancy, since the law should be designed to apply only to people who are at least minimally rational and have a reasonable opportunity to conform their behavior to the requirements of law. As we will see, however, there are good reasons for the law to resist incorporating the full range of morally excusing considerations. Excuses recognized by the criminal law are bound to fall short of what a reasonable morality would affirm as mitigating factors, and this alone does not indicate a problem with the law. Accordingly, we cannot assume that a person who is eligible for punishment is morally blameworthy for her criminal act.

This conclusion goes against the grain of popular thinking about criminal justice among legal theorists, moral philosophers, and the general public, at least in a punishment-heavy society like the United States.[6] That should not inhibit us from taking a critical stance. Thinking carefully about the limits of moral blame's relevance to criminal law should lead us to resist popular moralizing about people who are convicted of crimes. Showing that we can take wrongdoing seriously without morally blaming wrongdoers bolsters the case against retributive accounts of criminal justice and other theories of criminal justice that are heavily invested in moral blame. Retributivists and nonretributivists alike have reasons to be compassionate, or at least less morally severe, toward wrongdoers.

Blame

When we evaluate people, we don't merely appraise what they do; we judge *them*, personally, in view of how they act. We relate a person's actions to her qualities as a person.[7] Our moral appraisal of people is signaled by judgments, attitudes, and behavior we direct toward them. For example, criticism of a person for selfish behavior is signaled by disapproval, corrective interventions, or distancing oneself from her. Blaming responses include the "reactive attitudes" of resentment and moral indignation and the tendency to engage in retributive behavior. Such responses are commonly associated with condemning and punishing. But blaming responses might also be understood, more broadly, to include less retributive sentiments, such as disappointment, sadness, or resignation. Although they are not oriented punitively, these attitudes respond to an agent's wrongdoing and take it seriously. They may be accompanied by responses such as calling for an explanation or apology, lowering or otherwise changing expectations regarding future interactions, breaking off a relationship, trying to make the wrongdoer feel guilty, requiring that she make amends, and so on. These responses, as I understand them, do not necessarily or even typically involve commitment to the idea that the wrongdoer should suffer pain or some other deprivation as a matter of justice. Still, they qualify as blame when they accompany or express moral criticism of a person for her wrongful actions and are thought to be deserved.[8]

Specifically, blaming responses accompany moral criticism of a person for harboring judgments or attitudes that interfere with other people's moral confidence in her. Blame points to a person's moral flaws and connects them to aspects of character, disposition, or personhood, on the one hand, and some deserved response to those flaws, on the other. The moralized anger, demands for contrition, emotional disengagement, or punitive responses typical of blame are thought to be responses a person deserves because the damage she has done to her relationships with other people reveals that she has morally objectionable personal qualities, and she is responsible for having those qualities. Clearly, blaming is morally significant: it changes relationships and has lasting effects on them, as well as on the self-understanding and self-esteem of the people involved.

Thus far I have suggested that perceptions of morally flawed behavior steer blaming responses. But things can work in the opposite direction, too. Our sense of the appropriateness of blame may solidify our judgment that a person has acted wrongly.[9] Blaming responses may sharpen our attention to what exactly a person has done wrong. Feeling affronted may prompt a person to focus on how she has been mistreated. To be clear, I do not endorse a view that would reduce judgments of wrongdoing to those of blameworthiness.[10] A tiger escapes blame for the same reasons that it cannot be said to engage in wrongdoing, but the same is not true of people. A person might display the moral agency involved in wrong-doing without qualifying for blame. A guiding interest of my approach is in how judgments of wrongdoing and blameworthiness can be sepa-rated, as well as in how they interact. The interaction of these distinct judgments is morally illuminating because it helps us to understand the depth and variety of morality's norms, from private to public, limited to general, and hypothetical to categorical.

I will group retributive and nonretributive responses together, broadly, as blaming responses when they are taken to be responses that a wrong-doer is thought to deserve for her personal moral flaws, flaws exemplified in wrongdoing. Not only is there a variety of responses that can be counted as blaming behavior. The variation in blaming responses we find appro-priate to similar transgressions is also striking. Some people are blamed more harshly than others, not because the wrongs they commit are worse, but because of dissimilarities in their motivations for acting, as well as differences in their responsibility for having these motives. People who act from spite, jealousy, selfishness, hatred, or prejudice, for example, ordinarily seem more blameworthy than people who act out of fear, low self-esteem, resistance to injustice, or a desire to protect the innocent or to rescue the vulnerable. Persons whose actions are produced in part by physical pain, mistreatment, and mental distress also inspire sympathetic responses. Battered women who kill their abusers have a credible claim to be treated more sympathetically than other people who commit entirely unjustified acts of violence; this claim is to some degree recognized in law.

Some variation in blaming responses has to do with the position a blamer occupies in relation to a person under moral scrutiny. T. M. Scanlon and others have described the positional nature of blame as a matter of the *standing* a given person or group has to blame some wrongdoer.[11] We might feel less entitled to blame the battered wife, partly because the abuse she endured is facilitated by morally objectionable aspects of gender-based relationships that we do not consistently reject, even though we should. We might feel that we, collectively, have let her and others like her down by failing to protect her rights or properly empower her with opportunities. We may feel that we lack an appropriate position from which to blame her; sharing in the blame, even remotely, may seem to disqualify us from dishing it out. Engaging in moral criticism under the circumstances seems evasive and morally distasteful.

The positional nature of blame can mostly be segregated from judgments of blameworthiness. Determinations of blameworthiness, while not detached from human relationships, are less positional. It can be inappropriate for some people to engage in assessments of a person's blameworthiness, much less blame her, because, for example, doing so gives the impression of distracting from their own complicity. Imagine fans judging that football players should blame their team's coach for his indifference to the danger of brain injuries in the normal course of the game, though the fans themselves disregard evidence of harm to the players that would otherwise interfere with their enjoyment as spectators.[12] It might seem dishonest for the fans to recommend blaming the coach. But other people who are uninvolved may have grounds for believing that a coach, and perhaps the fans as well, have acted in ways that give injured players reasons to blame them.

Variation in moral responses—from blame to sympathy—can sometimes be attributed to moral pluralism: as we will see, differences in moral judgments and attitudes might be traced to differences in people's values. A plurality of values is compatible with full rationality, and differences in people's moral responses need not indicate that some people are morally biased, morally indifferent, or lack objectivity. But value pluralism does not explain the variation I am now discussing. Many people would agree that a person who is desperate for money to treat a sick child is less blameworthy for a theft she commits than someone who steals for the thrill of it. Most people would agree that child "soldiers" who murder or maim civilians are less blameworthy than their adult counterparts. Though we may disagree about where to set the threshold of relevant difficulty, we may agree that a person's difficult circumstances or psychological limitations have a bearing on evaluations of her blameworthiness. A person's circumstances and psychology may lead us, for good reasons, to find her less blameworthy than someone else for similar morally criticizable behavior.[13] Something interferes with familiar processes of inference from wrongful action to blameworthy agency. Wrongdoing, we think, is wholly or partly excused.

Some philosophical theories underplay the difference between moral appraisals of act versus agent. Peter Strawson maintains that excuses like acting under threat of physical harm, or some forms of ignorance, undermine the ordinary sense of an agent's having done wrong by demonstrating that there was no faulty moral judgment, disregard, or ill will on the agent's part.[14] This position, also defended by R. Jay Wallace, among others, has been influential.[15] According to Strawson and Wallace, excuses point to a missing link between an action and the agent's intentions and attitudes; her bad acts contrast with her "good will," or, at least, with the absence of bad will. We are all familiar with excuses like "She didn't mean it," "He didn't understand what he was doing," "She was only trying to help." One sort of excuse—"He was pushed"—shows that the agent did not really even act; agency was undermined by an external cause.

In fact, by undermining connections between action and will, excuses of this sort—complete excuses—divorce a person from her actions. Being pushed is a clear example of an act (if it even counts as an act) that a person does not intend, endorse, or identify with. Others include instances in which a person is tricked, manipulated, or intimidated into doing something. The result is that wrongdoing is only apparent: the excused agent hasn't really done the wrong, or the wrong is not appropriately attributable to her. It only seems otherwise until the excuse is unearthed. Excuses of this sort do not raise deeper issues about the difference between moral evaluations of act and agent. Rather, they imply that these evaluations are one and the same. What normally would be wrong is not wrong under these sorts of excusing conditions.

But complete or exonerating excuses are a special case. By contrast, there is a range of cases in which we draw a clear distinction between our moral appraisal of an action and our varying attitudes toward the agent. These are cases in which a person acts in a way that demonstrates moral disregard for other people, the act is clearly ascribed to the person, and it is not morally justified or permissible. An excuse in this kind of context does not threaten the notion that the agent acted wrongly, even if it establishes that she should not be blamed, or should not fully be blamed for what she has done.

Examples extend from the ordinary to the extraordinary: the parent under emotional strain who abuses her child, the child who is mistreated by her parent and in turn bullies someone else, the inmate who brutalizes another person to avoid appearing weak, the solider in a field of battle who shoots an unarmed civilian on orders from a superior, the alcoholic who drives after drinking, the compulsive who tells a lie, the paranoid schizophrenic who commits an act of hateful violence. We might excuse such agents, wholly or in part, from blame for their morally faulty actions. The circumstances or psychological vulnerabilities of these agents fit uncomfortably with blaming attitudes and judgments. Yet in each of these cases the agent acts intentionally and for reasons we can criticize on moral grounds.

The moral considerations illustrated by the cases I have in mind extend beyond the class of considerations recognized by the law as excuses from criminal liability. As we have seen, the excuses that are recognized as legal defenses are few and far between. Criminal law's recognized excuses are limited mostly to duress, coercion, and some mistakes when they show lack of *mens rea,* the mental element—intention, knowledge, recklessness, or negligence—of crimes. As we saw in Chapter 2, psychologically excusing abnormalities are largely limited to insanity, which is very narrowly defined. Insanity as a legal defense is a person's inability, at the time the crime was committed, to distinguish between right and wrong. So understood, insanity is an extreme and rare instance of the broader category of mental illness. Most morally disabling forms of mental illness, including significant impairments to moral motivation, empathy for others, and the like, are not recognized as legal defenses. Thus, a person who is not morally blameworthy can properly (so far as the law is concerned) be found guilty of criminal wrongdoing. The mental or circumstantial obstacles she faces may excuse her from moral blame, even though her intentional behavior violates criminal laws and renders her eligible for punishment.[16]

To be clear, then, I am interested in excuses that might not succeed as legal defenses against charges of criminal wrongdoing, or legal grounds for exemption from punishment, yet are relevant to how we think about criminal wrongdoers. Furthermore, I am interested in considerations that mitigate blame without providing a full excuse. That is, I am interested in the scalar nature of excuses—the spectrum of considerations that diminish accountability from a little to a lot. The aspect of law most connected with variation in the weight of excuses concerns whether punishment should be adjusted on the basis of mitigating factors. Typically these determinations are made in a separate sentencing phase of a criminal procedure, after the defendant has pled guilty or been found guilty at trial. In the sentencing phase, the defendant's character and circumstances may be introduced as bearing on how much punishment the defendant should receive. The legal practice that separates the sentencing phase from the finding of criminal guilt supports my contention that judging the blameworthiness of a person is and should be guided by a set of norms distinct from those we consult to evaluate the moral quality of a person's actions. Yet once we understand how distinct they are, we will see that considerations of blameworthiness do not constitute an appropriate basis for criminal sentencing. It is not enough for criminal law to segregate blame to the sentencing phase of a trial. A criminal justice system should get out of the blame game altogether.

In challenging Strawson's and Wallace's picture, I draw on the intuition that persons can be excused, in whole or in part, from blame, despite their wrongdoing. I will now identify moral reasons to maintain that an agent who is excused from blame can nevertheless have acted wrongly—the judgment that Strawson and Wallace resist.

Right and Wrong

A morality of right and wrong supports relationships of respect and consideration between people who may or may not care personally about one another. By offering criteria to guide our thinking, morality helps us to specify our mutual obligations, both personal and impersonal. Often, if not always, these criteria can be formulated as principles. Public recognition of moral principles eases conflicts between people that arise from the biases of self- and group-interest. The equal standing of persons under the scope of general moral principles promotes a sense of commonality, equality, and mutual sympathy. In these and other ways, social life is enhanced by principles of moral right and wrong, when those principles are justified.

The public and pragmatic dimensions of morality generate some pressure within moral thinking to handle exceptions to general principles by tempering blame rather than complicating action-guiding norms. Expanding principles of right and wrong to include their exceptions and qualifications is cumbersome. It requires either that we narrow our understanding of the relevant action-types captured by a moral principle in order to reflect contextual factors, or that we enumerate qualifications and exceptions to more general principles. Either of these strategies can detract from general principles that are intuitively appealing enough to capture our attention when we seek guidance from morality. To avoid this, we abstract, to some extent, in moral thinking from details that characterize differences in the circumstances to which we apply principles. Sometimes these details, including factors that make it difficult to act morally, have a bearing on what it is reasonable to expect people to do. It may not be reasonable to expect a person to deal forthrightly with someone who has betrayed her in the past, and we might not blame her for withholding or manipulating the truth. Or perhaps more obviously, we would not reasonably expect someone suffering from an attack of paranoia to refrain from making groundless accusations against other people, and we would be unlikely to blame her for her remarks. We might maintain, however, that the manipulation and groundless accusations were morally objectionable. It might be true that people hurt by these actions were done wrong. When we formulate norms that prohibit people from doing wrong, we meaningfully abstract from circumstances that mitigate blame.

We also abstract, to some extent, from differences in people's moral understanding and moral motivation. Affirming moral standards of right and wrong makes sense when many people are responsive to them. Though some people lack moral understanding or concern and are unlikely to change, most people are capable of meeting moral expectations, generally and in the moment. Unfortunately, there are some people who have no capacity to respond to morality's demands. But this does not defeat the social purposes served by action-guiding principles that most people can and do abide by.

These abstractions might seem merely to represent pragmatic compromises to the justifiable content of moral requirements, but pressures to abstract and to generalize in moral thinking about right and wrong have the support of important normative considerations. There are moral reasons to treat all rational persons as capable of moral action even though, in fact, some are not.[17] I will set aside the class of people who are incapacitated, generally speaking, to evaluate reasons for action of any sort: prudential, moral, or instrumental, even those concerning merely the means to immediate gratification. Such people are obviously irrational and unfit for practical directives of a reason-giving sort. This leaves us with the category of broadly rational people. In some cases, it might be difficult to distinguish between a person who can and one who cannot appreciate the difference between expressing angry feelings and abusing other people. And there is a moral difference between a person who is capable of impulse control and chooses not to and someone who cannot restrain herself. Psychologists recognize the difference between a narcissist and someone who simply chooses not to self-regulate, between a pathological liar and an ordinary dishonest person, between a kleptomaniac and a reprehensible thief. Still, it can be hard to tell whether a particular person has or lacks moral responsiveness, especially since she might act in accordance with morality for reasons of self-interest.

In affirming standards of right and wrong action, we treat all people who are at least minimally rational as though they are capable of responding to the demands of morality, even though some people lack the capacity to understand or to be motivated by those demands. It is arrogant and disrespectful to presume to be able to tell who has and who lacks basic moral competence. Persons who are capable of guiding their actions with moral principles might reasonably object to being treated as though they are not, since this is bound to limit their relationships with other people. This gives us reason to accept that moral ought judgments presume moral competence.

Nevertheless, as discussed in Chapter 2, sometimes we have grounds to doubt that a person who fails to demonstrate the understanding or concern morality requires was capable of doing better. And we might worry that grounds to doubt a given person's potential to meet morality's demands should unsettle our confidence about how morally to understand her. While we might feel comfortable directing all rational persons to strive to meet moral requirements, when it comes to judging a particular person for what she has done, we might hesitate. It might be that in some domain of action, a person does not understand or care about moral directives—moral reasons have no "authority" for her. Either she cannot cognitively grasp them or they do not resonate motivationally with her. Someone who lacks empathy for the suffering of people she professes to love might be experiencing a reaction to her own feelings of vulnerability. This might signal more than a moral flaw; it may represent a limit to her capacity for morally healthy relationships. Now assume that she was not, in fact, capable of appreciating the hurtful nature of her insensitivity. Does she wrong the people she hurts? I believe so, though Strawson and Wallace worry about whether it makes sense morally to criticize a person's action (or inaction) when it is true that she could not have acted well.

Contra Strawson and Wallace, I believe it makes sense to hold all minimally rational persons to common standards of moral right and wrong, even though the limits of a person's moral capacity are real. There are minimally rational persons who do not and could not act as they morally should, yet there is a clear sense in which any wrongdoer ought to have

acted better than she did. The moral ought, as I understand it, is fixed
by what a morally motivated person would do. The reason to fix a standard for evaluating actions in this way is that only this standard properly
acknowledges the moral costs, to victims, of wrongdoing. It is morally objectionable to claim that, because someone could not have treated another person as she ought to have, that person has not been wronged.[18]
Moral assessment of behavior must respond to the harms people suffer
as a consequence of the type of behavior in question. It should ask whether
those harms could be justified to people who suffer them. Action types
that reasonably are or could be objectionable to persons harmed by them
are wrong, whether or not the agents who commit those wrongs were capable of acting well. Since I am passing over cases of persons who are not
even weakly responsive to reasons, what I am affirming is the relevance
of moral standards for evaluating the behavior of people who are at least
minimally rational. A morality that is not pointless because it effectively
guides many people can be used to evaluate any minimally rational person's acts. In formulating such a morality, we have reason to separate evaluations of an agent's blameworthiness from the evaluation of her actions.

The distinction between wrongdoing and blameworthiness bears a certain affinity to the structure of some moral dilemmas. In some situations,
a person must choose between a set of bad options and may reasonably
choose the least bad or least objectionable of all the options available to
her. Thomas Nagel imagines having to twist the arm of an innocent child
in order to rescue injured friends.[19] While doing this might be, on balance, justified, Nagel's point is that it cannot so clearly be justified to the
child. From the child's perspective, the arm-twisting might only be excused and perhaps not entirely; the action is not without negative moral
remainder. There is an affinity here with the normative structure of excuses, though not an exact parallel. In Nagel's example, the arm-twister
wrongs the child, while not acting wrongly, overall. The harm to the child
is excused by a justifiable aim. In the cases of excused wrongdoing that
interest me, there is no such purpose. The common element in Nagel's
scenario and the one I am considering is the insistence on not subsuming
costs to the victim in an overall calculation of what it is reasonable to
expect a moral agent to do. Those costs are instead highlighted in a deontological assessment of the agent's act.

Tort law is instructive on this point. It offers a framework that distinguishes between judgments of wrongful harming and blameworthiness. Victims of a tort are entitled to collect damages when they offer adequate evidence that harms they have suffered were wrongfully caused by some other party, regardless of whether that party intended harm, demonstrated ill will in causing the harm, or brought about beneficial consequences, on balance, by so acting. In fact, the tortious conduct might have been morally commendable along these dimensions: motivation and wider consequences. A person who is praiseworthy for a heroic act, such as saving a life, might nevertheless be liable for compensating the owner of property damaged in the course of her act.

Tort law aims to compensate victims for harms wrongfully caused by the defendant. Facts about the defendant's mental state or the further consequences of her act are not necessarily germane to the victim-centered, rights-based focus of judgments of tort liability. For the tort of negligence, which imposes liability for injuries caused by careless conduct, the notion of carelessness or fault required to establish the defendant's liability is "objective." A defendant is vulnerable to liability for negligence if the actor breaches a duty owed to the plaintiff to take due care—the care a person of ordinary prudence would exercise under the circumstances—to avoid causing one of several sorts of setbacks that the law deems to amount to a cognizable injury (death, physical harm, property damage, economic loss, and so on).[20] A defendant might be found to be at fault for harms that are wrongful, in this sense, despite the fact that she is less reasonable than other persons, that she did her best to take care not to harm others, that she minimized harms overall, or that she was responding justifiably to a morally urgent problem.

In tort law, the relevant standard of fault is a generalized standard: it describes the conduct of a reasonably prudent person in situations of a similar kind. This standard is used to establish that a victim has been wrongfully harmed and should be compensated even though the harmdoer's mental state is virtuous and despite the fact that, in a particular case, beneficial consequences of the defendant's tortious act might accrue to other persons or even to the victim herself. There is arguably an affinity between the dynamics of morality and the structure of tort law, as some legal scholars have discussed. In particular, John Goldberg and

Benjamin Zipursky have defended the objectivity of negligence law's fault standard. They argue that there are good reasons for tort rules of conduct to be phrased simply and objectively so as to enable them to guide behavior and to compensate victims appropriately. They claim that the fact that torts are always wrongful injurings of another calls for an inquiry into responsibility that is particularly attentive to the interests of victims, and thus less accommodating to injurers by, for example, setting objective standards that most of us will not be able to meet on every occasion and that some people might even be regularly unable to meet.[21]

Putting aside individuals with demonstrated incapacities to appreciate reasons of any sort—hedonistic, prudential, or moral—we should extend the action-guiding requirements of morality to everyone else. Moral ought judgments extend to people who discount the importance of moral reasons, provided that they are capable of appreciating reasons of any sort—prudential, egotistical, or otherwise.[22] Their rational faculties make them candidates for moral obligation, whether or not morality will or could be effective in directing them. Morality effectively moves many people, and that is enough reason to maintain moral standards to assess action. Victims and potential victims of wrongdoing are morally entitled to the regard that morally motivated persons would give them.

Mitigating Blame

We have good reasons to believe that most people are capable of acting morally and that all minimally rational people are subject to morality's demands. While morality presumes general compliance, it does not presume the possibility of universal compliance. Among people who do not comply are some who are not morally competent: they are people who cannot understand or are not moved by morality, perhaps because they are mentally ill or morally corrupt. Yet general compliance gives us good reason to maintain moral standards, and we should address those standards to all rational persons, even though not all are morally competent.

The general (but not universal) presumption of moral capacity suggests a role for excuses, though I will argue that role is misconceived: excuses point to the limits of an individual's moral capacity and to the relevance of these limits for assessing her blameworthiness. Excuses point to reasons for doubting that a person whose behavior we morally judge to have been wrong was in fact capable of having acted better. While wrongdoing does not depend on the wrongdoer's capacity to have acted well, blameworthiness does. Blameworthiness presupposes a more robust moral capacity than minimal rationality: it depends on an agent's capacity to withstand serious challenges to moral understanding and moral motivation. Excuses point to the absence of such capacity, or to conditions that interfere with its exercise. Those who are excused could not (or probably could not) have acted for moral reasons.[23] While we might judge their actions, we should not blame them for acting badly. Call this analysis of excuses the Incapacity Thesis.

In fact, Strawson and Wallace use a version of the Incapacity Thesis to demarcate a class of cases in which an agent intentionally acts contrary to morality yet is not to blame. They do not, however, understand such cases as ones in which excuses operate. Instead, they place these cases in a separate category in which persons are *exempted* from moral responsibility because they are defective as agents. Insanity as defined by law belongs to this class of cases; as we have seen, it applies to persons with particularly severe cognitive defects. Regarding moral exemptions, Wallace writes, "Whereas excuses inhibit responsibility for a particular act by showing that a morally accountable agent has not done anything morally impermissible in the first place, exemptions block responsibility for a particular act by showing that an impermissible act has been done by someone who is not, in general, a morally accountable agent."[24] On this line of thinking, an agent is exempted from accountability because that person lacks, in a broad way, what Wallace refers to as "powers of reflective self-control." These are the agent's powers, generally speaking, to understand moral reasons and to regulate her behavior on their basis.[25] Agents who are exempted from responsibility have a defective capacity to grasp and comply with moral reasons, either permanently or for a limited period of time.[26] Involuntary intoxication is an example of a time-limited exemption from responsibility.

Appealing to this model of defective moral agency does not do justice to the range of cases I have specified. While there are some cases of intentional wrongdoing in which the agent lacked the capacity to recognize and respond to moral reasons, either at the time or more generally, not all cases in which blame is misdirected fit this description.

Consider political protest by an oppressed people that turns violent and results in property damage. While defective agency makes sense of mitigation by reason of mental illness, it does not address the mitigating nature of oppressive personal and social circumstances. Some cases in which blame is mitigated are those in which the agent may have demonstrated a healthy-enough capacity to grasp and to abide by moral reasons, and has not lost this capacity, even under the excusing conditions. Protestors might have expressed their anger with violence even if they could have refrained from doing so, in the psychological sense of "could" relevant to assessing individual moral agency. If their culpability is diminished, I am supposing, it is not because their psychology is compromised. These are important cases, and they reveal that Wallace's strategy of using moral incapacity to mark off the class of cases, in which an agent intentionally does wrong but is not to blame, will not work. I propose, instead, that excuses function by undermining what are normally reasonable expectations about how a person should be motivated.[27] Excuses serve to render morality itself more understanding and less severe in response to hardships people face.[28] I will explain what I mean by considering some examples in detail.

In 2007, football player Michael Vick was arrested for illegal dogfighting. The case provoked public outcry at his treatment of dogs, and he was charged with two felonies—mistreating dogs and promoting dogfights—each with a possible five-year prison sentence. Vick served twenty-one months in prison and two months of confinement to his home. Details of his case focused attention on dogfighting as a moral issue. On the National Public Radio show *Fresh Air*, Dave Davies interviewed Sean Moore, a former dogfighter in Chicago who now works with the Humane Society's campaign to end dogfighting.[29] Moore describes the role of dogfighting within the poor urban community where he lives. He helps the listener understand why a person might be drawn into dogfighting, what he himself personally got out of it, and why he eventually abandoned it. He does all this without minimizing the moral problem of animal cruelty. In fact, his concern for dogs, as well as his desire to stop urban violence, motivates him to work with the Humane Society.

> *Moore:* What got me involved with dogfighting was . . . these bully guys. They had German shepherds back in my day and Great Danes. . . . And a lot of guys with these German shepherds and Great Danes . . . used to chase us through the neighborhoods and bully us a lot. . . .
>
> So this one particular day, I was in the alley, and here come these bully guys with these two German shepherds, and this one German shepherd ran up on me and my dog, and my dog grabbed it and instantly locked up on his neck and killed it.
>
> I had to go get my uncles to release my dog from this other dog, and which built the reputation for me in the neighborhood to be a tough guy, a gangbanger. . . . It was like us guys in these urban communities, we born into negativity. We got to work our way out of it. . . .
>
> *Davies:* So having that animal that could kill was status? It was power?
>
> *Moore:* Oh yeah. You know, coming from where I come from, status means a lot, especially on the negative side, because you don't want to walk down the street and be bullied, get your money took and beaten on as a punk in the neighborhood amongst a lot of criminal activity. . . . Having dogs . . . led me to a point to where . . . I could walk through the neighborhood, and people talking about me in the negative way, but it's positive for me.

Moral lack of concern with the plight of the dogs encountered no apparent resistance from authorities. Moore describes encountering the police with his bleeding and suffering dog. "The police, you know what they used to say to me? Like, did he win? Or, he look like a killer." Moore continues, "If the police don't do anything about it, we thinking it's OK. . . . If law enforcement telling me, oh, I look like I got a killer, then there's nothing wrong with doing what I'm doing."

Davies asks Moore to discuss concern and love for the animals, which is the most obvious basis of moral objection to dogfighting. Moore responds by acknowledging love for the animals and then bracketing that feeling as irrelevant to the fight and its context—the very context that eventually led Moore to reject dogfighting. Moore explains, "On my level, street level, it's not about the two dogs fighting. It's really the two individuals that argued for these dogs to fight that should be fighting, but we got the two dogs that do fight so we're going to let them fight. So it's never about the love of the dog."

Moore goes on to explain why he abandoned dogfighting himself:

> What particularly stopped me from dogfighting was this one kid in Chicago named Julian. I'm sorry, I can't give him his last name. But this one kid was walking down the street one day with his dog. Two dogfighter dudes drove up on him, say come fight your dog with my dog. So this kid go, say no. I don't want to fight. He walk away. He walk home. These gangbanger guys drove around the corner, came back, by this time this kid get home to his mother and tell his mother that these guys want to get him to fight his dog, they blew his brains out.
>
>   So that pretty much was 100 percent game-changer for me. . . . I don't want to be a part of that. . . . I don't want to be a part of that no more, so that's what changed my life around.

Moore doesn't attempt to excuse the actions of young urban dog-fighters, or the moral seriousness of choosing to fight their dogs, but his description of their life situation seems to diminish the blameworthiness of young men who fight their dogs for social status, money, and personal protection—even though their choices are harmful to animals and draw these men into closer proximity to further criminal activity. Understood in relation to very serious problems of socioeconomic deprivation and vulnerability to street violence, sacrificing the welfare of their dogs seems understandable, even though morally troubling. We could simply condemn these men for animal cruelty or associating with violent criminals, but that seems harsh and reductive. Unjust social circumstances threaten individual autonomy and responsibility, not in a sense that threatens the possibility of wrongdoing, but in a sense that confuses and unsettles moral blame.

The standard view among philosophers is that morality rightfully holds individuals accountable despite the influences on their actions of social or "environmental" causes.[30] A view to unjust social causes is pushed aside because, as we have seen, evaluations of individual responsibility for wrongdoing are typically focused on the quality of a wrongdoer's will—largely apart from the context and personal history of its formation. The moral question, according to these philosophers, is whether the wrongdoer acted for bad reasons, reasons that provide other people with grounds to object, and whether in so doing the wrongdoer demonstrated disregard for the rights or moral standing of others. It is the quality of an agent's will that is the focus of our moral reactions, not how or why the agent's ill will came about, whether under unjust social circumstances or not. What we care about is whether a criminal wrongdoer has bad attitudes, something that, according to this philosophy, calls for a moralized response including, in the most serious cases, punishment.

The quality of a wrongdoer's will is rightfully the focus of serious moral appraisal, and the personal history and wider social context of will formation does not negate the importance of that evaluation. Moore regrets and repudiates the cruelty of dogfighting. He cites both moral reasons, emphasizing the problem of urban violence as well as a concern for the dogs, and reasons of self-interest for young men in his community to put an end to dogfighting, notwithstanding its benefits. But philosophers interested in moral responsibility are typically interested in something other than the need to criticize and reform behavior. As we have seen, they are typically interested in rationalizing a condemnation of the wrongdoer—that is, rationalizing blaming responses that are thought to be deserved by wrongdoers, who have disappointed moral expectations.

Yet circumstances surrounding an agent's disregard for morality sometimes challenge the appropriateness of ordinary moral expectations by unsettling their presuppositions. This is the case if obstacles seem too much for the agent to bear without experiencing the inner conflict, ambivalence, or stress that might lead her morally to fail to act well.[31] Blameworthy people are people who we think should have remained committed to moral ends, despite difficult circumstances and internal psychological obstacles. We might think that, despite challenging circumstances, the relevant moral demand is not unreasonable. Those who are not blameworthy are persons whose commitment to morality is too much to expect in such circumstances—obstacles to success are too devastating.[32] To demand that the agent demonstrate moral resolve would be callous.

One way to express this rationale for excuses is to say that it seems unfair that the requirements of morality are so much harder for some people to meet. While our moral judgments of right and wrong reflect our acceptance of moral luck—the recognition that the moral rightness or wrongness of a person's actions depends on a range of factors beyond the agent's control—our judgments of blameworthiness are uncomfortable with it, and legitimately so, at least when moral bad luck takes the form of hard choices.[33] A person with the misfortune to be faced with tough moral choices might fail to act well. Our recognition of the difficult circumstances under which she acted in morally criticizable ways bears on our assessment of what her wrongdoing says about her. Obstacles to moral success challenge our sense that it is fair to blame, not because we lack standing or because we judge that a person's capacity to choose to act in line with morality has been defeated, but because her confrontation with significant obstacles to moral understanding or moral motivation calls out for our compassion. This is not to say that the moral costs of wrongdoing are not real or important. Our judgment of a person's acts as wrong acknowledges their seriousness. Compassion is, in this way, compatible with moral criticism.[34] But circumstances that call for our compassion can disturb our judgment that she is blameworthy even though they do not lead us to conclude that she was incapable of having done better at the time she acted.

Hector Black is an organic farmer in Tennessee. In the late 1960s, he moved to Atlanta, Georgia, where several civil rights organizations were located, because he and his wife wanted to be a part of the civil rights movement. He settled into a rural community, made his life there, and raised a family. Today he is in his eighties. Photographs show him wearing overalls; his eyes are soft, and his hair is gray.

In 2001, Black's daughter, Patricia Ann Nuckles, was murdered in her home. A man broke into her house to steal things he planned to sell in order to satisfy his drug habit. Black talks openly and matter-of-factly about the incident:

> We learned about what had happened in bits and pieces. She came
> home and he was hiding in the closet hoping to jump out the back

window and get away. But she opened the closet door and she fell backwards and he tied her hands behind her back.

And they had a conversation in the course of which she told him that he needed to get help with his drug habit. He told her to put burglar bars on the back window and always leave a light on. He asked her for sex and she said, "You'll have to kill me first." And so he did.

We were all just devastated. Nothing like this had ever happened. I mean, we'd known death but not like this. I'd never been in favor of the death penalty, but I wanted that man to hurt the way he had hurt her. I wanted him to hurt the way I was hurting.

Black's thinking represents the paradigmatic natural moral reaction described by Strawson's moral philosophy. His voice is steady and calm. He continues:

> But after a while I wanted to know who it was, what kind of a monster would do a thing like this and I learned a little bit about Ivan Simpson, which is his name. I found out that he was born in a mental hospital. And that when he was about eleven years old his mother took him and his brother and sister to a swimming pool and said God was ordering her to destroy them. He escaped and his brother escaped from her but he watched while his mother drowned his little sister.[35]

Simpson later told Black that he felt relief that his sister was not going to be tormented any longer.[36]

Philosophers mostly reject the relevance of psychological causes—the psychological context in which choices are made—to appraisals of moral responsibility, unless that context is extreme, that is, obviously abnormal. In that case, as Strawson describes it, we naturally shift to an "objective" perspective that involves placing the wrongdoer outside of the moral community as a problem to be treated or controlled. According to Strawson, this involves morally disengaging with the wrongdoer in a stark way. We refrain from blame, but at the cost of treating him as less than fully human. Black does not do this in response to Simpson:

> I couldn't help but think what I would be like, if the woman who brought me into the world had tried to destroy my life. It wasn't that I was trying to excuse what he had done, but I felt for him as another human being suffering.[37]

At the sentencing hearing, Black described Simpson as among the people who have been deeply wounded by Simpson's crime.

Black's response is unusual, but he is not making a moral mistake. He describes Simpson as fully human and, remarkably, as an equal—equally human, vulnerable, suffering, and struggling with grief. He does this without evading the enormity of what Simpson did. Black read a victim impact statement after Simpson's sentencing, in which he said, "I don't hate you, Ivan Simpson, but I hate with all my soul what you did to my daughter."[38] Of course, Hector Black is morally entitled to respond in any number of ways. He was deeply and wrongfully hurt, and we can recognize that, in his grief, there are many understandable reactions.[39] In fact, he himself experiences several different reactions, but eventually he settles on a response that is not illuminated by Strawson's moral philosophy. Black teaches us that Strawson's philosophy obscures at least one legitimate moral response—a response that is both morally serious and compassionate.

When we determine that circumstances can mitigate blame despite an agent's wrongdoing, we express morality's recognition that the stringency of its requirements varies from one situation to another in a way that can be unfair. Judgments of what it is reasonable to expect of a person, under the circumstances, are moral judgments regulated by norms that address unfairness in the distribution of moral demands. This normative appraisal of unfairness stands in tension with a deontological appraisal of the content of the demand the agent faces. Our compassion for the wrongdoer alleviates this tension, to some extent, by allowing us vicariously to share in the burden of those moral demands.

Hardships

I have stressed a distinction between two sorts of moral judgments, guided by two sorts of normative standards. The first concerns the evaluation of actions. Like the legal criteria of tort liability, judgments of actions as right or wrong are structured by principles that attain a certain generality. Moral principles should meet requirements of justification, especially to the victim, and their directives are expressed by our understanding of how a morally motivated person would act. I stressed a parallel with the role of objective criteria in establishing tort liability, criteria that refer to generalized standards of reasonable conduct. Both moral principles for evaluating conduct as wrong and legal criteria for judging conduct as tortious express general standards for regulating and evaluating behavior that are characterized by deontological considerations.

The second sort of moral judgment I have discussed concerns judgments we make about the extent to which we think it is reasonable to expect a particular person to overcome hardships that constitute obstacles to moral motivation. These judgments deal more directly with threats to morality in worldly circumstances and in our psychologies. Reasonable expectations about a particular person's moral understanding and motivation are regulated by considerations of fairness. Our perception that a particular person is unfairly burdened by contingencies the rest of us tend not to encounter triggers a judgment that compassion or other nonblaming attitudes make sense. Hardship tempers a person's worthiness of blame.

This claim about fairness and compassion goes against the Kantian view that we should expect a rational person to overcome the appeal of her inclinations and disinclinations when so acting would conflict with the demands of morality. This view depends on an uncompromising premise maintaining the autonomy of rational agents from psychological obstacles and, accordingly, asserting the categorical nature of all moral demands. I challenge the categoricity of morality's demand that rational agents demonstrate "good will."

The view I am suggesting, however, might seem too crude. It might be argued that it is not simply the relative difficulty of the moral task that triggers excuses, but also the origin of the obstacles an agent faces. When these obstacles themselves have resulted from the agent's morally flawed behavior, their presence may fail to incite our compassion or to constitute an excuse.[40] We feel less sympathy for someone who is struggling with the results of her own bad choices—for example, someone who gambles away her paycheck or who is incarcerated for committing a crime—than we do for someone whose troubles are not of their own making. This explains the ambivalence that many people feel about whether an addict's wrongdoing under the influence of her addiction is excused. While an addict craving a drug might lack a normal capacity to recognize and be motivated by reasons, this impairment might have resulted from bad choices she made at a time when she did not lack this capacity.

The account I am developing accommodates and analyzes the intuitions underlying our responses: we assess whether the circumstances creating the obstacles an agent presently faces are circumstances that the agent ought to have avoided and could have avoided without undue burden. We want to know whether the agent had a reasonable opportunity to have avoided the circumstances or conditions (poverty, addiction, and so on) that are now extremely difficult for her to overcome and may factor into bad choices. If avoiding the circumstances that now pose serious difficulties for her moral performance would have been too much reasonably to expect of her, then her blameworthiness is called into question. In this way, the analysis I am proposing applies genealogically. If, at the earlier stage, we find that a person did have a reasonable opportunity to have avoided present constraints on her choices, we may find her blameworthy, even though she now faces difficulties that would cause most people to falter. I believe this suffices to accommodate the intuition that people are accountable for problems they have caused themselves to have.

The Kantian view is reflected in Strawson's position that people who fail to act as a morally motivated person would act and are excused either did not really do something wrong or are defective as agents, incapable of responding morally to reasons. As we have seen, Strawson and Wallace maintain that when a person is excused from blame despite demonstrating ill will, it is because her capacity for reflective self-control is diminished. I am suggesting a different paradigm. Excuses do not necessarily indicate either lack of ill will or an agential incapacity. Rather, they point to obstacles that make it difficult for a person to do what she ought to do, and that therefore trigger our compassion. They help us to identify ways in which the requirements of morality can be very difficult to meet— not for everyone, but for some people and under some circumstances.

Sometimes wrongdoing is excused, even when accompanied by ill will, not because an agent lacks sufficient capacity for self-control, but because the seemingly simple task of doing the right thing (which often involves merely refraining from doing the wrong thing) is so difficult under the circumstances, be those difficulties internal or external.[41] When the obstacles the agent faces are significant enough, we should relax our notion of what, on a personal level, it is reasonable to expect, even though we may not relinquish our understanding of the actions morality demands.

I have proposed that excuses represent a threshold of reasonable expectations about the burdens we should expect people to bear in order to do the right thing. It can seem unfair to expect some people to endure serious hardship in order to meet ordinary moral requirements on action, requirements that are not difficult for other people, in other circumstances, to satisfy. Our judgments about whether an agent is excused, or is excused to some extent, connect with certain sentiments, and I have stressed a connection with compassion. Whether or not excused wrong-doers lack the capacity to meet morality's demands, we can recognize that the obstacles they face would be deeply unsettling to almost anyone.

This approach to understanding excuses makes sense of scenarios that trigger nonblaming responses, and it illuminates the value of those attitudes as we reckon with people who have made moral mistakes. They allow us to view a person's mistakes through the lens of a nonblaming normative standard for judging moral commitment. This standard recommends modesty and restrains moral high-handedness by urging us to refrain from holding other people to more stringent demands than those we ourselves would confidently meet. Conversely, for our own moral and psychological health and the vitality of our emotional relationships, we might better appreciate that it can be very difficult to live a life of moral principle.

Our sense that compassion is called for can also, strangely enough, help to confirm our sense that an agent has acted wrongly. Compassion expresses the painful realization that the outcome of the agent's action and, indeed, the action itself, was morally troubling. We share in the response that a morally sensitive agent would experience. We do this by recognizing that the agent was unfairly situated to anticipate or to take on this response. We feel it, in effect, on her behalf or, if the agent feels regret, to lessen its pain. Thus, unlike a compassionate response to the phenomena of "agent-regret," where an agent regrets the outcome of an action of hers that was not wrong, compassion in this connection adheres to our recognition that the agent's action was wrong.[42] We attempt to soften the connection between the agent and her wrongful act.

Realizing that a wrongdoer faced obstacles that would have led many or most people astray does not entail a normative requirement to feel compassion toward the wrongdoer. A moral requirement would be too strong, and not just because feelings cannot readily be willed. Requiring compassion as a response to moral wrongdoing would be unbalanced in relation to the harms suffered by those who were wronged. But although considerations that render compassion acceptable and even admirable do not require us to feel it, they do enable us to understand how and why someone could be worthy of it.

I have argued that excuses do not challenge our understanding of how a morally motivated person would act. For this reason, they do not challenge our evaluations of right and wrong action. Nor do they entail that the excused agent was incapable of having satisfied morality's demands.[43] The point of excuses is to address obstacles to moral motivation— including cognitive and emotional problems, but also circumstantial troubles such as those illustrated by Moore—and to do this based on a normative standard. The normative standard is a moral one, but the norms that regulate it are different from the norms that guide our appraisal of actions as right or wrong. In evaluating an agent's blameworthiness, we assess how reasonable it is to expect an agent to act morally in the face of difficulties she faces. At the margin, we might wonder whether we should retain our presumption of her moral capacity under those circumstances (or more generally), but this is the outer margin only. Within the scope of many excuses, we do not relinquish our belief that the agent could have avoided wrongdoing. Instead, we take it that morality itself requires that we relax our expectations that she should have.

We can treat wrongdoing seriously without blaming all wrongdoers and without visiting harm on them when they are culpable for their wrongs. Retributivists and nonretributivists alike have reasons to be compassionate toward wrongdoers who fail to act rightly under circumstances that would make it difficult for most people to do the right thing. We will see, however, that the context-sensitive account of blame I have proposed is not readily applicable to criminal law.

A philosophical conception of responsibility should be sensitive to social context and institutional justice—or injustice, as the case may be. It should enable us, more directly than most moral philosophies do, to address the role of social practice, institutions, and the bearing of social injustice on the moral evaluation of individual wrongdoers. It should also enable us to consider the impact of mental illness and other psychological problems on a person's moral choices without dehumanizing or condescending to moral wrongdoers. But, as will be discussed in Chapter 4, setting a standard of appropriate blame is a normative project that permits disagreement. A morally serious perspective does not demand blame as the only reasonable moral response to criminal wrongdoing. This means that justice requires the law to distance itself from the practice of public blaming.

FOUR

CRIMINAL JUSTICE WITHOUT BLAME

AMERICAN CRIMINAL LAW IS bound up with judgments of moral culpability. In our criminal justice system, we do not simply judge acts for their legality or illegality; we condemn people morally for what they have done. At least this is the public narrative surrounding our punishment practices, a narrative promoted by prosecutors, legislators, political commentators, court TV sermonizing, featured profiles of convicted felons, heated talk radio discussions, and cathartic blogging. Through these and other channels, we are exposed to, and perhaps participate in, public proclamations about the repudiation offenders morally deserve and the justice of making them pay for their crimes.

For example, in 2016 the Justice Department under President Barack Obama sought the death penalty for mass shooter Dylann Roof, citing his reprehensible motives as well as the harm he did. Attorney General Loretta Lynch explained, "To carry out these twin goals of fanning racial flames and exacting revenge, Roof further decided to seek out and murder African Americans because of their race."[1] Though Obama was wary of the death penalty, his administration requested it for Roof as well as for Boston Marathon bomber Dzhokhar Tsarnaev. In Tsarnaev's case, United States attorney Carmen Ortiz cited the "heinous, cruel, and depraved manner of committing the offense."[2] She also asserted that

Tsarnaev "betrayed his allegiance to the United States" and that he "demonstrated lack of remorse." The government staked its position on condemning these criminal wrongdoers for their motives, sentiments, and attitudes.

Serious crimes understandably provoke moral outrage. Crimes violate the rights of their victims, and even victimless crimes sometimes involve significant moral transgressions. Criminal convictions convey the moral importance of individually and collectively rejecting behavior that disturbs the moral conscience or otherwise violates important public moral norms. Punishing criminally guilty people provides a public means for expressing condemnation, and it might seem natural for these judgments to focus on a criminal wrongdoer's moral culpability. By moral culpability, to be clear, I refer not to a legal finding of fault, but to a person's moral blameworthiness, the sort of question underlying debates about whether Dylann Roof was "ill or evil."[3]

However, as we have seen, deciding whether to blame involves more than determining that a person committed a wrong—even a grievous wrong. Blame involves responding to a wrongdoer in view of her behavior. It depends on evaluating what her moral faults, as her wrongdoing reveals them, say about what sort of response she deserves. Determining that a person is worthy of blame depends on assessing her motives—for example, whether she acted out of disrespect, hostility, indifference, selfishness, or ignorance. We do not, generally speaking, need to know an agent's motives in order to determine that what she did was morally wrong. Assault or murder is morally reprehensible even when a perpetrator is not motivated by a desire to harm. But a meaningful evaluation of what an action tells us about the person who did it depends on why she did it.

This assessment can be a politically powerful instrument. Nancy Reagan stoked the "war on drugs" with assertions like "Drug criminals are ingenious. They work everyday to plot a new and better way to steal our children's lives, just as they've done by developing this new drug, crack. For every door that we close, they open a new door to death."[4] The "war on drugs" contributed to the rise of mass incarceration, and the demonization of crack sellers and users played a leading role in rationalizing the escalation of criminal penalties.

The moral difference motives make to blameworthiness presents a problem for retributive accounts of justice and, more broadly, any theories that assign a blaming function to criminal law. When we evaluate a person's moral culpability, we need to know why that person acted wrongly; we must understand the reasons for her actions. But information about a defendant's reasons for acting is rarely needed to establish criminal guilt. Criminal law is insensitive to individual motives. Prosecutors are not required to produce evidence about what motivated a crime in order to establish that it took place. In this way, determinations of criminal guilt differ appreciably from assessments of moral accountability for wrongdoing.

There is a compelling rationale for this difference. The public nature of criminal justice differs from personal morality. Blame as a response to wrongdoing contains an element of personal choice. It is morally optional, at least in many cases, and people who engage in it do so in a personal way. By contrast, the rules of criminal justice apply coercively to all members of society, and legal rules should be supported by public reasons—reasons that all members of society could accept.[5] But since there are morally serious perspectives that do not require blame as the appropriate moral response to criminal wrongdoing, the institutions of criminal justice should not mandate public blame. Moral blame does not provide us with public reasons for criminal punishment.

The state may forbid us from acting against the interests of society, but it risks overstepping its proper bounds when it scrutinizes people's motives and condemns them for their personal moral flaws. Even those who regard blame as an appropriate response to wrongdoing have reasons to resist appointing the state to evaluate our moral worth as persons.

The Irrelevance of Motive to Criminal Culpability

Motive encompasses the reasons for which a person acts, as well as the cognitive and emotional state in which she acts. It includes a person's aims in acting together with her reasons for adopting those aims. We care about motives because they help us to understand *why* a person did what she did. A person might steal because she is greedy. Someone else might do so out of a sense of boredom, to express dissent, or because she is hungry.

Sometimes motives are complex, as a person may have several reasons for what she does. We must take on this complexity in order to assess what a person's wrongdoing says about *her*. The relationship between a person and her wrongdoing is naturally viewed through an examination of her motives and the connection of her motives to her standing characteristics: her dispositions, beliefs, judgments, attitudes, behavioral patterns, personality, and character traits. In this way we investigate the relationship between an action and a person's will.

Our assessment of what wrongdoing says about a person's will bears on the question of how ethically to respond to her wrongdoing and, in particular, whether to blame her for it. As we have seen, the most popular philosophical theory ties wrongdoing to *ill will,* understood to include a complex of cognitive, emotive, and dispositional factors. A wrongdoer is taken to be the object of blame for the ill will that motivates her wrongdoing. Specifically, according to standard accounts of blame, wrongdoers are to blame whenever they have demonstrated disregard for other people's moral rights or moral standing. In violating another person's rights, criminal wrongdoers have, through insensitivity, for example, egoistic self-concern, or animosity, disregarded that person's interests.

On the standard philosophical analysis of blame, people who actively seek to harm other people in response to their own feelings of envy, jealously, vulnerability, desire to dominate, and the like are blameworthy for the disregard of other people that their wrongdoing expresses, provided that there is no serious reason to doubt a wrongdoer's responsibility for her desires, dispositions, reasoning, decisions, or actions. Of course, there is disagreement about what counts as serious reason for doubt. I take up this matter in some detail shortly. But, generally speaking, considerations that break or weaken the link between wrongdoing and ill will are commonly accepted as considerations that mitigate blame. For example, people whose harms to others are inadvertent, impulsive, or thoughtless are taken to be less blameworthy than people who commit deliberate, studied acts of hostility, even though the less deliberate and less overtly hostile acts also transgress moral prohibitions. Harms to others are sometimes excused altogether when no ill will is present, or when a person entirely lacks the capacity for rational thought and action.

The approach to thinking about blame I have endorsed revises the standard picture by focusing on hardships. *It shifts our focus away from the difficult problem of distinguishing between capacity and incapacity, since even morally competent agents can be excused for their wrongdoing under conditions of hardship.* Still, it directs moral attention, as does the quality-of-will approach, to an agent's motives.

In American criminal law, motive is not relevant for establishing subjective fault, at least for most crimes. There are exceptions to the criminal law's disregard for motive in assessing criminal liability. Hate crimes involve group-based hostility. Treason involves desire to assist the enemy. Various "unlawful purpose" statutes exist in some U.S. states. In most cases, however, including murder, assault, and robbery, motive is not at issue in finding criminal fault. Robin Hood is as guilty of theft as a common thief. Homicides are catalogued by reference to finer grades of intention than are required to establish many other crimes, but the reasons behind these efforts to specify homicidal intent are usually immaterial to criminal guilt. Distinguishing between purpose, knowledge, recklessness, and negligence might reflect the law's attempt to grade a person's ill will,[6] and thus to reflect his or her blameworthiness, but an ethical assessment of action and intention without reference to an agent's motives is too coarse-grained to assess blameworthiness adequately. Intentional acts vary greatly in their moral quality, depending on what motivates them. Euthanasia is not similar to a sadistic murder. And reckless behavior might reflect utter disregard for the welfare of another person, or it could reflect an understandable, though not justifiable, distraction of attention. A similar point holds across categories—reckless behavior might be pernicious while intentional or knowledgeable wrongdoing may be, and frequently is, driven by economic need, ignorance, impulsiveness, or emotional distress, rather than by a deeper hostility, aggression, hatefulness, or disregard. Considered apart from motive, a scale of knowledge and purposiveness in the case of criminal acts is an unreliable guide to blameworthiness even if, generally speaking, there is reason to suppose that immoral acts are ill motivated. Even hateful motives, as in Roof's case, can be morally confusing, since the chances that a person with those motives is emotionally disturbed are great.

The role of motive in some *defenses* against criminal charges presents a further exception to the observation that criminal liability does not depend on motive. For example, provocation—such as a state of anger or fear caused by the commission of a serious crime against a family member—can function as a mitigating circumstance that reduces an intentional homicide to manslaughter. Motives that are evidence of mental illness can also reduce charges. Evidence of mental illness might establish that a defendant was incapable of forming the relevant intention and hence that he lacked the mental state belonging to a specific intent that is required for an offense, such as assault with the intent to commit rape. But these examples of the relevance of motive or its absence, while significant, are limited and specific, and they are compatible with criminal liability to lesser charges (manslaughter but not murder, assault but not assault with intent to rape), charges in which motives are irrelevant.

It is true that motive is sometimes introduced in the sentencing phase of a criminal trial, although more often as an aggravating than a mitigating consideration. Evidence of cruel or greedy motives can serve to increase the penalty, according to some sentencing guidelines. Overall, however, the legislation of mandatory sentences and other restrictions on judicial discretion counter efforts to individualize sentences in response to a defendant's motives, and motive has increasingly come to be treated as irrelevant to sentencing, at least in the United States. In principle, considerations of motive could more consistently and more deeply be brought into the sentencing phase.[7] Courts might more carefully consider mitigating or aggravating factors—factors that affect moral blameworthiness and thus might be thought to affect the suitability of a particular sentence for an individual defendant. This could help to address skeptical concerns that uncoupling culpability and motive threatens to undermine proof of a defendant's blameworthiness. If motive is a factor in sentencing, the skeptic might be assuaged to some extent.

I will not, however, pursue this line of reasoning, because I believe an attempt to calibrate punishment to moral blameworthiness faces a further problem. This problem concerns a mismatch between criminal liability and moral blameworthiness, in principle. The public role of criminal justice institutions does not morally license the use of criminal justice as an instrument of moral blame.

Quality of Will

A careful examination of the relationship between ill will and what brings it about reveals that the standard prescriptive view of how to understand and respond to wrongdoing is too narrow. The popular "quality-of-will" interpretation of blame neglects the relationship between a wrongdoer's ill will and her life circumstances, and this truncates the range of morally reasonable responses to a wrongdoer's demonstration of ill will.[8] Underestimating the possibilities for a morally sensitive response also obscures the fact that opting for one of these reasonable responses involves a personal choice that shapes possibilities for the future relationship of the people involved. Respecting the autonomy of individuals to negotiate the moral meaning of personal relationships requires the state to step back from legislating or judging in that domain of personal choice. The state should not usurp our moral prerogative to decide whether to blame, to forgive, or to engage, or not engage, morally with a wrongdoer in some other meaningful way.

P. F. Strawson describes the personal significance of blame in his classic article, "Freedom and Resentment."[9] The analysis Strawson sets forth has become the standard philosophical interpretation of blame. There are subtle differences between the views of those who claim to inherit Strawson's insights, but the broadly shared premise is the notion that blame attaches moral meaning to ill will. Blame conveys the relational significance of the ill will that others bear toward us, as displayed in their attitudes and actions.[10] It represents, claims Strawson, "the kind of importance we attach to the attitudes and intentions towards us of those who stand in . . . relationships to us."[11] Blaming responses signify the meaning of a wrongdoer's morally flawed behavior for relationships in which she is involved.[12] They attest to a person's moral unreliability and, more broadly, her unsuitability for the intentions and expectations that morality requires. Blame traces her unfitness for moral expectations to standing aspects of her character, dispositions, will, or personhood, which are revealed in her wrongful actions and the damage they have done, and holds her responsible for those deficiencies. A person is held accountable in the sense that she is taken to deserve blame for her shortcomings. Blame is expressed in behavioral adjustments the blamer makes to reflect the significance of those flaws for the blamer's relationship with the wrongdoer. Blame makes a difference to how we think, feel, or act toward someone who has done wrong.

By Strawson's description, blame is typically expressed through a moralized set of "reactive attitudes": resentment, indignation, and a desire to inflict harm on the blameworthy agent.[13] Strawson's characterization of the reactive attitudes has a distinctively retributive flavor, but analytical accounts of blame need not understand blaming responses as retributive. Blame is not limited to persons who deserve it, in a retributive sense, nor must it be conceived as a kind of retributive hurting. Some philosophers have helped to clarify the nonretributive dimensions of blame. For example, T. M. Scanlon revises Strawson's focus on punitive responses. He argues that blame is deserved when a person's judgments or attitudes interfere with her reliable prospects for acting in conformity with morality, but not because we think a person deserves to suffer on account of her wrongdoing. Rather, blaming responses are appropriate or fitting acknowledgments of the damage the wrongdoer has done to relationships in which she is involved.[14] Scanlon rejects the retributive thesis understood as the view that punitive forms of treatment "are appropriate, and even good things to occur, in part *because* wrongdoers have reason to dislike them." But he accepts that "fitting" attitudes have negative social and psychological consequences for wrongdoers that are justified and even desirable "simply by the faults displayed in the wrongdoer's conduct."[15] In addition to anger, moral indignation, and resentment, moral blame might include disappointment, sadness, regret, grief, and a disposition to renegotiate, restrict, or break off a relationship, or to demand an explanation or apology. This wider, nonretributive class of negative reactions, and the self- (and other-) protective behavioral changes they support, should be recognized as expressions of blame.

The common element in retributive and nonretributive accounts of blame is the notion that culpable wrongdoers deserve the negative emotions, attitudes, and behavioral responses that constitute blame.[16] Furthermore, as both Scanlon and Strawson emphasize, blame involves interpersonal engagement. Only people who stand in a relationship to a wrongdoer are in a position to blame her. While historical figures may be blameworthy, Scanlon argues, as our distance from those figures increases, blame is attenuated and replaced by less engaged attitudes of disapproval, that is, unless we have some special reason to be concerned about what a particular person was like.[17] Person-to-person blame might be intimate, or it might take place between people who do not know one another, as in a relation between citizens, but it is always relational, and it is personally experienced and enacted.

Excuses Revisited

Focusing on the quality of an agent's will supports a certain understanding of the limits of blame—factors that would excuse a wrongdoer from blame. As discussed in Chapter 3, the standard view is that excuses typically work in one of two ways. Either they point to the absence of ill will or they exempt the agent from responsibility by pointing to a defect in her will, what we might refer to as moral incompetence. Regarding assessments of incompetence, Strawson stresses that exempting an agent from blame by pathologizing her will places her outside of the moral community. He thinks that while blame describes a morally engaged response to wrongdoing, excusing conditions steer us toward the objectifying and morally detached attitudes of treatment and control. This makes it sound like blame is the more humane approach.

Actually, the suggestion that blame represents a morally involved response to wrongdoing that retains the ties of community should be resisted. Nathaniel Hawthorne plausibly describes the stigma of moral blame in terms that are similar to Strawson's account of the exclusionary effects of evaluations of moral incompetence. The scarlet letter stitched into to the dress of Hester Prynne, Hawthorne writes, "had the effect of a spell, taking her out of the ordinary relations with humanity and inclosing her in a sphere by herself."[18] As Hawthorne describes it, blame— at least its more punitive realization—is a moralized form of social condemnation that sets the morally culpable apart, either temporarily or permanently; the moral engagement of blame belongs to a form of social control that bears a close relationship to the exercise of social expulsion.

We have seen that the "quality-of-will" paradigm is challenged by scenarios in which a member of the moral community acts wrongly and demonstrates ill will, yet engages our compassion, understanding, or sympathy, at least to some extent. Examples extend from the ordinary to the extraordinary. We might be inclined to excuse, if only partially, a depressed friend who makes a false promise, a prejudiced child from a racist family, a disadvantaged teenager who joins a violent gang, a pedophile who was abused as a child, or a terrified person who participates in mass violence. We include among the morally significant challenges to acting well certain psychological obstacles—misdirected fears or immoral and intense desires, preoccupations, and impulses—that are engendered by personal histories of abuse, neglect, disease, violence, or misfortune, when such a history has seriously harmed a person and affected her prospects for acting well. It is reasonable to feel sympathy for individuals who encounter hardships—present or past—to acting well, and we might excuse such persons, entirely or partly, from blame for their morally faulty actions without finding them incapable of moral action or outside of the moral community and appropriately subject only to the detached and "objectifying" attitudes of treatment and control. The circumstances, history, and psychological vulnerabilities of these agents are at odds with our blaming attitudes and judgments. But their wrongdoing is not in dispute, since in each of these cases the agent acts intentionally and for reasons we can criticize on moral grounds. We treat such a person as a moral agent, yet we excuse her, wholly or in part, despite her ill will.

Factors that excuse a person's wrongdoing do this by mitigating her ill will. Consider a person with a hard life—basic needs unmet, unjustly restricted opportunities, and negative peer pressure. Suppose this person commits a violent crime. It is not unreasonable to hold that his psychological vulnerabilities give us reason to feel compassion, understanding, empathy, or concern, even as we acknowledge that he committed a crime intentionally and for reasons we can criticize on moral grounds. The quality-of-will interpretation of blame does not help us enough to understand this response. To make sense of it, we need to look more broadly at the context in which the person's intentions and attitudes were formed. We must consider a person's ill will in relation to her circumstances and life situation.

I have proposed that, in deciding whether or not to blame, we respond not to ill will per se. Rather, we evaluate a person's failure to negotiate

motivational or cognitive obstacles to acting well. Blame signals our belief that it was reasonable to have expected the wrongdoer to overcome
the obstacles she faced, in view of our awareness of the difficulty of doing
so. We evaluate the meaning of her ill will, not just by judging whether
her intentions and attitudes toward other people are open to moral criticism, but also by situating her intentions and attitudes in relation to her
character, situation, and personal history. *We consider both how a person's
attitudes arose and how difficult it would be for her to alter them.*

   Situating ill will more broadly within a person's psychology and life is
complex. It involves acknowledging obstacles the agent faced at the time
of acting as well as past difficulties that have influenced the development
of her attitudes and dispositions. Some hardships are identifiable as factors
that have been imposed—pressure from other people, deprivation of
needed resources, threats and sources of fear, social marginalization.
Others have sources that may be at least partly genetic, including, for
example, mental illness. Whether difficulties have been externally or in-
ternally generated, blame implies that the obstacles encountered—strong
impulses, obsessive thoughts—were manageable threats, although the
wrongdoer in fact failed to manage them well. Blame implies that it was
reasonable to have expected the agent to manage them better. People we
excuse from blame, on the other hand, are people who might reasonably
not have been expected to act as they morally ought to have acted, either
because their agency is undermined or because the obstacles encountered
were understandably, although not justifiably, mishandled. The latter
judgment is compatible with a person's basic moral competence.

   An appraisal of blameworthiness draws upon a general standard. It depends on a generic judgment about how fair it is to expect a person who
is a suitable candidate for moral expectations to have responded to adversity the wrongdoer encountered.[19] The presence of obstacles mitigates
blame in the sense that it gives us reason to view a wrongdoer's disposition to act badly as having been relatively weaker than the disposition of
a wrongdoer who did not face such troubles. The will of the person who
did wrong without recognizable and understandable incentives to wrongdoing is open to stronger moral criticism than the person whose
wrongdoing was prompted by significant impediments to acting well,
that is, incentives to wrongdoing that would be difficult for ordinarily

constituted persons to resist.[20] Morally flawed attitudes and intentions are viewed in relation to the difficulties a wrongdoer faced; they might not indicate blameworthy character traits or standing dispositions. Even irrational thoughts or feelings need not be regarded as personal defects, at least in relation to certain causes, like trauma or hunger. In many cases, we have the moral option to depathologize a person's faulty attitudes by considering them in relation to hardships. The standard for what counts as a hardship is generic, though it is also controversial.

The quality-of-will view can feasibly be broadened to accommodate attention to problems an agent faced at the time of acting. Encumbrances to the formation of moral dispositions in a person's history, by contrast, are more difficult for a theory of blameworthy agency to accommodate on a quality-of-will approach.[21] A person's past experiences and genetic qualities may have led to the formation of morally criticizable attitudes or dispositions whose strength, generally speaking, is not cast into doubt by the presence of incentives and pressures to do wrong at the time the agent acts. Obstacles to healthy moral development may affect what a person is like, causing vicious attitudes and dispositions to become characteristic of the person. As a result, causes of wrongdoing may be intrinsic to a person. This indicates blameworthiness, on a quality-of-will view, since a person's wrongdoing reflects what the person's beliefs and attitudes are really like.[22] But we might not rest easily with a judgment of blameworthiness or the blaming that this assessment seems to render appropriate. Understanding the causes of an agent's attitudes and dispositions can shift our moral perspective—engaging our compassion by highlighting weaknesses we share, namely, our common human vulnerability to mistreatment and misfortune—and this unsettles blaming responses.[23] In particular, it upsets our sense that a wrongdoer deserves to be scorned, publicly condemned, or dismissed as a "bad person." It is hard to believe a person could deserve to suffer harm for behavior caused by factors that would lead many, perhaps most, people to falter morally.

More broadly, compassion and understanding might affect our tendency to blame, whether or not we endorse the value of retribution. While not disabling anger, disappointment, distrust, disrespect, and even resentment or indignation, understanding might make engaging in blaming responses painful by undercutting a blamer's inclination to experience a sense of moral righteousness. More radically, grasping the causes of a person's moral flaws might interfere with the judgment that it is the wrongdoer's faulty agency that is "the cause" of moral disruptions to her relationships with other people. With a broader view of the causes of her wrongdoing we might cease to endorse the relevance of blame. Instead, we might view her agency as itself an ongoing form of engagement with a larger set of circumstances: we relate her faulty attitudes to other causes that interest us morally. In particular, causes we view as hardships may soften our reactions, rendering us more compassionate toward the wrong-doer. Repositioning ourselves accordingly bears on the sort of future relationship with the wrongdoer we find morally possible and compelling. For example, we might make strategic efforts to avoid aggravating circumstances rather than hold the wrongdoer fully accountable. These are options that are morally open to us.

I have proposed that excuses should be understood to express a judgment about what it is reasonable to expect in view of the difficulty many people would face in overcoming the influence of impediments to the formation of good will, adversity some wrongdoers actually faced. Subjection to stress, violence, abuse, subordination, addiction, deprivation, and illness may contribute to the formation of ill will in ways that are particularly difficult to resist. These problems present serious difficulties for the potentially virtuous and nonvirtuous alike. Contending with them interferes with the possibility of moral motivation, judgment, and action, although, of course, they do not always have that result. Some people maintain moral integrity under even extremely unfavorable conditions. This is what makes the Nelson Mandelas of the world so heroic. But for other people, that is, for most of us, mistreatment and other troubling experiences are obstacles to acting rightly—they interfere with the consistent realization of a moral disposition, including moral motivation and reasonable moral judgment.[24]

Sometimes hardships are generally disabling: they damage the agents who suffer them. When adversity is recognized in accounts of moral responsibility as "exempting" damaged agents from moral responsibility, it is typically the *disability* or incapacity rather than the *hardship* that is regarded as the excusing condition. "Insanity" is the paradigm exemption in law. But to focus primarily on insanity and other pervasive forms of mental dysfunction biases our understanding of morally excusing conditions. My focus is on the hardship, whether or not it disables the agent. The suffering caused by subjection to violence, abuse, oppression, illness, or poverty may provoke morally troubling reactions from people who are not generally morally disabled. Hardships may be a cause of intense anger and resentment, hostility, suspicion and distrust, lack of empathy, self-deception or other forms of dishonesty, and the impulse to engage in violent or abusive behavior. They are a source of trouble in personal and interpersonal settings, such as those that involve dynamics of intimacy, authority, trust, confidence and vulnerability—dynamics that characterize the setting of morality, generally speaking. Sometimes morally troubled and troubling responses lead to criminal wrongdoing. My point is that wrongdoing sometimes describes understandable, though not justifiable, reactions to unjust circumstances and disturbing experiences. Hardships muddy the waters of blame.

While blame highlights an agent's failure to act well despite the factors contextualizing her ill will, excuses indicate factors that render her failure understandable, if not reasonable. Excuses point to conditions that make it unfair to subject a person to ordinary moral expectations. Excusing conditions might not incapacitate the excused wrongdoer. More relevant, ethically, is our belief that the agent faced obstacles that would be very hard for most people to overcome. We need not confirm epistemic worries about a person-specific judgment of moral incompetence, nor need we insist that excusing or mitigating conditions prompt behavior that is atypical for the agent. The focus of blame and excuse, as I understand it, is an evaluation of the strenuousness of morally acceptable behavior under the pressure of factors and circumstances that help us to make sense of the agent's failure, including the intensity of her psychological aversion to a morally justifiable course of action and the history of the formation of her ill will. This interpretation of moral accountability tells a story that differs from the quality-of-will thesis, as it is ordinarily understood.

The possibilities Strawson envisages for understanding and responding to wrongdoing are too narrow. Evaluating an agent's will in connection with its context and causes broadens our moral options for nonblaming responses. It shows how evaluating an agent's ill will can

lead to empathy rather than blame. Through our understanding, we acknowledge that moral expectations might reasonably be adjusted in view
of difficulties besetting a person, whether psychological or social. More
radically, we could refuse to blame by suspending the agential perspective
altogether and concentrating on a view of persons as part of the natural
causal order. Blame is debilitated when we focus on natural causes that
threaten the agency of all of us. This might lead us to decide to restrict
the morally relevant sense of the possible to the actual. We would then
find that the moral course of action was impossible for any wrongdoer.[25]
But acknowledging mitigating and excusing considerations does not
imply that conclusion. We need not believe that to be excused, a wrongdoer must have been incapable, either generally or at the time, of having
acted well. Excusing a wrongdoer from blame by understanding her
misdeeds and faults in relation to hardships that have shaped them is
compatible with ascribing to her the capacity and, in the morally requisite sense, the freedom to have acted well.

Rejecting Blame

Though the standard for what counts as a hardship is generic, a decision
to blame or to refuse blame is largely personal. The subjective dimension
of blame—its noncategorical character—shows us that the question of
whether to blame not only extends beyond whether a person has done
something wrong, but also stretches past appraisals of the significant
moral faults behind an agent's wrongdoing. Neither the facts about a person's wrongdoing and moral flaws, the likelihood of her future wrongdoing, nor the requirements of morally healthy relationships demand a
blaming response to moral wrongdoing. In fact, the morally relevant
facts do not require any particular response. Though blame is inappropriate when it is directed toward a person who is not at least minimally
rational, above the threshold set by minimal rationality, there is room to
negotiate blame, morally speaking, or to opt for a nonblaming response
to wrongdoing. A morally sensitive person is free to choose from a range
of reasonable moral responses to another person's wrongdoing. Though
a person whose rights have been violated might not feel morally free to
choose a response, since reactions can be highly emotional, a number of

responses are morally possible. Responses might be unforgiving or merciful, angry or detached, sorrowful or withdrawn.[26] Each in a variety of moral positions has different personal and interpersonal meaning and consequences, and the moral enactment of a response implicates the responder in ways that are significant but not morally required.

When we consider the full range of morally engaged relationships, not all of which involve blame, we should conclude that criminal law institutions should not be in the business of blame. There are morally reasonable responses to wrongdoing that do not force us to choose between blaming and a disengaged, objectifying stance of treatment and control, the only two options presented by much of the current philosophical literature on blame and excuse. Instead of reacting with blame, persons who are mistreated might instead come to believe that the obstacles the wrongdoer encountered—circumstantial pressures, strong impulses, personal trauma, social alienation—were understandably, although not justifiably, mishandled. Though it is easiest to accept that it is the victim who is morally permitted to refrain from blaming, others who are involved might also suspend blame. Even grave moral wrongs might be viewed as tragic for everyone involved.[27] This response is compatible with morality. A nonblaming response can acknowledge the reality and personal impact of wrongdoing. Persons who suffer moral wrongs are morally free not to blame, at least when the wrongdoer has struggled with hardships, as many criminal wrongdoers have done. But if it is acceptable for victims to refrain from engaging in blame, then it is implausible to think it should be morally required for us collectively, through actions by the state, to blame people who are criminally guilty. And since the retributive theory insists that there is a punitive blaming response required by justice, we should reject the retributive theory.

Consider the following analogy between the morality of blame and how we might think about liability in tort law. Tort law addresses disputes between private parties concerning wrongful harms and losses.[28] On one normative understanding of tort law, a view I find appealing, the liability of a tortfeasor (an agent responsible for the violation of a legal duty to refrain from wrongfully injuring another[29]) is a function of a victims' right to seek recourse.[30] One party is due compensation from another party for a wrongfully inflicted loss only when the harmed party decides to seek compensation.[31] Tort law aims (or should aim) to empower those who have suffered wrongful losses to seek compensation, if they so choose. This "civil recourse" interpretation of tort law differs from a "corrective justice" approach that stresses the impersonal value of ensuring that tort victims are compensated.[32] Corrective justice maintains that parties who have caused wrongful losses thereby have a duty to compensate their victims. On a civil recourse interpretation of tort law, by contrast, a normative claim about liability has subjective conditions. The law empowers victims to seek damages without ethically mandating tortfeasors to offer them. Civil recourse theorists John Goldberg and Benjamin Zipursky write, "We do not conceive of the state itself as *aiming* to see to it that compensation is paid by tortfeasors to victims. The normativity of liability-imposition lies in the empowerment of plaintiffs to obtain redress if they choose."[33] On this way of thinking, the law is not set up to track a pre-legal moral conception of corrective justice. Rather, civil recourse theory emphasizes the importance of the fact that tort victims are entitled by law to seek compensation but are not required by justice to do so.[34] Tort law provides (or should provide) people who suffer a wrong at the hands of another party with a tool to redress that wrong. Negligent and other wrongful harm-doers are liable only when plaintiffs exercise their right to make them liable.

In parallel fashion, I am claiming that morality provides victims with a normative structure within which they might chose to express their sense of having been wronged through blame, but it does not require them to do so. The appropriateness of blame as a response to wrongdoing is a function of the wronged party's moral entitlement—not obligation—to insist upon the reasonableness of her expectation that the wrongdoer would have acted better, despite the difficulty of doing so. The exercise of this entitlement morally shapes the relationship in which they stand, without being directed by moral imperatives. At a personal level—judging a wrongdoer blameworthy and engaging in blame—closes off some relationship possibilities by, for example, solidifying feelings of mistrust, diminishing interest in friendship or intimacy, and prompting feelings of anger and resentment or a desire to meet injury with injury. The exercise of a prerogative to blame might also deepen relationships by insisting that the wrongdoer answer for her wrong by providing an account of it, a meaningful apology, the expression of good intentions going forward, and so on. Contemplating hardships that mitigate blame, on the other hand, might open up other avenues for engagement: greater psychological understanding, feelings of compassion, empathy, and the painful yet binding intimacy of confronting a moral misdeed together.

The personal dynamics of blame extend to people who do not know one another. Anger, retributive sentiments, and a desire to secure an apology are common responses to wrongdoing between strangers. A desire to understand is also common, and feelings of empathy that might follow an effort to understand are natural. My point is that blame is not required—we have no grounds for criticizing a victim who does not blame—when compassion is a morally reasonable option, and that this is the case more often than most blame theorists suggest. In particular, it is the case when it comes to assessing criminal behavior, since much criminal behavior is causally related to significant hardships faced by the agent. The moral relevance of, for example, trauma, illness, or social injustice is incompatible with an obligation to blame criminals for their unlawful actions, and we demonstrate respect for victims by permitting them room to decide how to manage their own moral response to the crimes they have suffered. Many moral philosophers fail to see this because their account of the ethics of blame is grounded in a categorical assessment of the moral meaning of wrongdoing: wrongdoing that is not offset by defective moral agency on the part of the wrongdoer demands blame. We should reject this view—it is too uncompromising, too rigid.

The position I am elaborating is compatible with maintaining that there are limits to a reasonable range of moral options for responding to wrongdoing. There are cases in which moral blame is misdirected. An agent might be so immature or impaired, or her circumstances so disabling to moral motivation, that either agency ought not be attributed to her, or her actions, while hers, do not reflect her values, dispositions, motives, and characteristics—that is, what she is like. I have also argued that when a person fails to meet minimal standards of rationality, moral blame is inappropriate. These sorts of cases might be thought to be represented, in a rough way, by the function of nominate excuses in criminal law. Excuses recognized by criminal law offer grounds for limiting criminal liability by serving as a defense against criminal charges. We have considered insanity, immaturity, duress, and necessity. These criminal defenses represent an "objective" standard through being very strict—imposing a high bar for a defendant seeking to invoke them to avoid punishment.[35] For example, as we have seen, the defense of insanity requires proof that the defendant had, at the time of acting, no knowledge of the difference between right and wrong. When the relevant standard is met, defendants are not guilty of the criminal charges. Excuses as criminal defenses are seldom successful.

Failure to secure a nominate excuse leaves considerable latitude for contemplating excuses that are compatible with criminal wrongdoing and might reasonably trigger compassion or otherwise justifiably quell vindictive and righteous moral sentiments and dispositions. I have argued that excuses, in this wider domain of moral assessment, depend on an important subjective element—a choice about whether and how to relate to a wrongdoer, above the threshold set by legally-recognized excuses or, more specifically, the moral threshold of basic responsibility those excuses represent. The subjective dimension of excusing means that imposing criminal punishment should not be used as an opportunity for the state to express blame. An individual's sentence should not be a function of a victim's subjective disposition to blame, or of the state's supposing the moral necessity of a blaming response.

Of course, some defendants do not appear to have suffered any hardship. Relatively privileged people, who have been treated well, enjoyed opportunities to satisfy their needs and develop their interests, and are psychologically healthy—or at least not very unhealthy—seem like excellent candidates for blame. Suppose such a person commits a crime. In the absence of any evidence of hardship, might we be required to blame him? Naturally, these cases would not include criminal activity that is deranged, cruel, or compulsive. Perhaps psychologically healthy defendants who have acted out of "ordinary" dishonesty, jealousy, greed, egoism, bias, or selfishness deserve moral blame. Whether they deserve retribution is a further question, one that was considered and rejected in Chapter 1. But a refined retributive thesis that applies only in cases like this would be more palatable and also radically constrained, though it might often attract nagging suspicions that the people it targets suffer more serious problems that are not obvious.

Thus, above the lower limit set by nominate excuses, the possibility of blame for criminal behavior is negotiable, at least in a wide range of cases. Available moral responses have subjective conditions, and if the subjective conditions of blame are as I construe them, collective blame is not morally obligatory. We are each morally entitled, within the relationships in which we stand, personal and impersonal, to blame those who have done us wrong. We are similarly entitled to decide, within reasonable limits set by the acknowledgment of wrongdoing, that blaming does not fit our stance or interest within a relationship. This important domain of moral choice enables us, in myriad ways, either to distance ourselves from or to confront the psychological and interpersonal dynamics of wrongdoing, something about which we can have differing interests and aptitudes without offending morality. While there are limits to what counts as a reasonable stance—that is, a stance compatible with recognizing that a moral wrong was done and that the wrongdoer met minimal conditions of rationality—within those limits lies the negotiable territory in which moral relationships take shape and evolve. The ethical value of a prerogative to blame or to excuse by engaging the wrongdoer's psychic world with compassion and understanding is evidence for the contingency of blame. In many instances of wrongdoing, a range of attitudes, more or less engaged, more or less demanding, more or less angry or righteous or sympathetic or compassionate are morally permissible. The appropriateness of a response depends on whether the respondent chooses to relate to the wrongdoer as righteous judge, empathetic partner, retrained bystander, or from some other morally acceptable position.

The conditional nature of blame—the subjective aspect of a decision about whether and how to position oneself in relation to a person who has done wrong—entails that blame is a poor foundation for criminal punishment. Though the relationship between a person's ill will and her life circumstances sets some limits to how other people may permissibly respond, it is not the state's job to guide or force us in that personal domain of moral choice. Blame is not required as a matter of law or justice. The subjective dimension of blame does not fit well with the general form of criminal law. Not only does a blaming stance fit poorly with the criteria of criminal liability, divorced as they actually are from an evaluation of motives; it also fits poorly with the public nature of criminal law: the collective nature of our obligation, through law, to redress violations of individual rights. In criminal law, redress is formulated in terms of the public's interest and obligation, which is to make it clear that certain types of behavior are forbidden and intolerable, to discourage people from engaging in those types of behavior, and, when available, to take other measures, such as restitution, to address harms to victims. A duty to redress criminal wrongs generalizes across the citizenry, even though the heaviest burdens appropriately fall on people who have been convicted of crimes.[36] In these respects, the criminal law enterprise is driven by the public moral importance of rights and the equal moral status of right-holders. Its basic function is to guide people's actions, generally speaking, in a way that respects and protects rights, not to engage or disengage moralistically with the meaning of wrongdoing for assessing a wrongdoer's personhood.[37] This is to say that criminal law is rightly act-focused, rather than attitude-focused. We can and should reject behavior that violates public moral norms that are legitimately codified in criminal law. We are responsible for maintaining a standard of behavior consistent with the basic rights of all individuals and with important shared interests, and our collective obligation to protect the basic rights and liberties of our fellow citizens supports the permissibility of burdening criminal lawbreakers with punishment when doing so is necessary to defend our basic rights. But there is no blaming stance we are required, as citizens, to take toward criminal wrongdoers.

Deploying the state's power to condemn the personification of "evil" has historically not gone well. From the Salem witch trials, to fabricated rape charges against Black American men perceived as threats to white women (and white male sexuality),[38] to extreme sentences for "crack pushers,"[39] to dubious legal provisions in the war on terror—such as the indefinite detention by the U.S. government of "enemy combatants" and abuse of the Material Witness Law to incarcerate suspects indeterminately[40]—persons in positions of power have too frequently permitted or manipulated our moral commitments and our fears to rationalize abuses. A criminal justice system that remains focused on evidence of wrongdoing could avoid abuses like these.[41] We could insist on evidence of wrongdoing and dangerousness before applying criminal sanctions, and we could calibrate those sanctions to that evidence. Of course, people who commit heinous crimes should be brought to justice. Yet using the moral language of evil to motivate the point of criminal justice is, morally speaking, a highly risky prospect, especially in a society characterized by racial injustice, serious socioeconomic inequality, and an inadequate safety net.

A legitimate democratic state must defend, with fair defensive measures, the equal rights of all citizens. But it does not need to blame people who are found criminally guilty in order to take measures to do so. Furthermore, the moral basis of a state's permission to burden criminal wrongdoers with punishment does not license its morally righteous condemnation of them. It is enough that it criticize, even condemn, their criminal acts. Punishment can and should remain act-focused. Doing without blame fits better with the actual basis of criminal liability in criminal law. Forgoing blame would also enable us better to reintegrate people into society after they serve their sentences, and to consider alternatives to prison when incarceration is not necessary to further the legitimate aims of criminal justice. This reorientation would, however, require a significant revision in the public moral discourse surrounding criminal convictions—a revision that is long overdue.

FIVE

RETHINKING PUNISHMENT

A JUST SOCIETY WOULD not prosecute criminal wrongdoing for the sake of retribution. Its criminal justice system would have a different rationale and other priorities. When people break criminal laws, they would be liable to criminal punishment, when and because criminal sanctions help to protect the equal basic rights of all members of society. The rationale for punishment in a just society would be harm reduction. The practice of punishment would be used only to prevent and to redress the harms caused by criminal wrongdoing, especially the criminal violation of individual rights. It would also be subject to other restrictions. Punishment would be limited to defendants whose guilt has been established, and provided only that the defendant had a reasonable opportunity to comply with the law, as determined by standards of minimal rationality and basic distributive justice.[1] Furthermore, punishment would not be excessive, by a measure of proportionality that incorporates an evaluation of the wrongfulness of the criminal act, the urgency of deterring it, and the severity of the sanctions.

I will count as punishment any court-ordered sanctions that depend on criminal conviction. This includes but is not limited to incarceration, monetary fines, probation, restitution, community service, and mandated treatment programs for mental illness or substance abuse.[2] Any of these penalties would count as punishment, if a court orders them as a consequence of criminal conviction. We should resist the tendency to equate criminal punishment with incarceration. Instead of assuming that equation, we should seek alternatives to prison.

Harm reduction is, in fact, the most a criminal justice system can achieve. A criminal justice system cannot ensure that punishment is allocated only to people who morally deserve it, much less that all wrongdoers get their just deserts. Nor can it cure a society of violence, stealing, cheating, and other forms of antisocial behavior. In order to "solve" the problem of crime, a society would have to make a commitment that goes beyond criminal justice.[3] It would need to address the causes of crime, which is something a criminal justice system does not do.

Harm reduction is accomplished by affirming the moral importance of the rights that are violated by criminal acts and by implementing measures to incapacitate, to deter, and to reform people who have committed those acts. It also involves adopting measures, such as restitution, to redress harm done to victims. Responding to the criminal violation of rights is morally urgent. But the goal of protecting a system of rights must be advanced in a way that is also fair to people who are burdened with punishment. A system of punishment must achieve "just harm reduction."

A criminal justice system can accomplish just harm reduction even when it does not presuppose the moral capacity of every criminal wrongdoer to have avoided his crime, and even though it does not calibrate blame for criminal transgressions on a scale of moral desert. Just harm reduction is cautious and morally modest. It attempts seriously and responsibly to respond to criminal wrongdoing without exaggerating the responsibility of wrongdoers, and in keeping with the inability of the criminal justice system to address the causes of crime. It maintains a humane and respectful attitude toward all people, including people who perpetrate and are convicted of crimes.

Distributing Punishment Justly

What permits us to criminalize certain types of wrongful behavior? Reasoning about the permissibility and limits of punishment can be understood to rely on a principle of distributive justice. This principle states that when another person unjustly threatens harm to us, we are permitted to shift harm onto that person in order to prevent unjust harm to ourselves. We are permitted to redistribute the unjust threat to the aggressor, provided the harm we impose on the aggressor is not excessive.

I borrow this idea from Daniel Farrell, who has argued that the right (strictly speaking, the "privilege") to use force against another in self-defense instantiates this principle of distributive justice. The right to self-defense entitles each of us to avert imminent threats to certain of our basic rights by harming, if necessary, people who threaten us.[4] Farrell writes:

> To see this, notice that in cases of the relevant sort, the victim is faced with a choice of two ways of distributing certain harms: she can refrain from resisting the aggressor, thereby sparing the aggressor harm while suffering harm herself, or she can resist, thereby saving herself from harm (at least if her resistance is successful) by subjecting the aggressor to harm.[5]

Farrell argues that when an aggressor has made it the case that a victim must make this choice, "justice entitles the victim to choose that the aggressor, rather than the victim, will suffer the harm that, by hypothesis, one or the other of them must suffer."[6] Based on this principle, he reasons, we have a right to self-defense.[7]

Actually, Farrell defends a broader right to self-defense. He proposes that justice permits us not merely to shift harm onto aggressors in order to negate the immediate threats they pose to our basic rights. We are also permitted to threaten them with retaliatory harm in advance of their acting to harm us, in order to prevent them from harming us. I am entitled to warn someone who threatens unjustly to attack me that if he attacks me, I will break his arm. Or, more realistically, I might tell him that if he harms me, he will face legal consequences. A threat of retaliatory harm is a step beyond the *direct* self-defense we have just considered, but it is a short step. Threatening retaliatory harm aims to prevent harm that is unjust, and it involves no harm to an unjust aggressor, beyond the discomfort of being subjected to a conditional threat. Farrell classifies this as a form of *indirect* self-defense, and he appeals to the moral permissibility of indirect self-defense in order to justify the threat of criminal sanctions to dissuade people from violating other people's rights.

Farrell's argument is interesting, and the following considerations support it. The threat of punishment is felt as a significant burden only by a person who is tempted to commit a crime. The threat of punishment functions as a disincentive to do something that a society has determined that people should not do. And the burden the threat imposes is largely defeasible. The threat of punishment operates by giving a person who is threatened a good reason not to commit the crime.[8] What the person is being threatened with could be avoided if the person chooses to comply with the law, either for moral or merely self-interested reasons. On these grounds, Farrell's extension of indirect self-defense to justify the use of threats is plausible.

Farrell also argues that we are permitted to *harm* unjust aggressors, when they have harmed us, in order to prevent them from doing further harm to us.[9] This form of indirect self-defense is more complicated to justify, since the harm we impose on an unjust aggressor is not, by hypothesis, necessary in order to prevent imminent harm. It is future-directed: it involves harming now—for example, with physical restraint or by causing fear—in order to prevent a future harm. Our aim in harming, in this context, is to deter an unjust aggressor from what he is on course to do at some future time. Farrell invites us to accept the legitimacy of this kind of indirect self-defense by imagining a case in which it is the only available means to prevent future unjust harm. Farrell reasons as follows: If I *know* to a certainty that someone will unjustly harm me tomorrow unless I harm him today, I would seem to be justified in harming him. Indirect self-protection that harms unjust aggressors is reasonable for us to take, Farrell thinks, when the alternative is suffering future unjust harm.[10] He continues his line of thinking like this: if I have the right to defend myself in this way, surely the state has the right to act comparably on my behalf. He concludes that the reasoning that justifies our individual right to indirect self-defense in the face of threats to our basic rights can be extended to the state's use of punishment for the sake of specific deterrence; criminal punishment is permissible as an indirect form of collective self-defense.

Specific deterrence involves the application of sanctions to a particular person to induce that person to refrain from engaging in harmful
behavior. It contrasts with general deterrence, in which we threaten or
harm a person in order to deter *other* people. As we will see, specific
deterrence is easier to defend than general deterrence but, as stated,
Farrell's argument for preventative measures against future harms is
unconvincing, even as an argument for specific deterrence. In crucial
respects, criminal punishment, including incarceration, is unlike self-
defense. If someone tries to steal my bicycle, I might be permitted to push
him away or to strike him, in order to defend my property, even if my
defensive action harms him. But I am not permitted to confine him for a
year, a month, or even a *day,* in order to prevent him from stealing my bicycle.[11] Now, it could be that what this scenario reveals is that confinement
is always unjustifiable for petty theft. But even when another person
threatens to do physical harm to me, the permission to confine that
person on grounds of self-defense is not so clear. If someone threatens to
assault me, am I morally permitted on grounds of self-defense to lock that
person in my garage for a month, or even a week, in order to prevent him
from assaulting me? I doubt it. Something other than a right to self-
defense is needed in order to justify the permissibility of a punishment
practice like incarceration, if it is ever justifiable.

Furthermore, a right to self-defense involves the right to use coercive
measures to protect some of our rights but not others. It concerns, primarily, a permission to threaten and to inflict harm on a person who poses
an immediate and forceful threat to our person or property. It is doubtful
that the harms self-defense permits us to inflict on another person could
be used to prevent someone from swindling or slandering us, for example. We need a broader account of the source of our permission to
impose harms on people in order to prevent them from harming us in
those ways. We might construe self-defense in a broader way—as the
defense of our basic rights through a state system of incapacitation and
deterrence—but this presentation would lose the intuitive connection
with ordinary self-defense cases that Farrell uses to launch his argument, and it is not clear why our right to self-defense, in the familiar
sense, would justify it.

Retributivists argue that what makes punishing a criminal wrongdoer permissible is that a criminal wrongdoer deserves to be punished. They argue that there is no other plausible basis from which to explain why it is justified intentionally to inflict harm on a criminally guilty person but not on a person who has committed no crime. Even Farrell, who rejects the "fierce" retributive argument that a wrongdoer *must* be punished, suspects that the idea that wrongdoing makes a crucial difference to how one may justifiably be treated involves at least a weak form of retributivism.[12]

Others resist this conclusion. Victor Tadros rejects the value of retribution and fills the apparent gap in the argument with the notion that wrongdoers incur a special remedial duty to those they have harmed, a duty that can be discharged by submitting to punishment.[13] Short of positing such a duty, he does not see how we could allow the punishment of someone who cannot be said to deserve it. But ascribing a special duty to criminal wrongdoers adds an unnecessary complication to the justification for punishment. A principle of just harm reduction does not need to rely on the notion that criminal wrongdoers have personal obligations to their victims to accede to being harmed. Furthermore, conceiving of punishment as something that allows individual wrongdoers to discharge special obligations to their victims places the state in the position of facilitating private morality. The state is cast as an enforcer of private, pre-legal duties and obligations, and this fails to account for the public nature of criminal law, which stands for the interests of society, not just the people most directly affected by a criminal wrong.

I reject strong retributive claims, weak retributive claims, and the idea that the permissibility of punishment depends on the notion that wrongdoers incur remedial duties. Farrell's characterization of criminal sanctions as instruments of indirect self-defense is also unsatisfactory, yet he is right to think that what underlies the deterrent use of criminal sanctions is a broader principle of which self-defense is one application. The principle is that of just harm reduction. It allows us to criminalize certain acts and to apply sanctions when doing so prevents, reduces, and remedies harm in the least objectionable way. It permits self-defense and other defensive actions and criminal justice policies, including the imprisonment

of criminals who are dangerous. It also supports efforts through criminal justice institutions to redirect criminal lawbreakers to law-abiding
lives and to increase their chances of meeting law's requirements. Courts
might do this, for example, by requiring people who are convicted of
crimes to perform restitution or community service, to engage in media-
tion, or to enroll in treatment programs for mental illness or substance
abuse.[14] If their victims desire it, the courts might offer defendants the
option to engage in a process of restorative justice.[15]

Recall that Farrell defends the permissibility of indirect self-defense
by arguing that the infliction of harm on an unjust aggressor is justified,
in advance of his aggression, where it is the would-be victim's only available means to prevent the harm. The problem with Farrell's argument is
that it does not incorporate sufficient regard for the aggressor's capacity
for choice. A potential aggressor could decide not to aggress, whether or
not he is harmed. By constructing the thought experiment to rule out the
possibility that a potential aggressor will change his mind, Farrell distorts
the moral dimensions of the situation he describes. Unlike scenarios permitting direct self-defense, in the indirect case there is time and reason
for a potential aggressor to decide not to commit a crime. This fact generates an independent restriction on the acceptable use of coercion. If the
infliction of harm is permitted, it is permitted at least partly on grounds
of persuasion, rather than mere prevention, and to that extent it differs
from the use of force in self-defense.

Just harm reduction must be sensitive to a person's capacity to make
choices that satisfy the requirements of law, even when a person has disregarded those requirements in the past. The action-guiding function of
criminal law, when it is reasonably just, recognizes that actions are morally significant in ways that mere happenings are not, even though actions
and passive responses, such as thoughtless reactions, cannot always
be clearly distinguished. As moral agents, we are, generally speaking,
capable of guiding our choices with practical reasoning, including
reasoning that takes the requirements and sanctions of law into account. Our capacity for practical reasoning and decision-making, and the
difference that exercises of this capability normally make to what a person
does, renders choice salient to law.[16] When law is just, it expresses rea-

sons most people can and usually do take into account, reasons that guide rational and reasonable people to act appropriately.

Because a legal system that is at least minimally just is designed for human beings who can recognize and guide themselves by relevant reasons, moral or prudential, the law's default position should be one of rational address. Threatening an unjust aggressor with retaliation counts as a form of rational address, since its aim is to change the aggressor's self-interested calculation: the prospect of retaliation makes unjust aggression irrational, or so we aim to persuade the aggressor. The deterrent use of force also functions in this way, when it serves to impress upon a wrongdoer the cost of wrongdoing and aspires thus to influence future decision-making. A deterrent strategy treats a criminal wrongdoer as capable of acting better, and should not be viewed as treating her future criminal behavior as otherwise inevitable.

A principle of just harm reduction permits us to apply criminal sanctions to a person who has committed a serious wrong in order to protect, to reduce, and to remediate harm to the basic rights of other people. The mere threat of sanctions has not achieved deterrence. This gives us reasons to take stronger deterrent measures, when a criminal wrongdoer might be convinced by further disincentives to avoid violating the law. Furthermore, when the criminal agent has done harm that might, in some ways, be remedied, we have reason to require such remediation. We cannot say these things about a person who has committed no crime, however worried we may be that he will do so. Each of us has a basic right that our vulnerability to criminal sanctions depend on our voluntary behavior. This right is enshrined in legal doctrine as well as exemplified in a reasonable public morality: the state is prohibited from sanctioning a person who has committed no crime. Penalizing people in order to deter them from committing future wrongs is permissible only when they have already committed criminal acts.

We do not, however, need to rely on claims about moral desert or personal remedial duties in order to justify the use of criminal sanctions to protect shared interests. We may rely instead on a moral appreciation of choice together with the consequences of a person's decisions—how things, in fact, turn out. The quality of a person's choice is of interest to the criminal law, but the impact of a person's actions on other people matters greatly, too. A person is answerable for the consequences of her criminal wrongdoing, at least when they are reasonably foreseeable. Her crime and its harmful effects are attributable to her and provide public reasons to apply coercive measures to dissuade her from future criminal acts, whether or not she is to blame for her morally wrongful action or owes remediation for it. Respect for other people's rights and interests is a central demand of morality, and a person's failure to demonstrate this respect is a matter of reasonable collective interest and concern. We normally can and do regulate ourselves as individuals to meet reasonable public standards of accountability, and when we fail to do this, our fellow citizens are justified in pursuing coercive measures to protect equal basic rights and shared interests, including the use of sanctions to influence people who have committed criminal wrongs to make better choices. People who fail to respect the rights of other people or the fundamental interests of society may be held accountable to action-guiding norms—provided that they are not obviously incapable of satisfying normative demands— whether or not they were, in fact, capable of acting better when they committed a crime. Because a just set of public norms can generally be effective for guiding the behavior of minimally rational beings, it makes sense to design a system of law to attend to the relationship between a person's choices, her actions, and other people's basic interests and rights.

In this way, and provided that they meet relevant criteria of public justification, legal standards comprise a subset of morally justifiable norms—norms that aim to guide people's behavior in mutually justifiable ways. Beings capable of purposeful action might be persuaded by reasons to refrain from acting in ways that violate one another's rights—stealing, assaulting, cheating, et cetera—even if, for some people, the motivating reason is simply to avoid criminal sanctions. When it is possible to take meaningful action, the criminal law may also aim to redress harms a criminal wrongdoer has caused by, for example, forcing a person who steals to return the stolen property. It is the state's duty to require this or other measures of harm reduction. When a principle of just harm reduction authorizes the state to require a defendant to redress his wrong in a particular way, the state's permission to do this does not depend on a criminal wrongdoer's personal duty of redress.

I submit that people concerned to formulate laws that meet public standards of justification would endorse a principle of just harm reduction that permits the application of criminal sanctions to prevent and to remedy the violations of rights and other important collective interests, at least when any harm imposed on wrongdoers does not greatly exceed the harm they have caused. This proportionality constraint (which is not a cost-benefit analysis) expresses a plausible conception of responsibility for harms that are the reasonably foreseeable consequences of a person's choices—a responsibility that permits the state to shift comparable harms onto a criminal wrongdoer in order to prevent further harm and to remediate harm he has done, provided that he is minimally rational.[17] This notion of responsibility is in line with the importance of securing equal basic rights, and with the aims and public function of law to achieve that protection. It would be reasonable for each of us to agree to a system of punishment that has this set of aims, even with the risk of liability it imposes.[18] Criminal sanctions, so understood, would burden people only as a result of choices they make, and only for choices that could be avoided were they to attend to good reasons they have to make better choices. Furthermore, the burden it shifts onto them would not be excessive in relation to the crimes they have committed. For these reasons, the distribution of harms permitted by the principle is not unfair.

Of course, there are some puzzles here, prompted by the notions of reasonable foreseeability and comparable harm, and by reliance on these notions to set standards that some people will not be able to meet. I will address these questions below. But first I take up a prior concern about general deterrence.

I have argued that a burden-shifting principle of harm reduction permits us to apply criminal sanctions in order to deter people from committing criminal acts. That is, the principle supports measures of "specific" deterrence, in which we threaten, or coerce, in order to deter the person being threatened or coerced. Now I will explore how we might bring in an element of "general" deterrence, which is the practice of punishing criminally guilty individuals in order to deter *other* people from committing crimes. Though deterrence is only one component of just harm reduction, it is an important aim of a criminal justice system. I will introduce general deterrence by way of some thoughts about fairness, due process, and the shared responsibility of people who have committed crimes for the consequences of their crimes. These considerations, together with the broader burden-shifting notion of just harm reduction I have been defending, bridge the gap between specific and general deterrence.[19]

The Trouble with Deterrence

General deterrence is an unsettling rationale for criminal justice. It is hard to justify because it seems to involve "using" someone by making an example out of him in order to discourage *other* people from committing crimes. Many people's moral intuitions lead them to balk at the moral permissibility of using someone in this way—as a "mere means," as Kant would put it. We do not normally view ourselves as responsible, at the cost of our liberty, for preventing other people from acting wrongly.

A specific deterrence rationale for threats and sanctions is not subject to this worry. We do not use a person as a mere means if we threaten him, within reasonable limits, in order to stop *him* from acting so as to violate someone else's rights. The aim is to guide his action and, in particular, to discourage him from acting in a way that we have good reason to prohibit. Within reasonable limits, this does not seem objectionable, or so I have argued. I have also argued that we are allowed to avert harms to potential victims by penalizing wrongdoers in order to deter them from aggressing. People who have violated other people's rights are candidates for punishment when their actions suggest that they stand in need of further incentives to comply with the law. By imposing a penalty—for example, incarceration, a monetary fine, community service, or involuntary treatment for addiction—we permissibly aim to guide them to comply with the law in the future, and we relieve potential victims of a threat to their rights.

Thus understood, the aim of punishment is not to give criminal wrongdoers the suffering they deserve but, rather, to provide them with incentives to refrain from reoffending. We must, of course, restrict candidates for punishment to people who have broken the law, not only because requiring a person to serve the general good at severe cost to her personal liberty cannot be squared with that person's individual rights, but also because the effectiveness of a system of threats and penalties is undercut when persons lack confidence that they could avoid sanctions by complying with the law. Moreover, we may punish only people who have faced the threat of punishment; justice requires giving people advance warning that they face a penalty for certain acts.[20] This is a basic element of due process and legality. Provided that these and other relevant conditions are satisfied, the threat and use of criminal sanctions seem among the least objectionable means of protecting each person's basic rights and liberties, short of addressing, more comprehensively, the causes of crime.

A feature of this argument for specific deterrence is that the voluntariness of a criminal act is a criterion of liability to the threat of punishment—not for its connection with moral blameworthiness, but for its connection with the rationality of the threat and use of punishment as a deterrent.[21] Punishment is justified as an incentive to make choosing to comply with the law a rational choice for potential lawbreakers. For persons who cannot understand or be influenced to avoid a criminal sanction, the threat of it cannot function as a disincentive.[22] Minimal rationality is a condition I am endorsing for justified liability to punishment. Therefore, liability would not obtain under some excusing conditions. Certain legally recognized excusing conditions—insanity and deception, for example—point to conditions that undermine the possibility of informed, reasoned choice to comply with the law. When a person's agency is so compromised by mental illness that she fails to meet the most basic requirements of rationality, punishment is not justifiably addressed to her. Nonpunitive forms of behavior control and crime prevention, such as mental health treatment that is not premised on criminal conviction, should be pursued instead. Punishment is properly directed only to people for whom it could rationally count as a disincentive. While there are defensive measures that give us reasons to incapacitate individuals who have demonstrated their dangerousness, and while their confinement might be justified by reference to their dangerousness and inability to be deterred, a criminal justice system will not be viable unless this group is small. A system of law could not function efficiently and with a basic measure of justice unless it offered rational incentives to most of its subjects.

The threat of punishment is also ineffective as a deterrent for people who expect to be punished, whether or not they make reasonable efforts to comply with law. In some neighborhoods it is routine for young people to be harassed and arrested by the police.[23] "Stop and frisk" policies, supported by a low threshold for arrest (such as loitering, or an expansive notion of "disorderly conduct," or "failing to obey a police order"), create an expectation of arrest and punishment. More broadly, a "broken windows" approach to law enforcement, (which recommends aggressive responses to minor offenses, allegedly to contain crime,) together with stringent conditions of probation that might include, for example, a requirement to pay court fees or child support, results in ratcheting up from noncustodial offenses to crimes punishable by incarceration. Just deterrence is undermined by such policies and practices.

These cautionary notes are important because it is crucial that people who are liable to criminal sanctions have a reasonable opportunity to avoid criminal sanctions by choosing to comply with the law. We have seen that the justification and effectiveness of punishment depend on whether a person who is subject to it has a reasonable opportunity to avoid the sanction and good reasons—other-regarding or self-interested—to avoid committing a criminal act. When people lack such reasons, because they are incapable of perceiving the threat of punishment as a rational disincentive, or because they expect to face criminal sanctions regardless of their choices, the threat and use of sanctions against them cannot be justified. In other words, we must acknowledge and support the legal recognition of some morally excusing and mitigating conditions. When such conditions do not obtain, we can say that a person's criminal act could have been avoided in this sense: it was committed under conditions in which that person had good reasons and a reasonable opportunity to avoid breaking the law. The point of punishment is to motivate a person to avoid doing something he ought not do and has a reasonable opportunity to avoid doing.

The construal of reasonable opportunity I have offered, however, may seem to raise a difficult objection—indeed, a version of the objection that made retributivism seem implausible. Standard excusing conditions of the sort we have admitted—such as deception, insanity, ignorance, mistakes, and accidents—may seem to be too limited. Suppose a person regards the threat of punishment as a disincentive for committing a crime, yet fails to be deterred. Her decision to commit a crime is a product of what she is like as a person—which, I argued in earlier chapters, is influenced by genetic and environmental factors beyond a person's control. Sometimes those factors represent hardships that mitigate blame, though they do not fit the legal definitions of excusing conditions, and the criminal justice system does not recognize them. Why is it not plausible to argue that such a person lacked a reasonable opportunity to avoid committing a crime?

A plausible answer is found in the idea that the relevant notion of reasonable opportunity generalizes across persons. Fairness requires us to evaluate and respond to individual infractions with standards that extend to relevantly similar cases. Consider two people, each of whom takes another person's property, though they steal under different circumstances and for different reasons. Normally, it is permissible to charge both with larceny and, if they are found guilty, to sentence them similarly. Here, as discussed in Chapter 1, the law ignores most individual differences. Treating like cases alike, or at least with reasonable similarity, requires some abstraction.[24] (Ironically, of course, if we did not abstract from these differences, the cases would not be alike.)

Both positivist and nonpositivist legal philosophers have recognized the importance to law of treating like cases alike. H. L. A. Hart refers to it as part of the minimum moral content of law, and Ronald Dworkin calls it a matter of integrity in the law.[25] We can understand the rationale for this notion of fairness to connect with the purpose of law as a general and reliable guide to social cooperation. The criminal law, which functions primarily as a constraint on people's behavior, articulates a standard of what it is reasonable to expect of people generally, and it prohibits forms of behavior that are important to discourage and reasonable to discourage using force. A plausible understanding of reasonable opportunity is shaped by the general action-guiding purpose of the law, together with an understanding of the rights, liberties, and interests it is the purpose of the law to protect. Reasonable opportunity is established when behavior that violates these rights or interests is justifiably criminalized and when penalties designed to prompt compliance meet the following conditions: they are applied only in response to the criminal nature of a person's behavior, and they are effective, generally speaking, for discouraging people who are inclined not to comply. If, as I am arguing, this plausible understanding of criminal law's ambition permits and limits punishment, the relevant measure of effectiveness will refer to the average offender.

With the exception of evaluating insanity, a principle of fairness maintaining that like cases be treated alike largely directs us to turn away from the question of what it is reasonable to expect of a particular person, given his individual situation and psychology, and to look instead to the typical circumstances in which other people face the same apparent choice about whether or not to comply with the law. We are to think about what it is reasonable to expect of most people who stand in relevantly similar circumstances. Principles of criminal justice tailored more specifically to realistic expectations of particular individuals would fail to serve as general guides to behavior and protections for common interests. The purpose of the rules imposed by the criminal law is a normative and practical one that is determined by a conception of justice that we have reason to believe people generally are capable of respecting. This means that the rules of criminal law should be pitched according to the normal capacities of people who are at least minimally rational, and that the imposition of penalties may be justified even though some minimally rational individuals do not and perhaps could not comply with the law's directives. We owe one another reasonable security for our basic rights and liberties, but not necessarily every measure of protection against committing crimes.[26] There are good reasons for the law to tailor its excuses narrowly.

The nature and purpose of criminal justice, as I have elaborated it, implies that people who have committed crimes should be considered as members of a group: the group of criminal lawbreakers who, with adequate incentive provided by criminal sanctions, would typically not reoffend, or at least would be significantly less likely to reoffend. Nevertheless, a line of defense should be open to some individual defendants, namely, those for whom the threat of punishment does not function as a rational incentive to comply with the law.[27] The defendant could argue that, despite the fact that he committed a crime, he should not be placed in the group subject to punishment.[28] If the defense can provide evidence to unsettle a presumption of rational competence, the burden of proof is on the prosecution to demonstrate that the defendant had the capacity to perceive the threat of punishment as a rational incentive to comply with the law. I have argued that lacking moral capacity would not be adequate to establish that the burden has not been met. The defendant would have to be unresponsive to the incentive on any rational ground, including a calculation of self-interest.[29] A defendant capable of self-interested calculations would be held criminally liable.

I have argued that fairness in the law requires reasonable parity in criminal liability: people who commit the same crime under similar circumstances are candidates for the same criminal charges and penalties. Individuals should be treated as members of a group—the group of persons who have committed the same type of crime under similar conditions. I have reached this conclusion without relying on considerations of general deterrence. As we have seen, general deterrence is troubling, for it involves restricting the liberties of some people in order to prevent other people from committing crimes. General deterrence seems inconsistent with the foundational commitment of liberal democratic institutions to people's equal basic rights and liberties. We can now see, however, that an interesting consequence of aiming for parity in criminal liability is that in calculating our threats to deter people from reoffending we are, in effect, calculating the general deterrence value of the punishment. The rationale is specific deterrence, but the effect is general deterrence.

Proportionality and its Limits

There will be some people who are not at significant risk of reoffending—less than the average person and perhaps not at all. We need to know whether and how a society could justifiably punish them without embracing retribution or falling into the problems with general deterrence. The problem concerns sentencing. Defendants convicted of the same charges are eligible for the same punishment. But on a harm reduction approach, people who are unlikely to recidivate are poor candidates for punishment.

The considerations of fairness I have introduced suggest that exempting people who are unlikely to recidivate from punishment might be resisted. As we have seen, integrity in the law prescribes that like cases be treated alike. Those who have committed similar crimes are eligible for comparable sentences. Fairness counsels punishing those who are more easily deterred with penalties needed to deter the average offender. Still, fairness may seem to conflict with justice: it is difficult to reconcile a principle of fairness requiring that like cases to be treated alike with a principle of justice requiring that no one's rights be compromised in order to increase overall social utility. This conflict appears to be an unavoidable consequence of a difference between the penalties needed for general deterrence and those allowed on grounds of specific deterrence.

We may connect this worry about punishing the nonrecidivist with a broader concern that nonretributive, consequence-sensitive theories permit punishing too much. Worries about scapegoating and over-punishing are commonly directed toward utilitarian accounts. The account I have begun to develop is not utilitarian, for reasons I will elaborate below, yet similar worries might seem to apply. Consider the matter of scaling punishments for different types of crimes. The account I have proposed thus far suggests that the groupings—the crime types—and the relative seriousness of the corresponding penalties be justified by appeal to how to reduce the harm that crime does overall. What, then, is to ensure that a certain type of crime is not punished too harshly? Many people share the intuition that harsh penalties, such as a prison sentence for misdemeanors like turnstile jumping, truancy, or public drinking, are disproportionate and unjust, even were it the case that a weaker penalty would have less deterrent value.[30] Can this intuition be accounted for in nonretributive terms?

Appealing to deterrence to calibrate sentences could also leave objectionable disparities in the severity of punishment across types of crimes. The deterrent value of a threat is a function of both the severity of the penalty and the chances of being apprehended. This opens up the possibility that less harmful crimes that are unlikely to be detected require stiff sentences to achieve effective deterrence while more harmful crimes that are easily detected could be deterred with light sentences. Appealing to the value of deterrence does not seem to provide adequate protection against disparities in the rank ordering of penalties according to the gravity of crimes. Nor does it guarantee that the punishments for different crimes are adequately spaced. If one sort of crime is only slightly more serious than another, it is inappropriate for the penalty to be considerably more severe.

Retributivists deal with these concerns about proportionality in sentencing by claiming that sentences should be proportionate to the gravity of the crime, for only then are the penalties deserved. The difficulty comes in evaluating gravity by reference to what the defendant deserves. Andrew von Hirsch and Andrew Ashworth write, "The gravity of a crime depends upon the degree of harmfulness of the conduct, and the extent of the actor's culpability."[31] I have raised skeptical doubts about the reliability of our assessments of individual moral culpability. But there is a further problem. Often the gravity of a crime is a function of factors that extend beyond assessments of individual culpability and harm done. A crime's gravity may be influenced by other people's crimes.[32] Let me explain.

When the cause of general deterrence requires a harsher penalty than what is required to achieve specific deterrence, we might think of the penalty as warranted by extending the defendant's liability in order to accommodate penalties that would deter typical offenders of the crime in question. We may do this in order to achieve purposes that correspond to the reasons we have to criminalize acts. One reason is to prevent intolerable harms that the acts in kind typically bring to individual victims (and the people who care about them). This may be a priority apart from the number of people affected. Certain acts, such as rape or murder, are deplorable, however many offenses of their kind we anticipate. These harms are violations of people's most basic rights, and we have reason to use the threat of criminal punishment to discourage people from such wrongdoing. Even if few people are tempted to engage in a certain type of behavior, such as mutilating corpses, the act may be morally serious enough that it makes sense to take steps to solidify our intolerance with measures to discourage those who might be tempted.

The other reason to criminalize a certain type of act is to prevent harm that results from the combined effect of acts of that type. The social disruption or fear generated by a certain type of crime can be a matter of the aggregate effects of many people's actions. A single tax evader may seem

innocuous enough, but the combined effect of many is damaging to a
society's infrastructure and to programs in need of tax support. Moral
appraisal of an individual delinquent in isolation provides inadequate
insight into the reasons for criminalizing his action and the relative
importance of discouraging it. When a person commits a crime, he con-
tributes to a larger problem. This can be true of violent crimes as well.
Fear of assault or robbery that impinges on people's personal freedom to
walk alone at night, for example, is the product of a pattern of violations.
The scale of the larger problem provides grounds to penalize a crime type,
beyond the moral significance of the harm a particular wrongdoer causes
his victim.

We must be careful here. It would be unfair to hold each person who
is convicted responsible for the total effects of his crime type. But it does
not seem unfair to hold each person equally responsible for a *share* in the
total effects of his crime type. We can think of this as responsibility for
the threat of harm, distributed across the population of criminal wrongdoers. Sometimes it is also true that the number of people who engage in
a certain type of crime influences a potential lawbreaker by figuring into
his perception of the likelihood of getting caught. A person may exploit
the fact that others are likely to engage in the sort of crime to which he is
drawn by attempting, in effect, to hide among their numbers. A person
who is tempted to speed may be more likely to do so on a busy highway
with fast-moving traffic.[33] Other drivers may be similarly inclined, resulting in more dangerous highway conditions overall. This weak sense
of coordinated action strengthens the case for maintaining that criminal wrongdoers share responsibility for the aggregate effects of their
type of crime.

An individual's liability should be understood to encompass these considerations. Legislation aiming for general deterrence can be understood
to involve holding each of those who contribute to a social harm similarly
responsible for the typical effects of their crime—taking the typical effects
on individual victims together with a share in the threat to persons generally, measured across the population. A criminal wrongdoer is treated
as a member of a group of people who, together, are responsible for serious harms—harms measured in the typical instance and for a share
in their aggregate effects. A society is permitted to penalize members of

this group in order better to protect the basic rights and interests of its members by establishing an effective scheme for preventing crimes of the kind in question from reoccurring, as well as for possible remediation once a crime has occurred. A burden-shifting principle of harm reduction permits this in order to protect the rights of potential harm victims and, more broadly, the collective interests of society. How intense harm reduction efforts, for a given crime, should be would be a function of how important the society decides it is to deter and remediate crimes of the sort in question. The procedures for making this decision should be fair and inclusive, and the populace should be well informed about the schedule of proposed penalties.[34] A penalty should not exceed what would be reasonably effective for deterring people tempted to commit the crime in question.

Our obligation to refrain from criminal activity is robust enough to warrant extending our liability to punishment in this way. Criminal liability is the corollary of obligations that we have not to act in ways that cause or threaten to cause serious harms, either directly or when combined with the acts of other people. Criminalization acknowledges, formally and publicly, the links between certain kinds of conduct and certain kinds of harms. People are criminally liable when their criminal acts, acts they were on notice to avoid, have contributed causally to an aggregate social harm or to the violation of a person's rights. This notion of criminal liability fits together with what I have presented as a requirement of fairness: that like cases be treated alike. The risk of being held accountable together with other people is a consequence of criminal behavior, something made clear by the law in advance. Punishment can thus be reconciled with the rights of criminal defendants.

As I have described it, responsibility for the effects of crime distributes to individual lawbreakers in the sense that each may be punished. Yet what makes the penalty appropriate is not an evaluation of what a person deserves as a matter of his individual blameworthiness or the impact of a crime on a particular victim. The proper penalty, or at least its upper bound, is scaled instead to the typical harm caused by the sort of crime the defendant committed. Crimes that are typically more harmful may be punished more harshly than less harmful crimes since solving the problems posed by those crimes is more serious. Once a society sets its priorities, provided that they are morally defensible, we have the basis for establishing an upper limit to how much a given crime maybe punished, even when further punishment would be efficacious for achieving greater deterrence.

In considering the upper limit to an entire rank-ordered scale, it is important to bear in mind that the idea of liability for harm done differs strikingly from the goal of maximizing social utility. The goal I am advocating is to promote a legitimate social order after serious criminal activity has disturbed it. I have proposed that the utility exacted by the punishment should be scaled by deciding how important it is to avert the relevant type of harm. Since the harm is measured across a crime type and responsibility for the harm is distributed over the group of people who cause it, proper scaling would refer to the deterrent effect of imposing a penalty on the average person who has committed the crime. I have argued that this seems a fair way to distribute the burden across the group of persons who have committed a crime of a certain sort. The punishment is not calculated to maximize crime prevention by, say, targeting the most determined offenders—a goal that could violate an apt rank ordering of penalties according to the gravity of their crime-type.[35]

Still, sometimes there are factors, like duress, that characterize the circumstances under which a defendant committed a crime and provide reasons to think it is less likely, generally speaking, that defendants who commit crimes under conditions of that sort, would recidivate. These conditions include coercive situations that increase the likelihood that an ordinary person would commit a crime. Suppose someone credibly threatens to harm my daughter unless I drive the getaway car in a burglary. I might consider doing it, though I would otherwise have no desire to become involved. The presence of duress and other forms of coercion can make standard penalties excessive because those penalties are not needed for deterrence. More generally, penalties designed to deter people from committing crimes under conditions like these seem unfair.[36] Some legally recognized excuses—duress, provocation, and entrapment—can be understood in these terms, and a just harm reduction rationale would accept this. Sometimes seemingly like cases are not alike. Yet we can recognize situational factors that mitigate punishment without invoking a retributive theory of criminal justice.

Once retributivism is rejected, there are several considerations that exert pressure toward moderation overall in punishment. Incarceration has devastating effects on incarcerated persons, their families, and their communities.[37] The importance of minimizing these costs counts against marginal gains in deterrence value.[38] In addition, incarceration brings with it serious costs for the broader society, since locking people up is expensive.[39] When other social problems are also pressing, money may be better spent to solve them. Small gains in the marginal deterrence of criminals may not be worth the cost of scarce resources.

This point gains force in view of studies indicating that harsh sentences tend not to produce greater deterrent effects.[40] More effective for deterring crime is the likelihood of getting caught.[41] Limits to general deterrence would then be set by the value a society places on individual liberty and privacy, since crimes could be more easily detected by compromising those protections. A liberal political culture would be reluctant to permit such compromises.

As to the minimum for the scale overall, a minimum punishment for any crime could be preserved by a default shift to the broader deterrence aim of maintaining respect for the law—provided, of course, that a system of law is just enough to be worthy of respect. The burden of helping to maintain norms of law-abidingness is something that might reasonably be required of all lawbreakers, provided that the penalties tied to this general deterrence aim are modest enough to leave room for an ordinal ranking and spacing of crimes by severity. Such modest penalties could be seen in effect to anchor the entire scale.

Once the upper and lower limits are set for the scale overall, it is tempting to conclude that the sentence for each crime is established by its place in an ordinal ranking by severity. But without the goal of retribution there is no moral imperative to punish up to the point allowed by the rank an offense occupies. In fact, on the rationale I have given, punishment is permissible only as part of a broader strategy of crime reduction and remediation. Thus we must accept a serious caveat to the moral requirement that punishments be rank-ordered according to a crime's gravity. Penalties should be rank ordered and spaced according to the social harmfulness of the crime, but only provided that harm reduction could reasonably be achieved by imposing these penalties. Penalties that arc not effective for reducing or remediating crime should not be imposed. If an appreciable measure of harm reduction is achievable with minor penalties, despite the gravity of an offence, this could compromise the rank ordering and spacing of penalties. There are good reasons for this. Further efforts at harm reduction are not desirable and retribution does not justify additional penalties.

The reasoning I have presented, including the argument from fairness, *permits* punishment but does not *require* punishment. For example, the eligibility of all convicted shoplifters for punishment does not require us to punish them equally. A public record of conviction is, of course, a penalty they all receive. Even if we were to reduce, or even to eliminate, the stigma of public blame, a record of wrongdoing is socially significant, as we have seen, in potentially myriad ways.[42] Above the threshold of that burden, the unfairness of punishing some people more than others is not worse than the problems generated by mandating punishment in a heavily punitive society. There are urgent considerations that favor scaling down: namely, the importance of reducing our investment in punishment, especially incarceration.

Morally Rejecting Crime

I have argued that a criminal justice system should aim to establish and sustain an effective, credible, and fair system of threats, with the aim of protecting people's basic rights and liberties by incapacitating criminal wrongdoers, deterring crime, reforming lawbreakers, and redressing harms. The social goal of harm reduction sets this account of punishment apart from retributive views. Furthermore, the nonretributive orientation of my approach is evident in the measures I introduced for evaluating the gravity of crime types. For example, I argued that the moral gravity of an offense might be influenced by the combined effects of its many instances. Thus a criminal wrongdoer's liability to punishment may come apart from his moral blameworthiness and be influenced, in a measured way, by other people's wrongdoing.

I also argued that liability to punishment does not presuppose a person's moral capacity to have complied with the law. A person can be faulted for having done something wrong in the sense that the act was his and he committed it under conditions in which he had a reasonable chance to avoid doing it. But the relevant criteria of reasonable opportunity do not ensure that a criminal lawbreaker had the *moral* capacity to avoid criminal wrongdoing. This means that criminal liability cannot establish that someone deserves to suffer. Some retributivists disagree. They take choice under fair conditions to establish that wrongdoers deserve to be harmed. Determinants of choice—strong emotions motivating choice, for example—are regarded as factors for which a person can rightly be held responsible because they are a part of who he is.[43] In previous chapters, I argued that this retributive position is open to serious doubts about the bases of responsibility for self. My account of criminal justice is much less vulnerable to these worries.

Despite its nonretributivist character, the rationale I have given for criminalization and punishment incorporates certain communicative aims. In fact, it seems naturally to incorporate a morally expressive function. We punish to discourage certain kinds of wrongdoing, and in so doing we express our disapproval of acts of that kind. The relevance of a person's fault, if not his blameworthiness, opens the way for his punishment to communicate a moral judgment. The object of the moral judgment, as I have construed it, would be the wrongdoer's act.[44] A criminal act is judged to be incompatible with other people's basic rights or with important collective interests. In judging an act to be wrong and worthy of criminal sanctions, we display publicly our moral rejection of acts of that type and call attention to the reasons we take them to be objectionable. This public expression stands independently of our assessment of any particular individual's blameworthiness for failing to take moral reasons into account.

While morally judging an act to be wrong differs from morally condemning a person as blameworthy, it does make room for public acknowledgment, in moral terms, of harms done to crime's victims. This public acknowledgment may be important to many people. Moreover, it may serve such important aims as strengthening the ties of community, vindicating the law, and increasing mutual respect for individual rights.[45] These aims would seem naturally to be served by a public demonstration of commitment to increasing the safety of potential victims by using the criminal justice system to incapacitate, deter, and rehabilitate criminal wrongdoers and, when possible, to redress the harmful effects of crimes on their victims. These purposes together constitute a morally adequate response to victims. I submit that victims have no right to a retributive form of justice that would reach beyond these aims.

An account of justice that permits the use of criminal sanctions and aims to treat defendants fairly must reckon with the substantial power and discretion of prosecutors, especially in an adversarial system. In the American system, prosecutors have wide latitude to decide whom to charge and what to charge them with. Our current system—in which the vast majority of criminal prosecutions are resolved by plea bargains, and in which sentencing guidelines reduce the ability of judges to adjust punishments to fit the particulars of each case—has effected a transfer of power from judges to prosecutors: the charges that the prosecutor chooses to bring, and the deal that he or she offers the defendant, pretty much determines the defendant's punishment. The imbalance between prosecution and defense of resources and control over the criminal justice system is very concerning, and the abuse of prosecutorial power is dangerous. Mandatory minimums, "three strikes" laws, and life without parole are major drivers of mass incarceration. Moreover, evidence shows that mandatory sentences have been imposed at a higher rate on defendants of color—a consequence of a prosecutor's decision about which charges to bring.[46] In view of these problems, we should repeal draconian and mandatory penalties and view parity in sentencing as a presumptive guideline for judges and prosecutors, rather than a formal constraint on judges.

Still, there is always a danger that ethical pressure on the criminal justice system to treat like cases alike will lead to corrections in favor of more punishment. This result would stand in tension with a reasonable requirement of parsimony in punishment, but political realities can be stubborn, and philosophers should be cautious. In a punishment-happy society like the United States, scaling up is always a threat. We should counter it with deliberate attempts to scale down. This book belongs to that effort. It is my assessment that a "lock 'em up" mentality and the excessive punishment it supports are undermined by rejecting the blaming function of punishment, and by criticizing the political manipulation of public sentiment as well as systematic racial bias in prosecution and sentencing. The requirements of fairness I have stressed are not likely to be distorted in favor of more punishment were we to reject the blaming function of punishment and to address systematic injustices. Appropriate skepticism about the blaming function of punishment would lead us to be more hesitant to punish *anyone* beyond what is minimally required by reasonable harm-reduction goals. Just harm reduction directs us to relinquish our infatuation with public forms of blame and to work toward a society in which all persons subject to law are treated as worthy of respect. For example, eliminating prison uniforms and offering incarcerated people some measures of privacy—standard practices in some European systems of criminal justice—are appropriate acknowledgments of individual dignity.[47]

The main danger of deterrence as a rationale for criminal justice is its vulnerability to excessive fear of crime.[48] Harm reduction in response to crime is but one among numerous social goals that serve our basic rights, liberties, and collective interests. A balanced political agenda will understand criminal justice as one aspect of a broader commitment to social justice. This broader commitment includes ensuring adequate opportunities for all members of society to enjoy education, health, a decent income, and political influence. Fear of crime should not be allowed to offset the importance of our shared responsibility to advance this broader social justice agenda. There is a disturbing tension between our shared responsibility to address the social injustice underlying much criminal behavior and the retributivist's focus on individual culpability for crime. Our understanding of criminal justice should not be at odds with our collective responsibility to secure the broader terms of social justice.

Clearly, the notion of reasonable opportunity I have endorsed, together with its limited range of excusing conditions, falls considerably short of the fair opportunities for education, employment, health care, and the like demanded by social justice. On the rationale I have presented, criminal punishment may be permitted in a society even when that society is characterized by serious social and material inequalities, which are unjust and help to explain criminal behavior. The permissibility of punishment signifies the priority that protecting basic rights and certain collective interests has within a conception of social justice. The wider context of social injustice, of course, demands redress, and it challenges our blaming attitudes toward people who have been convicted of crimes.

It is possible that systematic conditions of social injustice consistently undermine the rational force of punishment as a disincentive for certain crimes. Uniform evidence of the failure of deterrence for members of a marginalized social group would be symptomatic of a loss of institutional legitimacy. It would reveal a breakdown of respect for law and order in that segment of society.[49] The legitimacy of criminal sanctions for the sorts of crimes in question—for example, certain property and drug crimes—would be called into doubt, since the law would have become a system of coercion lacking public justification.[50] I now turn to a discussion of these serious matters.

SIX

LAW ENFORCEMENT IN
AN UNJUST SOCIETY

I NCARCERATION IS A SERIOUS, life-debilitating experience imposed most frequently on racial minorities and the poor—the very population most vulnerable to social injustice prior to incarceration. We have seen that the use of incarceration as punishment requires careful justification, even in a society whose institutions are basically just. In reality, things are more complicated, because most societies are burdened with one or another serious injustice. What relevance, if any, does systematic social injustice have for thinking about the moral permissibility of law enforcement or the use of incarceration in a society like the United States?[1] Social injustice—which includes poverty, racial discrimination, and the persistence of historically rooted inequalities—presents special problems for philosophical theories according to which the liability to punishment depends on the state's moral authority to blame people with criminal convictions for their criminal acts. When the state has failed to redress the unjust social circumstances surrounding many criminal convictions, the state's standing to blame is undercut. This provides further reasons for rejecting punishment as a form of blame, which is an understanding of punishment that is uncritically accepted too often by too many people.

Social injustice also presents a problem for *any* theory of punishment, including an account of punishment focused on harm reduction rather than retribution. When it is serious, social injustice can undermine the democratic authority of the state to enforce legal rules, whether or not punishment functions to express blame. This is because it is objectionable for people to be to be burdened with serious, harmful consequences for breaking the law when they are not treated, in basic respects, as equal members of society. This objection is serious enough to unsettle the conventional presupposition of law's moral authority.

A Nest of Problems

The vast majority of people locked up in the United States are poor, and not just because they are in prison. A 2014 study analyzing data from the Bureau of Justice Statistics found that incarcerated people in all gender, race, and ethnicity groups earned substantially less prior to incarceration than their nonincarcerated peers. In fact, they were found to concentrate at the very lowest end of the national income distribution. The median pre-incarceration income of the largest segment of the incarcerated population, ages twenty-seven to forty-two, was $19,185—41 percent less than the income of nonincarcerated people in the same age group.[2]

Sociologist William Julius Wilson describes the economically most vulnerable population in American society as "the truly disadvantaged."[3] The truly disadvantaged live in areas of concentrated poverty—urban areas with a high percentage of poor people—and they come from families with a history of poverty. Neighborhoods afflicted by concentrated poverty are socially and economically isolated, and they tend to be racially segregated as well. People who live in these neighborhoods are troubled by joblessness, crime, delinquency, drug trafficking, broken families, and dysfunctional schools.[4] The joblessness rate reveals that a substantial proportion of the adult population is either officially unemployed or has dropped out of the labor force.[5] The distinction between unemployment and joblessness is important. The official unemployment rate does not capture the rate of joblessness because it does not include people who have stopped looking for work or never entered the job market. The rate of joblessness for Black American men, in particular, is especially high in areas of concentrated urban poverty, and it has grown

significantly in the last four decades. Wilson reports that in the traditional Black Belt area of Chicago's South Side, where Black migrants
from the South settled in the early twentieth century, 64 percent of all
males fourteen and older were employed in 1960, whereas only 37 percent
of all males sixteen and over were employed in 1990.[6] Nationally, between 2000 and 2004, the average real annual earnings—earnings adjusted for inflation—of twenty-four-year-old Black males who were in
the bottom quarter of the earnings distribution (that is, the twenty-fifth
percentile of earnings) were only $1,078, compared with $9,623 for Latino
males and $9,843 for white males.[7] Many of these men have low levels of
education, and their life prospects—how well they can expect to do in
their life course—are severely limited.

Racial minorities are disproportionately represented among the truly
disadvantaged, and they are also disproportionally represented among the
incarcerated. Two out of every three people in prison are people of color.
Incarceration rates for Black non-Hispanic adult males are nearly seven
times that of non-Hispanic white men, and among Hispanic men the rate
is approximately three times the incarceration rate of white men.[8] More
than a third of Black men without a high school diploma are currently in
prison.[9] These are shocking numbers for a society that promises liberty
and justice for all.

The politics of crime has been hard on the truly disadvantaged. By "the
politics of crime," I am referring to a punitive law-and-order approach to
social problems. This includes the "war on drugs" as well as a political
climate favoring increasingly harsh sentences for violent crimes.[10] The
United States has dramatically intensified its punitive policies in recent
decades. Between 1980 and 2001, the average time served for a drug crime
increased 71 percent—from fourteen to twenty-four months—and the average time served for a violent crime rose 60 percent—from thirty-three
months to fifty-three months. The number of drug arrests almost tripled
(from 580,900 to 1,579,600), and the number of prison admissions per
drug arrest rose six-fold. The arrest rate for violent offenses increased only
slightly, but prison admissions per arrest more than doubled (from
13 percent to 28 percent). Regarding property crimes, the arrest rate per
offense remained steady but the time served almost doubled (from sixteen
to twenty-eight months).

This escalation of punishment in America bears no consistent relationship to the crime rate. In other words, the crime and punishment rates are not inversely correlated. Numerous studies of the deterrence and incapacitation function of punishment yield no consensus on the relationship between more incarceration and less crime.[11] As political scientist Marie Gottschalk concisely summarizes the empirical findings, "We have long known that crime rates move up and down independently of punishment practices."[12] Contrary to popular opinion, punishment seems to be driven by a logic of its own, apart from its effects on crime. This gives rise to complex and interesting questions about the causes of punishment, questions that go beyond the scope of this book. It is the contention of this book, however, that *a punitive, moralizing conception of individual responsibility provides, at the very least, a cover for public acceptance of a harsh and unforgiving punishment culture.*

The politics of crime has disproportionately burdened the truly disadvantaged for many reasons, among them the following. Residing in an area of concentrated poverty increases one's chance of arrest and incarceration for criminal activity, real or suspected. Police have targeted urban neighborhoods with "stop and frisk" policies, leading to sweeping arrests of low-level offenders. Federal cash grants to state and local law enforcement agencies have supported and rewarded this "broken windows" approach.[13] Furthermore, the government has promoted aggressive police tactics through military-style training and technical support. From 2006 to 2015, the federal government provided $2.2 billion worth of military equipment to state and local law enforcement agencies, including M16 and M14 rifles, riot shotguns, airplanes, helicopters, armored trucks and cars, mine detecting sets, grenade launchers, bayonets, and swords.[14] Clearly a military-style "war on crime" hardly conditions a moderate and balanced approach to law enforcement and criminal prosecution, and the least well off members of society pay the heaviest price for a maximalist approach.

Generally speaking, defendants from poor neighborhoods, and especially people of color, are more likely to be charged with serious crimes, less likely to receive favorable plea agreements, and more likely to receive harsher sentences, including the death penalty. Though Black men have higher rates of involvement in crime, especially violent crime, this does not suffice to explain existing differences in incarceration rates.[15] For example, Blacks are no more likely to use drugs than whites, yet they are much more likely to be arrested and imprisoned for drug offenses.[16] Racial prejudice influences the behavior of police, prosecutors, judges, and juries, and other factors also disproportionately burden defendants from areas of concentrated poverty. For example, in densely populated inner-city neighborhoods, criminal activity is more likely to occur in proximity to schools, a fact that can be used by prosecutors to increase sentences. Urban schools are themselves more likely to have police presence, and data indicates that schools that employ police are more apt to take a law enforcement approach to student misconduct.[17]

When a poor defendant faces criminal charges, a lack of resources makes mounting a criminal defense difficult and increases a defendant's odds of going to prison. The 1963 Supreme Court decision in *Gideon v. Wainwright* promised legal representation to all defendants facing felony charges, yet the promise has proven hollow. The public defender system is woefully underfunded, understaffed, and, in some jurisdictions, non-existent.[18] Public defenders are burdened with enormous caseloads, which compromise their ability to provide professional services to their clients. It is not uncommon for indigent defendants to meet their lawyer for the first time only a few minutes before a hearing or trial, and sometimes as a group. Some public defender offices have no budgets for case investigations, unlike district attorneys, who work closely with the police. As defense lawyer Stephen Bright sums up the dismal situation, "The U.S. criminal system is not truly adversarial because prosecutors possess broad, unchecked power and therefore determine results in criminal cases with little or no input from the defense."[19] Faced with bleak prospects for a fair trial, and often a lack of money to post bail, the vast majority, roughly 95 percent, of criminal defendants resolve their cases through a plea bargaining process in which defendants are threatened with sometimes outrageous sentences unless they accept "deals" offered by the prosecution.

Prisons themselves are brutal places with very few support services, despite the needs of the incarcerated population. Addiction and mental illness, common among the incarcerated, receive little attention. According to a report by the National Center on Addiction and Substance Abuse at Columbia University, "Of the 2.3 million inmates in U.S.

prisons, 65 percent—1.5 million—meet the DSM-IV medical criteria
for alcohol or other drug abuse and addiction."[20] Yet only about
11 percent of the addicted population receives any treatment in prison.
Mental illness is also rampant among the incarcerated, and treatment
is sparse.[21]

The injuries and trauma imposed by incarceration are little studied or
addressed by the medical profession or our health care system. There is
a growing literature in psychiatry on post-traumatic stress disorder, with
scant attention to prisons.[22] Juveniles are especially vulnerable to the
traumas associated with incarceration, and will reckon with the scars of
prison for the majority of their lives. A wrenching example is the story of
Kalief Browder, a teenager who was incarcerated for three years at New
York's Rikers Island while awaiting trial.[23] Eight hundred of those days
were spent in solitary confinement.[24] Ultimately, charges against Browder
were dropped for lack of evidence, and he was released. He died by suicide two years later.

Currently, 2.3 million people are locked up in the United States, and
we demonstrate little concern about the psychological damage this does
to them. To the contrary, prison seems designed to inflict psychological
distress and suffering beyond the anguish caused by the deprivation of
freedom.[25] The use of solitary confinement is one disturbing example of
a particularly brutal and psychologically damaging practice that has
prompted outcry by human rights groups.[26] People imprisoned in solitary confinement live twenty-two to twenty-four hours per day, for weeks
and sometimes years, in small, often windowless rooms, with little to no
human interaction. Researchers estimate that in 2014 between 80,000 and
120,000 people were held in solitary confinement on any given day.[27]

The harm of incarceration extends beyond damage to mental health
and self-esteem. Criminal arrest and conviction carry with them serious
and lasting social stigma. This stigma is often accompanied by the permanent retraction of important entitlements and rights, such as eligibility for student loans, housing assistance, food stamps, and the right
to vote. Felony conviction can lead to deportation in the case of noncitizens. Licenses in many professions and occupations are unavailable to
people with felony records. For example, in the state of California, a
person with a record of conviction for *any* felony is ineligible to be li-

censed as a nurse, social worker, optometrist, landscape architect, contractor, psychologist, marriage or family therapist, Department of Motor Vehicles employee, home-care aide, or professional photocopier.[28] The stigma of criminality supports the law's verdict that it is not illegal to discriminate against felons who apply for employment, admission to college, mortgages, or housing. As a result, felons are more likely to be jobless, poor, uneducated, and homeless—all factors that are correlated with recidivism and reincarceration.

These are very serious burdens imposed on socioeconomically disadvantaged people whose prospects for leading satisfactory, law-abiding lives have been seriously and unjustly compromised, even apart from the harms inflicted on them by the criminal justice system.

In the next three sections of this chapter, I discuss the problem social injustice presents for the state's authority to blame. Then I turn to the broader problem of the conditions of democratic legitimacy for a criminal justice system. We will find that when law enforcement lacks democratic authorization, this compromises the normative authority of the criminal law. It disturbs the presumption that law is rightfully enforced and should be obeyed. A criminal justice system that lacks democratic authorization has no authority beyond what is supported by a moral calculus of relevant costs and benefits. Law enforcement has no authority beyond the good it does, and when it does no good, it does not morally demand our respect and deference.

A(nother) Problem for Retributive Theories

In earlier chapters, I showed that a retributive theory of criminal justice cannot justify the practice or doctrine of Anglo-American criminal law. I also presented compelling reasons to reject attempts to reform the law in a retributive direction. There is no satisfactory public justification for organizing our criminal justice system around the aim of retribution. This chapter adds a new argument against the retributive theory: in a system that consistently and unfairly denies important opportunities to members of certain groups, criminal punishment of members of those groups cannot be justified on grounds of retribution.[29] People who defend punishment as retribution tend to do so in a "siloed" manner, without reference to the social, political, and economic context in which individuals are deemed to "deserve" their punishments. They are mistaken to do so. Indeed, retributivists who have acknowledged the interdependence of criminal and distributive justice have recognized that distributive injustice can remove the state's basis for administering a scheme of retribution. *Just as the permissible use of criminal punishment depends on the minimal rationality of defendants, it also depends on social conditions of basic distributive justice. When these conditions are not satisfied, the state lacks standing to administer punishment on the basis of anything like desert and retribution.*

The central claim of the retributive notion of justice is that justice requires culpable wrongdoers to pay a price for their culpable wrongdoing. In particular, the retributive view maintains that justice requires the suffering of culpable wrongdoers, and that culpable wrongdoers ought, morally speaking, to be harmed in proportion to their wrongdoing. According to a retributivist, this proportional suffering is not a cost that is outweighed by the good criminal punishment does. It is valuable and itself required by justice, apart from its consequences. Consider two different versions of the retributive view. First, there is Jeffrie Murphy's "fair play" notion of desert.[30] According to Murphy, those who disobey the law gain an unfair advantage over those who obey voluntarily. A lawbreaker gains the benefits of the system—other people's obedience to law—without accepting the burdens of self-restraint. Punishment restores a proper balance between the benefits and the burdens of the system for each person. According to Murphy, "If a person chooses not to sacrifice by exercising self-restraint and obedience, this is tantamount to his choosing to sacrifice in another way—namely, by paying the prescribed penalty."[31] Punishment takes from a criminal something that he owes—it exacts a debt, and thereby balances the scales of justice. According to this view, punishment is a fair price to pay for lawbreaking.

As Murphy points out, this justification supposes that law abiders are advantaged by their participation in a reciprocal system of benefits, which outweighs the disadvantage of self-restraint. But under conditions of social injustice, this might not be true. Those who are socially disadvantaged might not gain an unfair social advantage through their criminal activity. In that case, according to Murphy, they could not be said to deserve punishment. Murphy imagines an armed robber "whose whole life has been one of frustrating alienation from the prevailing socio-economic structure—no job, no transportation if he could get a job, substandard education for his children, terrible housing and inadequate health care for his whole family, condescending-tardy-inadequate welfare payments, harassment by the police but no real protection by them against the dangers in his community, and near total exclusion from the political process. Learning all this," writes Murphy, "would we still want to talk—as many do—of his suffering punishment under the rubric of 'paying a debt to society'? Surely not. Debt for what?"[32] Murphy's point is that injustice in the basic structure of society can undermine a fair play source of obligation to comply with the law. We will see that this claim is plausible when the structural injustice is broad and serious, and that it challenges nonretributive as well as retributive conceptions of criminal justice.

Murphy's version of this worry supposes that claims about moral desert depend on distributive justice, so much so that under conditions of distributive injustice, many wrongdoers could not deserve retribution. Not only are the disadvantaged burdened by an unfair lack of socioeconomic opportunities; often they do not receive adequate law enforcement protection, despite higher rates of crime in their neighborhoods. In fact, residents of poor urban neighborhoods may hesitate to call upon the police when they have been victimized by crime, and with good reason. The police concentrate on poor neighborhoods to detain and arrest suspects and to harass people on the street, but this does not have the effect of making residents of these neighborhoods feel protected and safe. The police intimidate law-abiding citizens, who fear arrest themselves if they call the police for assistance.[33] Members of disadvantaged neighborhoods receive few systematic benefits of a cooperative institutional system of law and order and are instead vulnerable to harm by criminal justice practices.

For example, in an August 2016 U.S. Department of Justice investigation of policing in the city of Baltimore, the DOJ concluded that the Baltimore police department "engages in a pattern or practice of (1) making unconstitutional stops, searches, and arrests; (2) using enforcement strategies that produce severe and unjustified disparities in the rates of stops, searches and arrests of African Americans; (3) using excessive force; and

(4) retaliating against people engaging in constitutionally-protected expression." Investigators describe unconstitutional searches as follows:

> During stops, BPD officers frequently pat-down or frisk individuals as a matter of course, without identifying necessary grounds to believe that the person is armed and dangerous. And even where an initial frisk is justified, we found that officers often violate the Constitution by exceeding the frisk's permissible scope. We likewise found many instances in which officers strip search individuals without legal justification. In some cases, officers performed degrading strip searches in public, prior to making an arrest, and without grounds to believe that the searched individuals were concealing contraband on their bodies.[34]

The report describes an egregious pattern of constitutional violations in the city's poor Black neighborhoods, in stark contrast with positive experience of law enforcement by the residents of wealthier neighborhoods. People living in the city's wealthier and largely white neighborhoods reported that officers "tend to be respectful and responsive to their needs," while residents of the city's largely Black neighborhoods "often felt they were subjected to unjustified stops, searches, and arrests, as well as excessive force." Evidence of systematic patterns of violations and abuse was largely uncontested. The report states that "almost everyone who spoke to us—from current and former City leaders, BPD officers and command staff during ride-alongs and interviews, community members throughout the many neighborhoods of Baltimore, union representatives of all levels of officers in BPD, advocacy groups, and civic and religious leaders— agrees that BPD has significant problems that have undermined its efforts to police constitutionally and effectively." The DOJ report and others like it add credibility to the notion that Murphy has identified a real problem for a fair play version of the retributive thesis, at least in places with similar law enforcement practices. Those who break the law in disadvantaged neighborhoods might not have received the benefits of a cooperative and reciprocally beneficial set of law and order practices. In that case, their law breaking would not amount to unfair "freeriding."

Let's now consider a different version of the retributive thesis. According to Michael Moore, morally culpable wrongdoers deserve to suffer.[35] This is a moral claim about desert that treats desert as a function of culpable wrongdoing, whether or not that wrongdoing occurs under conditions of social cooperation and reciprocity. The retributive ideal applies under *any* circumstances in which a person can act wrongly and be culpable for that wrongdoing. This version of the retributive view does not depend on claiming that the function of criminal justice institutions is to serve the interests of persons as free and equal cooperating members of society. Instead, the alleged purpose of criminal justice institutions is to give wrongdoers what they morally deserve. Since some actions are wrong even in the context of social injustice, social inequality does not necessarily challenge the legitimacy of criminal justice practices.

This formulation of the retributive thesis is not appealing. Moore rejects reciprocity as a premise of retributive justice, without replacing it with a plausible conception of individual responsibility. As discussed in Chapter 2, it is reasonable to believe that any notion of moral culpability robust enough to support the claims of retributive justice would imply, at least, that a culpable wrongdoer had a *capacity* to have acted better. Individuals could not plausibly be said to deserve penalties they were not capable of avoiding. Specifically, a person could not deserve to suffer by virtue of being the kind of person who chooses badly, unless that person were capable of making a better choice. Moore treats choice as the criterion of responsibility, but mere voluntariness—whether action is a function of choice without coercion, which is the core of criminal law's conception of free will—is insufficient to establish a wrongdoer's competence to have chosen better. If a retributive understanding of moral desert requires a wrongdoer's capacity to have chosen well, as I have argued, then many criminal wrongdoers—for example, the mentally ill and perhaps people who are unshakably selfish or cruel—will turn out not to be culpable for their wrongdoing.[36] Insofar as these individuals are not capable of altering their own psychological dispositions, they do not deserve punishment.

Seriously unjust circumstances also challenge relevant judgments of blameworthiness, at least regarding some crimes, because these circumstances substantially narrow a person's prospects for legal employment, remove important sources of social support, and impose psychological stress and harm. As discussed in Chapter 3, judgments of deservingness are challenged by circumstantial as well as "internal" factors, since a person's prospects for satisfying her basic needs, while leading a law-abiding life, depend on enabling social conditions as well as a healthy psychological disposition. Possibilities for empathy and understanding of criminal wrongdoers who have suffered difficult life circumstances help to show that retributive sentiments are not morally required in response to criminal wrongdoing, contrary to what some retributivists claim.

We are in the highly contested territory of legal theory debates. Some theorists will try to rescue the notion of retributive desert. It may or may not be worthwhile pursuing an argument with them. But, as I will now argue, even if the notion of moral desert could be rescued, there would be a serious problem with the practice of implementing retributive justice or, more generally, a view of punishment as morally deserved. I turn now to that problem.

Moral Standing to Blame

The problem is this: pervasive social injustice challenges the *moral standing* of authorities and, more broadly, the public to stigmatize criminal wrongdoers as deserving punishment. Here I am separating the question of whether criminally guilty individuals deserve punishment from the question whether authorities have the moral standing to blame them. Apart from whatever the truth may be about what criminal wrongdoers deserve, the administration of retributive justice requires that authorities have the moral standing to admonish them as individually responsible for their criminal acts. The administration of retributive justice expresses blame, and public authorities must have standing to deliver it.

The retributive view belongs to a family of views about criminal punishment that construes a finding of criminal guilt to involve a claim about the moral blameworthiness of a person who has been convicted. Not all moral theories that stress the moral blameworthiness of criminal wrongdoers count as retributive theories. Retributive theories add the further claim that blameworthy wrongdoers ought to be harmed, that justice calls for harming them because that's what they morally deserve. In other words, for retributivists, the imposition of punishment has a blaming purpose that involves harming. But this involves a claim that goes beyond an assessment of a person's blameworthiness. It accords a particular role to the state: to blame that person on behalf of us all by imposing sanctions. Theories in agreement on the point that the finding of legal guilt indicates (or should indicate) that a person convicted of a crime deserves moral blame might refuse a retributive understanding of whether or how that blame ought to be expressed and, in particular, whether a criminal sentence should be calibrated as a matter of moral desert. For example, Tommie Shelby argues that the finding of guilt exhausts the function of criminal justice institutions to express moral blame; the rationale for the infliction of punishment should be regarded as a separate matter that is justifiable only to further the social good.[37] According to Andrew von Hirsch, moral censure represents the primary purpose of punishment, but other aims, including deterrence, are also permissible. Punishment should be minimal, though, so it is not coopted by its secondary purposes.[38]

Differences aside, let's concentrate on the notion that either criminal conviction or punishment, or both, involve blaming. Blame involves shifting our moral view from appraisal of *act* to *agent*. Blaming expresses a negative moral appraisal of a wrongdoer in view of her wrongdoing. It imposes a moral stigma on the wrongdoer as a person. More specifically, blaming involves altering relationships and expectations to imply that a wrongdoer has disrupted relations of reciprocal concern and respect that form the basis of our moral expectations, and that this disruption calls for disapproving moral attitudes and repudiating behavior toward her.[39] We imply that a wrongdoer has willfully violated reasonable and mutual expectations of trust, good will, and consideration, and for reasons that reveal morally undesirable personal qualities, qualities for which the wrongdoer is accountable. Blame implies that we should now lower our expectations of the wrongdoer, qualify our good will toward her, and admonish her in a way that communicates the seriousness of the relational damage she has done. This is allegedly what the wrongdoer deserves, and this assessment is assigned to her moral character.

The social stigma of criminality—whether incurred via legal findings of guilt or the imposition of punishment—functions as a form of public blame. The stigma of criminality signifies a morally weighty alteration of social relationships in response to a negative moral appraisal of the wrong-doer in light of his criminal wrongdoing. As we have seen, criminal conviction alters a person's social status and opportunities in profound and lasting ways. The stigma and its rationale imply that this is what a criminal wrongdoer deserves. Yet the existence of social injustices that disproportionately burden people who end up in prison may seem to disrupt an analysis according to which moral blame presumes that the reasonable moral expectations the wrongdoer has violated were supported by morally viable relationships. Social injustice indicates morally dysfunctional social relationships. Of course, this is not to say that moral expectations always presume morally intact and healthy relationships. We can and do evaluate people for behaving badly in morally abnormal and even perilous situations. For example, we recognize ethical principles of conduct that apply in the context of war, we recognize proportionality limits to a principle of self-defense, and we are often comfortable enough evaluating the responses of individuals who are abused. Stressful and morally dysfunctional situations can mitigate blame without excusing the wrongdoer from it. Blame might still be fitting, even when its intensity is mitigated by attention to obstacles the wrongdoer faced. Nevertheless, the relevant point here is not about what a person deserves. It is that unjust circumstances disrupt the ordinary suppositions of *public* blame: namely, the proposition that our moral obligations to respect the rights of other people have the support of mutually and reciprocally beneficial political arrangements. In this way, social injustice wholly or partially disables the moral appropriateness of public blame, by exposing as fraudulent a premise of the state's claim to have moral standing to blame.

In an unjust society, the basis of mutuality and trust in social relationships is lacking. This lack of reciprocity is especially harmful to members of society who are least well off; they are the primary targets of mistrust, suspicion, and deprivation. In that context, blaming a criminal wrongdoer is morally unbalanced. It avoids attending to significant wrongs a disadvantaged person has suffered and the collective responsibility a society bears for those wrongs. By tolerating social injustice, the state and members of society who support it have demonstrated a lack of concern and respect for the just claims of the disadvantaged. A more measured perspective would include empathy for a person who has struggled with these difficulties, solidarity with a person's rejection of social injustice, and recrimination of the state. It would not be overwhelmingly punitive toward people who commit crimes.

To deepen the point: not only is the basis of mutuality and trust in social relationships lacking under conditions of social injustice, but the lack of mutuality and trust in social relationships has also been perpetuated by the state's own failure to remedy social injustice.[40] The state has violated its duty to provide mutually beneficial social institutions. By contributing to the establishment and maintenance of a system that denies reasonable opportunities for education, jobs, homes, health care, and legal assistance to a significant segment of the population, the state has failed to deliver even minimal justice. Prior to any criminal offense a disadvantaged person may or may not commit, the basis of trust in socially cooperative relations has already been disrupted by unjust background conditions that have been tolerated by the state and by people who confer a sense of legitimacy upon its institutions and practices—a sense of legitimacy that is used to perpetuate a culture of blame.[41]

The state's failure to deliver minimal justice damages its claim to moral authority.[42] Under conditions of social injustice, moral expectations among members of society cannot reasonably be supported by reasons to think that the state represents a shared perspective and common interests. The state's standing to blame is undermined when background injustice is severe: when the police are not trustworthy, when legal opportunities for a living wage are not reliable, when housing, health care, and social services are inadequate, and when people who live in poverty are not protected from crime. The case for this conclusion is strong in a society that could afford to satisfy the minimal requirements of justice were it to rearrange its priorities. Its failure to do so has implications for the moral standing of its officials.

Contextual Causation

In fact, the problem extends beyond the state's failure to secure reasonable expectations of trust and reciprocity between its citizens. The state is implicated in the problem of crime. Unjust governmental policies and a lack of institutional support for morally functional social relationships have wrongfully restricted opportunities and choices available to people who are seriously disadvantaged and have increased the appeal, and even sometimes the necessity, of criminal activity. In this respect, the state's injustice is a *cause* of the wrong for which a wrongdoer is blamed individually.

There are, of course, substantial epistemic impediments to determining what difference social injustice makes in any individual case, but that is not my point. I have already stressed epistemic obstacles to appraisals of individual moral capacity. The epistemic inaccessibility of the difference social and environmental factors make to an individual's decision to commit a crime has been a central theme of prior chapters. There is, however, no epistemic difficulty in showing that social factors make a difference to crimes rates. And if social injustice makes a difference to crime rates, members of society share responsibility for the problem of crime.

Causal claims about differential crime rates are supported by "ecological" theories of crime, which explain crime as the outcome of an environment of social structures, incentives and disincentives, opportunities and barriers.[43] Dominant explanations appeal to economic, psychological, institutional, geographical, and sociological factors. Findings indicate the causal relevance of failures on the part of the state to deliver justice. As I have suggested, because explanations operate at a macrolevel and focus on the crime rate rather than particular actions, they avoid deterministic claims about individual choices. The agency of individuals is not negated; rather it is placed in the context of an individual's life circumstances, which include important facts about institutions and social life.

Three different approaches are dominant in the criminology literature. An *economic* approach to thinking about punishment was introduced in the eighteenth century by Jeremy Bentham and also by Cesare Beccaria, and was elaborated by Gary Becker in the 1960s.[44] It illustrates the typical logic of deterrent approaches to criminal punishment, in which potential wrongdoers are presented with disincentives. An economic analysis of the crime rate represents individuals as rational agents who choose among available opportunities on the basis of self-interested calculations about likely benefits. Crime is understood as analogous to employment and other market activities: it is one line of work among others. People choose crime when the expected utility of doing so exceeds the expected costs. In this way, crime has a standard economic supply function. Social inequality means that some people have drastically lower returns to legal market participation than others and potentially higher ratios of reward-to-risk associated with crime. In other words, inequality is a causal factor in crime by changing expected utility. Unless punishment raises the cost of crime sufficiently, increases in socioeconomic inequality will raise the expected utility of crime for the less well off, causing increased crime.[45]

This framework yields some undeniable explanatory power, particularly regarding property crimes, but it is open to criticism for its psychologically thin representation of human agency as a utility function. Still, by portraying criminal choices as rational under some social circumstances, even under the threat of punishment, it highlights the state's abdication of its responsibility to ensure a decent menu of choices for all its citizens or, when that is not possible, to at least provide adequate social welfare for those who lack employment.

An approach centered more fully on the psychology of offenders is found in *strain theory,* according to which a cause of crime is a tension between the goods a society encourages its people to pursue and the inability of some people to attain those goods by socially permissible means, or to have a fair opportunity to attain them by such means. According to strain theory, inequality causes psychological harms when it is visible and unfair, which, in turn, leads the least well off to resent and reject the restrictions on the means by which they may pursue socially encouraged goals, like money, status, and respect.[46] The psychological strain produced by deprivation and social inequality produces oppositional subcultural norms that support deviant behavior and drive the crime rate up. This thesis is supported by some urban ethnographies.[47] Though psychologically and sociologically more complex than the economic approach, strain theory remains controversial for its emphasis on the power of culture. It does, however, importantly call attention to oppositional norms, the socially unjust circumstances that give rise to them, and their relevance for making sense of criminal behavior. Furthermore, it reveals the courage and pitfalls of people's daily struggles with entrenched conditions of deprivation and social injustice in truly disadvantaged communities, and it highlights the psychological stress suffered by people who are subjected to ongoing conditions of serious social injustice.

A third approach incorporates insights from strain theory with added attention to the social systems of societies, cities, neighborhoods, and communities. According to *social disorganization theory*, crime rates are best understood by reference to weak social structures as well as cultural adaptations.[48] The theory is that robust social structures, like stable families and community groups, mitigate crime by exercising informal control over their members and providing them with alternatives to crime. When people, particularly juveniles, lack family and community structures of supervision and oversight, opportunities for crime increase, and social costs decrease. Higher rates of crime are explained by, for example, higher rates of single parent households and low participation in community organizations, and these factors are understood in relation to governmental policies and their legacy. Public policies such as mass incarceration, residential displacement for commercial development, and highway construction through neighborhoods, disrupt family, friendship, and community structures.[49] Some U.S. cities have adopted deliberate policies of capital disinvestment in poor inner-city neighborhoods, predictably resulting in housing decay, population dislocation, and damage to networks of family and community. Relocation to stable neighborhoods is unrealistic for many poor and racially disadvantaged families. As a result, they must make do in poor neighborhoods with weak social structures.

The role of social structures in this analysis shifts individual responsibility talk. As William Julius Wilson and Robert Sampson emphasize, "When segregation and concentrated poverty represent structural constraints embodied in public policy and historical patterns of racial subjugation, notions that individual differences (or self-selection) explain community-level effects on violence are considerably weakened."[50] Overall, their finding is that concentrated disadvantage predicts higher rate of crime, and the role of structural factors softens explanatory appeals to deviant culture and values.

Certainly, elements of these different theoretical frameworks can be understood in ways that render them compatible, and together they offer a powerful set of ideas for understanding how social context bears on a society's crime rate. Sociologist Robert Sampson's study of the explanatory role of social mechanisms has prompted him to speak of "contextual causation."[51] We can make sense of the notion of contextual causation by understanding the point of criminology. What criminologists aim to answer is not a *legal* question about whether a person's behavior is "the product of the effort or determination of the actor," evaluated in relation to legal standards of law-abiding behavior—a query that leads us to identify "the cause" of a person's criminal behavior as his voluntary choice.[52] Instead, criminologists seek to explain why people in some social circumstances and not others commit crimes at a higher rate—a question about whether we can identify environmental factors that make a difference.

When we focus on individual choice in relation to legal norms, contextual factors bearing on choice operate as mere background conditions, but when we compare patterns of choices that differ across social groups, the role of individual choice is an uninformative common factor. What were in the legal context regarded as irrelevant background conditions—salient neighborhood differences that include entrenched poverty, racial segregation, lack of social cohesion, weak adult supervision, and strong peer pressure—stand out as factors that make a difference to the crime rate and hence have explanatory value.[53] They are *causes* of behavior. As Sampson puts it, "Neighborhood contexts are important determinants of the quantity and quality of human behavior in their own right."[54] H. L. A. Hart and Tony Honoré explain that "the distinction between cause and condition may be drawn in different ways in one and the same case according to context."[55] Criminal trials and criminology research count as different "contexts." A sociological perspective is broader than what is relevant to the courts, and it teaches us that it is it informative to understand the state's policies and omissions as causes of crime. We cannot otherwise explain variations in the crime rate in different neighborhoods.

Let us return now to the question of the state's standing to blame criminal wrongdoers. I submit that moral acknowledgment of the bearing of social injustice on people's life prospects is subverted when parties who share responsibility for the unjust social circumstances of criminal wrong-doing stand in moral judgment of disadvantaged persons who have committed crimes, and when the privileged group's representative authorities focus blame for a criminal act individually on the person who committed it. It is a moral distortion for a person to be held fully morally responsible for his criminal act by the state and its supporters, who are themselves to blame for unjust circumstances that engender crime by limiting people's opportunities and choices.

This is not to say that the state is *complicit* with a person's criminal act, at least in the familiar legal sense.[56] Complicity as a legal concept is otherwise known as "accomplice liability." An accomplice is a person who knowingly and substantially facilitates the commission of a crime. Accomplice liability is purposeful; the accomplice must aim to aid illegal conduct, and when *mens rea* is an element of the principal's criminal act, the *mens rea* requirement for liability applies to the accomplice as well as to the principal. For example, an accomplice to intentional homicide must purposefully and substantially facilitate the commission of an intentional homicide. Complicity is not a separate crime; it is a way of committing a crime—the same crime the chief actor commits.[57] In most American jurisdictions, accomplices can be charged with the same offenses as principal actors, and they are subject to the same penalties.

The state and its supporters, in an unjust society, are not like accomplices to criminal acts. Law enforcement officials and the public who support them normally do not intend to facilitate the commission of crimes. But they need not be complicit, in that sense, before we can say that their moral standing has been damaged. Policies and practices that help to explain the crime rate need not aim to promote crime in order to unsettle the moral authority their proponents have to cast blame on criminal wrongdoers. Even a looser and broader notion of complicity, one familiar in moral parlance, is not needed to show that the state has morally compromised its standing to blame criminal wrongdoers, if that moral notion of complicity implies that a criminal act is part of a joint plan, socially coordinated action, or socially accepted result.[58] It is enough to note that focusing blame individually is a moral diversion from morally and causally relevant factors. Individualized blame diverts attention from a relevant acknowledgment of shared responsibility for factors that help to explain why crime is committed. Though a person's choice to commit a crime may have been a morally bad one, limiting our moral attention to that fact is objectionable when institutional and social factors unjustly limit an agent's access to reasonable alternatives.

I conclude that the state's role in perpetuating or failing to address social injustice undermines its standing to blame criminal wrongdoers for their criminal acts. This claim depends on the injustice being serious. If social injustice is minor, it might make little difference to the distribution of responsibility for criminal wrongdoing.[59] It may thus have little impact on the state's standing to blame. In order to disrupt the familiar blaming function of criminal justice, the state's role in perpetuating social injustice, or failing to remedy it, must have disrupted the basis of mutual moral expectations, thereby throwing into doubt the notion that social, political, and legal conditions serve mutual interests and the common good. The state's moral failure is even more serious when it is the case that this moral breakdown bears on the rate of crimes that represent moral wrongs even under those conditions. Not only have the state's policies, such as a history of enforced residential segregation by race, contributed to joblessness and enduring poverty; they have undercut the stabilizing social structures and opportunities that help to prevent crime.[60] Under these circumstances, the state's moral failures are obscured by blaming and stigmatizing individual wrongdoers. Social injustice undermines the standing of the state to blame criminal wrongdoers, even when it does not undermine their criminal agency.

I have argued that when background injustice is grave and gives rise to criminal activity, even behavior that is morally wrong, the requirements of background justice bear on the blaming function of punishment. The basis for mutual moral expectations between members of society no longer includes reasons to believe that the state represents a shared perspective and common interests, and the unequal and unjust treatment of some social groups compromises the state's standing to blame members of those groups. Background injustice should be regarded as severe whenever a statistically disproportionate number of crimes are committed by or attributed to a disadvantaged group and we have compelling explanations for the increased crime rate that appeal to that group's socially unjust

life circumstances. In such cases, we may infer that members of the disadvantaged group lack a reasonable opportunity to lead satisfactory,
law-abiding lives. The state's role in sustaining that injustice presents a
forceful moral objection to the stigmatizing use of punishment.

A Problem for Law Enforcement

Injustice damages the state. The state's failure to deliver minimal justice
undercuts its claim to moral authority. In fact, damage to the state's moral
authority threatens even an account of criminal punishment that does not
depend on assigning a blaming role to punishment. Social injustice raises
a broad challenge to law enforcement. Apart from further undermining
the plausibility of retributive notions of criminal punishment, it challenges
the legitimacy even of a criminal justice system that operates on terms
consistent with a harm-prevention rationale of the sort I offered in
Chapter 5.

The question of institutional legitimacy concerns whether an institution—its rules, practices, policies, and officials—is worthy of moral regard and deference.[61] People's deference to law enforcement authority
typically carries an express presumption that authorities stand for shared
interests and the public good. In that sense, institutional legitimacy is
the legal expression of mutual moral expectations. This is important
because the healthy functioning of institutions, whether democratic or
not, depends on social cooperation. Stable social cooperation is organized and supported by norms that are collectively endorsed for moral
reasons; it is not achieved merely through pragmatic calculations on the
part of individual members about whether their individual and joint interests support compliance. Criminal law, as a case in point, functions
well only when people generally comply with it, even when their noncom-
pliance would not be detected and penalized. Criminal law institutions
depend on people's moral commitment to the interests and rights the
law claims to protect. Furthermore, the law's effectiveness depends on
the perception that moral reasons to comply with law provide reasons
to obey criminal justice officials. For example, criminal prosecutions require the cooperation of victims and witnesses. When people believe

they are unfairly treated in the practice of criminal justice, they are less motivated to cooperate with legal institutions, and when people lack respect for the practice of law enforcement, it is harder to maintain public order and security, at least in a society that is not a police state. In short, criminal justice institutions depend on their public endorsement for shared moral reasons as well as on the public's confidence in the conduct of officials. Legal institutions are *legitimate* when they are worth supporting, as against feasible alternatives, for moral reasons that persons subject to those institutions can appreciate.

Thus institutional legitimacy depends on a relationship of reciprocity between citizens, a relationship that supports deference to authorities who represent common interests. Otherwise construed, deference to authority is repugnant, since it lacks critical sensitivity to how the state's power is used. When institutions attain the public support that recognition of legitimacy affords, this has important consequences. The deference and compliance afforded to legitimate institutions expands the power and stability of those institutions and renders their functioning more efficient. Officials have the public's trust, and they can conduct themselves transparently, with latitude, and with minimal use of force. On the other hand, when institutions lack legitimacy, they misuse the public's support, and when institutions are not perceived to be legitimate, they may not function well. In some cases, they cease to function altogether.

Questions about legitimacy can arise for the full range of institutions: social, political, economic, and legal. Compromised institutional legitimacy is perhaps most stark in a society whose institutions claim democratic authority and permit dissent. It is not uncommon for people who are members of a society whose institutions claim democratic authority to demand, based on their equal citizenship and rights, a public justification of those institutions and how they function. Indeed, that sort of public pressure stands behind the Department of Justice's recommendations for law enforcement reform. Democracy requires not only that its institutions protect the equal rights of all citizens to participate in politics and freely to express their beliefs and values, but also that institutions protect, more broadly, the basic rights, interests, and equal status of all people as legal subjects.[62] A public justification of institutions in a democracy must affirm the equal standing, mutual interests, and reciprocal obligations of citizens. When the demands of public justification are not met, institutional claims to democratic legitimacy are unconvincing, and public dissatisfaction is typically open to view.

Democratic legitimacy renders coercive law enforcement acceptable, within reasonable limits, based on the collective authority of a democratic people to make and enforce laws that are reasonably designed to promote their shared interests.[63] When law is democratically authorized, law enforcement is permissible, provided that laws promote equal basic regard and are not egregiously unjust. Law enforcement is permissible because it expresses the democratic will of a people, furthers a reasonable conception of their common good, and exhibits the procedural protections afforded by democratic values. So realized, the production and administration of law reflects the equal status of all citizens, even when the content of law is not fully just, as, for example, when measures designed to advance security are objectionably invasive of privacy, or when measures designed to promote public health are overly paternalistic. If, on the other hand, institutions—their procedures and outcomes—are not consistent with the recognition of all members as social equals, the democratic authority of those who administer the institutions and the legitimacy of their directives are undermined. This was the case with the practice of "democracy" under American slavery and Jim Crow. The fundamental problem was not social division, understood as conflict between the interests of whites and Blacks. Rather, the problem was the exclusion of Black Americans, on the basis of their race, from full and equal membership in the polity and, more broadly, in civil society.

The causal bearing of social injustice on the crime rate and the unjust practice of law enforcement in some communities cast doubt not just on the state's standing to blame. It also casts doubt on the democratic authority of the criminal law in the United States today. A democratically authorized legal system cannot be one in which people are subjected to unwarranted searches, coerced into confessing, and sentenced disproportionately. It cannot be one in which poor people lack access to adequate legal representation, face retaliation for criticizing the police, and are powerless to challenge the abuse of prosecutorial discretion. It cannot be one in which significant numbers of people are convicted for acts that should not be criminalized. It cannot be one in which an entire segment of the population is deprived of adequate opportunities for education, legal employment, and mental health care.

A criminal justice system as troubled as this fails to display equal basic regard for all members of society, and thus it lacks democratic authority. It burdens members of some groups severely without providing them with access to benefits to which they are entitled. Absent democratic authority, the practice of law enforcement is not perforce worthy of collective support and deference. Criminal justice institutions that fail to display the collective authority of a democratic people to make and enforce laws that reasonably promote their shared interests and social good lose a powerful source of presumptive normativity.

When the moral permissibility of law enforcement does not follow from the democratic authority of law, that is, when legal institutions lack democratic legitimacy, a question arises about where the moral permissibility of law enforcement might come from and whether its legitimacy can be established on other grounds. There are accounts of institutional legitimacy that do not depend on claims to democratic authority. But these other candidate sources of normative authority—the ties of community, the familiarity and predictability of customary rules and practices, mutually self-interested reasons to prefer an organized state to a "state of nature," fair play obligations for benefits obtained, such as basic security—do not require treating all persons as equal members of society. These sources of "authority" permit the oppression of some groups. This makes these accounts of the state's legitimacy unconvincing, especially when there are, in fact, socially subordinated groups that are deprived of the benefits of a system of law. Unequal treatment blocks the *systematic* legitimation of an institutional scheme. While some people may have self- and group-interested reasons to comply with institutions, those reasons do not extend to everyone. And even when some reasons—such as brute advantages over a state of nature—extend to everyone, these reasons have limited scope and are inadequate to ground a broad moral assumption of legitimacy when more inclusive institutions are possible. The obstacle to more inclusive institutions is political will, and its existence should not be thought to lower the standard of political legitimacy to a threshold satisfied by almost any political institutions over a state of lawless brutality.

When there is no systematic presumption of legitimacy, the recognition of legitimate exercises of authority can be acquired only piecemeal: only parts of the law are permissibly enforced. The piecemeal justification of law enforcement does not support a claim on our allegiance to the criminal justice system per se. Law enforcement practices are worthy of our respect and cooperation only when they are reasonably successful at arresting and prosecuting people for committing what are and ought to be crimes, at morally acceptable costs to all parties involved, including defendants. Even an unjust society is morally permitted to attempt to deter and incapacitate people from committing wrongs like rape, murder, and assault. We may need law enforcement *even more* under seriously unjust conditions, since under those conditions we should expect the problem of violent crime to be worse. But serious social injustice implies that practices of law enforcement are morally legitimate and worthy of our cooperation only when they are reasonably successful, and at morally acceptable costs, in achieving harm reduction. In order to avoid morally unacceptable costs, law enforcement practices must at least respect human rights.

When the democratic authority of legal institutions is lacking, the scope of justifiable law enforcement is limited. Individuals are liable to punishment only for acts that are morally wrong; they cannot justly be subject to punishment for acts that are merely legally prohibited.[64] This does not necessarily limit the relevant criminal wrongs to *mala in se* crimes. *Mala prohibita* crimes might also represent moral wrongs, in view of benefits to society of compliance with the relevant rules. But mere legal prohibition generates no obligation to comply. This is because there is no basis for law's legitimacy or authority per se. When some groups do not enjoy the status and benefits of equal citizenship, the social bond of citizenship is broken; the law fails to represent the democratic will of equal citizens and loses its professed normativity. We are no longer (if we ever were) obligated to one another through collective acts of will, and the law's officials have no moral authority beyond what is required for them to discharge their moral responsibility—as individuals who have committed themselves to this responsibility—to take reasonable harm-reduction measures.

Even so, the use of incarceration as a means of harm reduction is morally troubling. Although a society does not need democratically authorized institutions in order to take defensive measures against serious wrongdoing, systematic injustice has significant implications for when it can be said that a person is not unfairly burdened by harm-reduction efforts. In Chapter 5, I argued that it would be reasonable for each of us to agree to a system of punishment the aim of which is just harm reduction, even with the risk of personal liability that system would impose. Criminal sanctions are designed to protect important rights and liberties, and they can be avoided by anyone who chooses, either for moral or for self-interested reasons, to comply with the law. Under those conditions, the burden of redressing one's violations of other people's rights, by accepting penalties designed to discourage the violation of those rights, seems reasonable. Yet this argument is inadequate when it comes to incarceration under conditions of social injustice. The serious personal harms imposed by incarceration, together with the social stigma and marginalization it imposes, are excessive for people who have not benefited from the legal system as democratic equals. Under conditions of severe social injustice, in which some people lack reasonable prospects for a satisfactory, law-abiding life, those who are deprived of reasonable prospects to lead a decent life are excessively burdened by incarceration.

Social injustice presents a dilemma for the prospects of criminal justice. We are torn between protecting some people's basic rights by incapacitating dangerous people and refusing unfairly to deprive criminal wrongdoers of their liberty when they have already suffered serious injustice. This dilemma for criminal justice cannot be solved in an unjust society.[65] A system of criminal justice cannot stand on its own; it requires the support of institutions of distributive justice.

If we opt for collective self-defense, even though it cannot be fully justified, incarcerated people are due compensation for the burdens we impose on them. This could take the form of delivering to them some of the social goods they have been denied, including education, health care, and job opportunities. By including elements of distributive justice in our criminal justice system, we acknowledge the rights, welfare, and humanity of people we lock up. We owe this to people whom we, as a society, have failed, and whom we are now asking to bear the brunt of our criminal justice efforts to protect other people's rights. We owe everyone who is subject to the requirements of law a reasonable opportunity to lead a decent, law-abiding life. People who were deprived of this opportunity prior to prison should have it after prison and, as much as is feasible, in prison. Our prisons should be humane institutions that provide basic social and health services and treat inmates with the fundamental respect owed to all persons. People who are incarcerated should not be treated as discarded members of society whose fate does not matter. A criminal justice system that brutalizes people, especially people who were already unjustly disadvantaged, implicates the society that supports it.

Limiting Punishment

I have argued that, as members of an unjust society, we have reasons to reject the familiar blaming and stigmatizing function of criminal sanctions, even when law enforcement is needed to protect important basic rights. The familiar expressive purpose of punishment cannot be justified under conditions of serious social injustice. Retributive justice can have no application under these circumstances, nor can, more generally, rationales for punishment that depend on expressing public blame.

There are at least two nonblaming but morally expressive purposes of criminal law that are available in a nonretributive, just harm reduction approach. The first emphasizes the value of criminal law in relation to the public's interest in producing and enforcing a democratic will—a set of democratically authorized rules to guide behavior. The second concerns the public's interest in criminalizing certain moral wrongs as a way publicly to reject those wrongs and to discourage members of society from committing them. The latter interest permits the use of criminal sanctions even when the former is not satisfied. Morally permissible practices of law enforcement do not depend on the democratic legitimacy of a criminal justice system. But when democratic authority is lacking and social injustice is severe, the use of punishment must be strictly limited and qualified.

A society that systematically protects the safety and welfare of some members of society at the expense of the basic needs, interests, security, and liberty of other members suffers from grave structural injustice. That injustice poses a deep challenge to the institutional legitimacy of anti-crime measures, even for violent crimes, when those measures are directed primarily at underprivileged members of society. Many violent crimes are moral wrongs, but law enforcement that burdens individuals and communities it does not protect expresses basic disregard for the rights, interests, and liberty of the members of those communities.[66] In that event, the use of punishment should be highly restricted, and those who, inevitably, are treated unjustly by the criminal justice system are owed compensation for harms they are made to suffer.

CONCLUSION

Civic Justice

U NJUST SOCIAL CONDITIONS, like poverty, lack of adequate social welfare, substandard schools, isolated and under-resourced
neighborhoods, and racially discriminatory law enforcement, make it
harder for people afflicted by these problems to lead law-abiding lives.
Some people who are encumbered in these ways will commit crimes.
Their actions are morally significant and so are their motives. Criminal
wrongdoers can be morally criticized for what they have done and why
they have done it. But their society is also morally implicated by how it
responds to their crimes. A society that is eager to blame and to punish
is dangerously out of balance.

Punishment is a massive industry in the United States. It is intense,
incarcerating 2.3 million people and employing almost 800,000 people.
And it is severe—frequently imposing mandatory sentences of years in
prison, sometimes without the possibility of parole. Criminal conviction
devastates the lives of people who are or have been in prison, as well as
those who avoid prison but cannot escape their public criminal records.
Incarceration also causes pain to families and communities, too often
walling people apart without any good reason.

When the use of incarceration is morally permissible, it is not shown
to be so by appeal to retribution. The attractions of the retributive theory

of criminal justice have been oversold. Though imposing punishment on criminal wrongdoers might provide a sense of satisfaction to some people, including some crime victims and their families, it ruins others and cannot be justified on the basis of claims about what wrongdoers deserve. The appeal of retributive justice has given punitive criminal justice policies a false sense of legitimacy.

The death penalty is the purest expression of punishment that aims at retribution. Retribution is the only tenable rationale for the death penalty, since its deterrent value is highly doubtful. At best, deterrent effects are minimal and present only under certain conditions.[1] Without a basis for confidence in the deterrent effects of capital punishment, death as punishment must be about what the condemned individual deserves. The worst of the worst deserve to die, or so defenders of capital punishment say. Yet, unsurprisingly, the "worst" also overwhelmingly tend to be the most disturbed and least equipped to deal with the world and their own serious problems.

Philosopher and legal scholar Joel Feinberg observes that people who have committed crimes that shock the public have come to be viewed not merely as sick; they are "sick, sick, sick." He describes a tension between judgments of "triple sickness" and appraisals of moral desert by exploring the relationship between believing that a person is deranged and describing that person as evil. Feinberg describes "pure wickedness" as the doing of evil acts that are "not means to any other end." Evil, done for no end beyond itself, is frightening and troubling, and we have difficulty making sense of it. The historical model for conceptualizing evil, Feinberg writes, "is not the sick human being, but rather the smoothly and rationally functioning nonhuman being, the subhuman animal (ghoul, ogre, beast, monster) or the superhuman (demon, devil, fiend)."[2] Evil creatures take willful delight in twisted acts.

Feinberg proposes that triple sickness bears an unstable relationship to evil. On the one hand, we resist equating these notions, since mental illness is taken to be a morally mitigating consideration, while evil is represented as calling for our strongest moral condemnation. On the other hand, these notions seem to be merely one beat apart, and then indistinguishable, and we are drawn to the conclusion that a person who is "sick, sick, sick" deserves our harshest moral response.

In fact, Feinberg takes this conclusion to represent a sea change in our attitudes toward people who are mentally disturbed. "Sick" has come to mean what "wicked" used to mean. Feinberg writes, "A sicko, like a weirdo and a wacko, by definition is sick in such a manner that his illness actually aggravates his moral guilt and deservingness of punishment. Instead of being a kind of softening excuse, mental illness has become in some quarters a kind of hardening aggravation. Instead of saying, 'He is mentally disordered, poor fellow, go easy on him,' some now say, 'He is a damned sicko, so draw and quarter him.'"[3] The rise of the retributive justice movement belongs to this sea change.

Contemplating evil within the ranking and scaling enterprise that is the hallmark of retributivist thinking has little to do with the practice of criminal justice in the United States, including capital punishment. States have not tried to identify which criminal wrongdoers are the most morally blameworthy, nor has the Supreme Court required them to do so.[4] The law requires eligibility for the death penalty to be established through aggravating factors or their functional equivalent, which ostensibly narrow the class of death-eligible murders, but in some states, including Arizona, over 90 percent of first-degree murders satisfy at least one factor. The death penalty is not restricted to the most culpable murders. Rather, it is disproportionately applied to defendants who are poor and Black, and the same is true of long prison sentences and most arrests, including high arrest rates for drug offenses, as well as for minor "quality of life" crimes like disorderly conduct.[5]

Proponents of the death penalty face considerable opposition, and public support for the death penalty in the United States has declined.[6] Yet advocates of capital punishment have succeeded in helping to normalize alternatives to it that are also extreme.[7] The death penalty distorts the entire schedule of criminal sanctions. It makes life without parole seem attractive, even reasonable. Defendants guilty of capital charges are "lucky" if they are spared death and instead face life in prison. In 2017, while approximately 2,800 inmates lingered on death row in the United States, more than 50,000 people were serving sentences of life without parole.[8]

Some notable cases have contributed to public opposition to the death penalty, including the story of death-row inmate Karla Faye Tucker. Tucker, known as the "Pickax Killer," was convicted in 1984 of a vicious double murder and sentenced to death. At the time of her arrest, she was callous and ruthless. She was reported to have bragged about deriving sexual pleasure from her crime.

Tucker had a terrible childhood. She was introduced to drugs at age eight, and by age ten she was injecting heroin. Her mother worked as a prostitute. When Tucker was fourteen, her mother prepared her for a similar life by taking her to "a place with lots of men." Recalling that day, Tucker said, "I wanted to please my mother so much. I wanted her to be proud of me."[9] Shortly thereafter Tucker was selling sex. She used drugs heavily until she was incarcerated. At the time she committed her crime, an act of angry revenge, she had been high on amphetamines for three days.

Tucker's case attracted media and celebrity attention. Though the state of Texas was executing more people than any other state in the country, it had not executed a woman since 1863. Tucker converted to Christianity after her arrest. During her fourteen years on death row, she studied the Bible and even married a prison minister. Her cause was taken up by the Christian Broadcasting Network's *The 700 Club*. Its evangelical host, Pat Robertson, was in favor of the death penalty, but he opposed it in Tucker's case. "If there was ever a truly rehabilitated inmate," he said, "it was Karla Faye."[10] Tucker publicly admitted guilt and expressed remorse. She conducted televised interviews and participated in antidrug videos aimed at youth. She talked about the crime and her feelings about it. In her plea to the Texas Board of Pardons, she wrote, "Even though I did murder . . . that night and not think anything of it back then . . . in the Frame of Mind I am in now, it is something that absolutely rips my guts out as I think about it."[11] The author of a book about her concluded that Tucker had worked hard to become "another, better version of herself."[12]

Clemency was denied to Tucker, and she was executed in 1998. Fred Allen, captain of Huntsville State Penitentiary's death row, participated in the execution chamber routine. His job was to spend the day with the condemned person and strap him or, in this case, her, to the gurney before the execution was performed. Allen participated in the execution of more than 120 men condemned by the state of Texas. After the execution of Karla Faye Tucker, he reversed his stance on the justice of the death penalty. He quit his job, at the cost of his pension. "No sir," he said, "no one has the right to take another's life."[13]

Another case that caught the public's attention occurred in the state of California. Stanley "Tookie" Williams was convicted of capital murder in 1979. Williams founded the Los Angeles Crips, a violent gang in South Central Los Angeles. Williams maintained his innocence of the murders for which he was convicted. He did, however, issue this apology for his gang involvement: "My apology firmly goes out to all of the grieving mothers who have lost a loved one through street violence. For many years, I have shouldered the heavy encumber of this madness that perpetuates your sorrow. Your suffering has not gone unnoticed. I acknowledged it. I feel it. With humility, I express my deepest remorse for each of you for having help[ed] to create this bloody and violent legacy."[14]

When he was in prison, Williams became an antigang activist. He spoke publicly against gang violence and wrote several children's books cautioning young people not to join gangs and to stay away from weapons and drugs. He drafted an initiative for brokering peace between violent gangs, and he created an international peer-mentoring program for high-risk youth. He wrote several books describing his life of crime and subsequent "redemption." His autobiographical writings describe his difficult childhood, his drug dependence, and his struggle with violence from a young age, such as being forced into street fights by adults who placed bets on him and other children.[15] Celebrities and activists, including actor Jamie Foxx, who starred in a movie about Williams's life, and Reverend Jesse Jackson, took up Williams's cause. Appeals to the governor were unsuccessful, however, and the state of California executed Williams in 2005.

What do these stories tell us? It is possible that Tucker and Williams were hopelessly bad people whose lives were not worth saving. But reflecting on what their lives were like before and after their crimes suggests otherwise. Their lives were very troubled, and they committed acts of violence at a young age, under the influence of drugs and alcohol, like so many other convicted felons. Though their lives were devastated by their own wrongful actions, they tried to salvage a measure of moral integrity, as we ordinarily expect people who have wronged other people to do. They are exceptional for changing as much as they did, and for their leadership and commitment while imprisoned to helping other people, but they are not unusual in demonstrating the complexity of a person's relationship to his or her own moral mistakes—even terrible wrongs. They are not extraordinary in demonstrating a human capacity to reflect and to change over time, especially with the help and support of other people.[16]

Rejecting retribution does not demonstrate indifference to the victims of crime or the suffering of people who loved them. Stepping back from the culture of blaming and the massive suffering it perpetuates leaves room to grieve with the victims of crime and to acknowledge their losses, which are not undone by the violence of retributive harm. Mourning is painful. It takes away our freedom for spontaneous joy.[17] Yet grief is a natural and appropriate response to loss. Being wronged by another person involves a particular sort of damage, an injury involved in recognizing that, at the time the wrong was done, a wrongful harm did not count for the wrong-doer as a reason not to do it. This is an excruciating kind of loss to suffer, and it makes grief difficult to experience. But mourning cannot be avoided through displacement, namely, by taking satisfaction in the suffering of the condemned.[18]

In his 2011 film *Into the Abyss: A Tale of Death, A Tale of Life,* filmmaker Werner Herzog interviews Lisa Stotler Balloun, daughter of Sandra Stotler and brother of Adam Stotler, both murdered in 2001, in Conroe, Texas, by Michael Perry and Jason Aaron Burkett. Herzog's film details the crime and concentrates on the suffering of several people affected by the murders, including family members of the offenders and victims. Prompted by Herzog's questioning, Balloun describes her reaction to seeing Perry strapped to the gurney in the execution chamber at Hunts-ville State Penitentiary. She says, "I remember walking in and thinking, 'This looks like a boy.' I had built this huge monster—evil, murdering monster—in my head, and he was just a boy. He was just a boy lying on that gurney."[19] We recognize that this is true, because we have seen Mi-chael Perry in the film. Though Balloun says she was relieved when Perry was gone, her statement that "some people just don't deserve to live" is hard to square with other perspectives we consider in the film, including that of Delbert Burkett, Jason Burkett's father, himself a convicted felon who is interviewed for the film through prison glass. Burkett says he is "doing fine . . . a little bit sick," but in the course of the interview he is overcome by guilt, shame, and remorse over his son's crime, sympathy for the victims' families, and loss at Perry's death.

Philosopher Bernard Williams wrote that blame involves a fantasy of retrospective prevention. We imagine that that the sting of blame might make it the case that someone who committed a wrong would have acted differently, as though our moral indignation had the power to wind back the clock and make it true that a person who was morally lost would have done better.[20] According to Williams, we ground our blame in an exaggeration of another person's freedom, representing her will paradoxically as free now, after our moral correction, to have acted otherwise at the time the wrong was done. We imagine that this impossible freedom to undo the past is unleashed by the power of our moral stance. It is a moral fantasy. Naturally, Williams's caricature of this fantasy utilizes irony and itself involves an exaggeration. But even so, it points, insightfully, if indirectly, to the anguish of uncertainty about whether a person's moral mistakes could have been avoided, and it captures an aspect of our investment in the power of blame, in relation to human freedom, as well as our reluctance to give that power up.

It is my hope that appreciating the limits of blame will help us correct a criminal justice system that is rife with excessive punishment, assuming that the criminal justice system really is supposed to function as a *justice* system—as compared, say, to a racialized system of social control or a modernized version of the lease convict system. Accepting the limits of blame removes a socially powerful rationale for overpunishment—a moral exaggeration about what criminal conviction tells us. No longer would we assume that criminal lawbreakers are morally blameworthy for their criminal acts and deserving of all the suffering we impose on them. We would stop righteously overreaching in our moral assessment of people who have committed crimes. Were we to refocus our moral perspective to fit the relevant legal criteria and moral circumstances, our approach to criminal punishment would be more reasonable, more appropriately limited, and more humane.

Understanding individual actions in relation to their many causes leads us away from the moralizing stance of a retributive morality and the condemnatory attitudes connected with the notion of moral desert. When we limit moral blame, we open up greater space for considering the social dimensions of responsibility. This could help us reckon in new ways with the moral significance of lawbreaking, even when it comes to illegal acts that are clearly morally wrong. Recognizing that society deprives some of its members of basic rights, fair opportunities, and the necessary means to satisfy their basic needs should move us to emphasize collective po- litical obligations—to rectify current injustices, to address the conse- quences of past wrongs, and to prevent future wrongdoing.[21] Taking that task seriously would be to redress not only criminal wrongdoing but also distributive injustice, including socioeconomic inequality and the shameful legacies of a long history of racial injustice. Crime requires re- sponses that reach beyond criminal justice. The fragility of individual moral agency demands a collective commitment to political and social equality.

Crime is the subject of political campaigns, private industry invest- ment, and infotainment. Though it is the subject of much talk, it is not often confronted with the honesty that is required to remedy it. Fighting crime means grappling with poverty, social stigma, and mental illness, aiming to understand the workings of injustice, placing racial subordi- nation in historical context—our society's history—and searching for ways to remedy it by cultivating what we might call *civic justice*. It is not enough to write institutional rules; we must transform the public culture. Seeking civic justice involves exposing the rationales behind which injustice hides and bringing to public consciousness how unjust practices, like excessive punishment, have influenced our thinking about what is normal.

A just society would think critically about how it treats its most vul- nerable members, which include people who are incarcerated and stripped of most of the rights and privileges other people take for granted. It would treat all of its members with dignity and respect, even those who have made serious moral mistakes. Moral outrage at their morally wrongful ac- tions should not lead us to brutalize their lives. We might consider the alternatives and ask ourselves: What sort of society do we want to live in? Which side of history will we be on?

NOTES

Introduction

1. Quotations from Winfred Rembert interview with Erin Kelly on April 28, 2015, and April 2, 2017.

2. Truth in sentencing requires that people sentenced to prison serve at least 85 percent of their sentence.

3. Three-strikes legislation requires that people convicted of three prior felonies receive an enhanced minimum sentence of twenty-five years and, in some cases, life in prison. The majority of U.S. states have three-strikes laws, including the state of Georgia.

4. See Whitney Benns, "American Slavery, Reinvented," *Atlantic,* September 21, 2015, https://www.theatlantic.com/business/archive/2015/09/prison-labor-in-america /406177/, and Steve Fraser and Joshua B. Freeman, "21st Century Chain Gangs: The Rebirth of Prison Labor Foretells a Disturbing Future for America's Free-market Capitalism," *Salon,* April 19, 2012, https://www.salon.com/2012/04/19/21st_century _chain_gangs.

5. On the moral hazards of social labeling, see Kimberley Brownlee, "Don't Call People 'Rapists': on the Social Contribution Injustice of Punishment," *Current Legal Problems* 69, no. 1 (2016): 327–52.

6. Chapter 6 considers the plausibility of claiming that an act that is illegal is thereby unethical.

7. P. F. Strawson, "Freedom and Resentment," *Proceedings of the British Academy* 48 (1962): 1–25. Reprinted in Gary Watson, ed., *Free Will,* 2nd ed. (Oxford: Oxford University Press, 2003). Strawson writes,

The preparedness to acquiesce in that infliction of suffering on the offender which is an essential part of punishment is all of a piece with this whole range of attitudes of which I have been speaking. It is not only moral reactive attitudes towards the offender which are in question here. We must mention also the self-reactive attitudes of offenders themselves. Just as the other-reactive attitudes are associated with a readiness to acquiesce in the infliction of suffering on an offender, within the "institution" of punishment, so the self-reactive attitudes are associated with a readiness on the part of the offender to acquiesce in such infliction without developing the reactions (e.g. of resentment) which he would normally develop to the infliction of injury upon him; i.e. with a readiness, as we say, to accept punishment as "his due" or as "just." (section, 6)

8. See R. A. Duff, *Punishment, Communication, and Community* (Oxford: Oxford University Press, 2003), and Anthony von Hirsch, *Censure and Sanctions* (Oxford: Oxford University Press, 1994).

9. Michelle Alexander, *The New Jim Crow: Mass Incarceration in the Age of Colorblindness* (New York: The New Press, 2010). See also James B. Jacobs, *The Eternal Criminal Record* (Cambridge, MA: Harvard University Press, 2015).

10. Victor Tadros, "Justice and Terrorism," *New Criminal Justice Review: An International and Interdisciplinary Journal* 10, no. 4 (Fall 2007), 671–72. See also Andrew Ashworth and Lucia Zedner, *Preventative Justice* (Oxford: Oxford University Press, 2014).

11. See *McClesky v. Kemp,* 481 U.S. 279 (1987).

12. See Carlos Berdejó, "Criminalizing Race: Racial Disparities in Plea Bargaining," *Boston College Law Review* 59, no. 4 (2018): 1187–1249. See also Michael Harriot, "We Told Y'All: New Study Reveals How Every Phase of Criminal-Justice System Favors Whites," *Root,* October 26, 2017, https://www.theroot.com/we-told-yall-new-study-reveals-how-every-phase-of-crim-1819880516.

13. See Jennifer L. Eberhardt, Philip Atiba Goff, Valerie J. Purdie, and Paul G. Davies, "Seeing Black: Race, Crime, and Visual Processing," *Journal of Personality and Social Psychology* 87, no. 6 (2004): 876–93, and Glenn C. Loury, *Race, Incarceration, and American Values* (Cambridge, MA: MIT Press, 2008).

14. Donald Trump has repeatedly characterized Mexicans as rapists and Muslims as terrorists.

15. The United States Sentencing Commission reports that in 2016 almost 16,000 people were convicted of illegal reentry. Of these, 98 percent received prison sentences of, on average, fourteen months. See https://www.ussc.gov/research/quick-facts/illegal-reentry.

16. See Alan Gomez, "Trump Plans Massive Increase in Federal Immigration Jails," *USA Today,* October 17, 2017, https://www.usatoday.com/story/news/world/2017/10/17/trump-plans-massive-increase-federal-immigration-jails/771414001/.

17. The vast majority of criminal cases in the United States are settled through plea bargaining. See Lindsey Devers, "Plea and Charge Bargaining: Research Summary," Bureau of Justice Assistance, U.S. Department of Justice (January 24, 2011), https://www.bja.gov/Publications/PleaBargainingResearchSummary.pdf.

1. Accountability in Criminal Law

1. Doris J. James and Lauren E. Glaze, "Mental Health Problems of Prison and Jail In-mates," Bureau of Justice Statistics Special Report, U.S. Department of Justice, Sep-tember 2006 (Revised December 2006), https://www.bjs.gov/content/pub/pdf/mhppji.pdf. See also KiDeuk Kim, Miriam Becker-Cohen, and Maria Serakos, "The Processing and Treatment of Mentally Ill People in the Criminal Justice System: A Scan of Practice and Background Analysis," Research Report, the Urban Institute, March 2015, https://www.urban.org/research/publication/processing-and-treatment-mentally-ill-persons-criminal-justice-system/view/full_report.

2. Statistics on the percentage of intellectually disabled individuals in the prison popu-lation are not well established.

3. *Ewing v. California,* 538 U.S. 11 (2003). For discussion see Michael Tonry, "Differ-ences in National Sentencing Systems and the Differences They Make," in *Sentencing Policies and Practices in Western Countries—Comparative and Cross-national Per-spectives,* ed. Michael Tonry (Chicago: University of Chicago Press, 2016).

4. *Rummel v. Estelle,* 445 U.S. 263, 274 (1980). In this case, the Court upheld a sentence of life in prison for a defendant convicted of a $120.75 theft.

5. See, for example, Douglas Husak, *Overcriminalization: The Limits of Criminal Law* (Oxford: Oxford University Press, 2008).

6. See, for example, Michael S. Moore, "The Moral Worth of Retribution," in *Respon-sibility, Character, and the Emotions: New Essays in Moral Psychology,* ed. Ferdi-nand Schoeman (Cambridge: Cambridge University Press, 1987), 179, reprinted in Michael S. Moore, *Placing Blame: A General Theory of the Criminal Law* (Oxford: Oxford University Press, 1997); Mitchell Berman, "Rehabilitating Retributivism," *Law and Philosophy* 32, no. 1 (January 2013): 88; and Douglas Husak, "Retribu-tivism in Extremis," *Law and Philosophy* 32, no. 1 (January 2013): 11. See also Her-bert Morris, "Persons and Punishment," *Monist* 52, no. 4 (October 1968): 475–501, reprinted in his *Guilt and Innocence* (Los Angeles: University of California Press, 1976).

7. Berman, "Rehabilitating Retributivism," 87–88.

8. Husak, "Retributivism in Extremis," 8.

9. See, for example, Moore, "The Moral Worth of Retribution," 184–85.

10. Moore, "The Moral Worth of Retribution," 213.

11. John Rawls, *A Theory of Justice,* rev. ed. (Cambridge, MA: Harvard University Press, 1999), 42–45.

12. John Rawls, "The Idea of Public Reason Revisited," *University of Chicago Law Re-view* 64, no. 3 (Summer 1997): 765–807, reprinted in John Rawls, *Collected Papers,* ed. Samuel Freeman (Cambridge, MA: Harvard University Press, 1999).

13. Some retributivists refrain from committing to retribution as the most important aim for a criminal justice system. Some of these count as "mixed" theories that incorpo-rate attention to the consequences of punishment. See Andrew von Hirsch, *Censure and Sanctions* (Oxford: Oxford University Press, 1994). Others point out that "all things considered," retributive reasons might be unsettled by other concerns. See

Douglas Husak, "Holistic Retributivism," *California Law Review* 88, no. 3 (May 2000): 991–2000, and David O. Brink, "Retributivism and Legal Moralism," *Ratio* 25, no. 4 (December 2012): 496–512.

14. Rawls, "Two Concept of Rules," *Philosophical Review* 64, no. 1 (January 1955): 3–32, reprinted in Rawls, *Collected Papers,* see 23. See also Vincent Chiao, *Criminal Law in the Age of the Administrative State* (New York: Oxford University Press, 2018), especially chaps. 1–3.

15. J. L. Mackie, "Morality and the Retributive Emotions," *Criminal Justice Ethics* 1, no. 1 (1982): 3.

16. Consequentialism is the moral theory that the moral value of an action, policy, or institution depends entirely on its consequences.

17. Mackie, "Morality and the Retributive Emotions," 5. See also G. W. F. Hegel, *Elements of the Philosophy of Right* (1820), ed. Allen W. Wood, trans. H. B. Nisbet (Cambridge: Cambridge University Press, 1991), §§82–103.

18. The "unfair advantage" view was proposed by Herbert Morris, "Persons and Punishment." See also Jeffrie Murphy, "Marxism and Retribution," *Philosophy and Public Affairs* 2, no. 3 (Spring 1973): 217–243, and George Sher, *Desert* (Princeton, NJ: Princeton University Press, 1987), chap. 5.

19. For criticism of the unfair advantage view, see Jean Hampton, "Correcting Harms vs. Righting Wrongs: The Goal of Retribution," *UCLA Law Review* 39, no. 6 (August 1992): 1660–61.

20. A similar analysis is found in P. F. Strawson, "Freedom and Resentment," *Proceedings of the British Academy* 48 (1960): 1–25, reprinted in Gary Watson, ed., *Free Will,* 2nd ed. (Oxford: Oxford University Press, 2003). See also John Stuart Mill *Utilitarianism* (1861), section 5.

21. Victor Tadros, *The Ends of Harm: The Moral Foundations of Criminal Law* (Oxford: Oxford University Press, 2011), 44–51.

22. Tadros, *The Ends of Harm,* 45. See also T. M. Scanlon, "Punishment and the Rule of Law," in *The Difficulty of Tolerance: Essays in Political Philosophy* (Cambridge: Cambridge University Press, 2003).

23. See, for example, Göran Duus-Otterström, "Why Retributivists Should Endorse Leniency in Punishment," *Law and Philosophy* 32, no. 4 (July 2013): 459–83, and Patrick Tomlin, "Extending the Golden Thread?," *Journal of Political Philosophy* 21, no. 1 (March 2013): 44–66.

24. Nicola Lacey, "The Resurgance of Character: Responsibility in the Context of Criminalization," in *Philosophical Foundations of Criminal Law,* ed. R. A. Duff and Stuart Green (Oxford: Oxford University Press, 2011), 152. Lacey provides a helpful and interesting discussion of the porous boundaries between these capacity-responsibility and character-based accounts.

25. See David Hume, *A Treatise of Human Nature* (1738), book 2, part 3.

26. Hampton, "Correcting Harms versus Righting Wrongs," 1689–90.

27. As Hampton sees it, perpetrators implicitly assert their superiority over their victims. Their crimes are an affront to a victim's dignity, and the state is obligated to counter

this message. By making the perpetrator suffer in ways that correspond to the victim's suffering, the state takes away from the guilty offender any claim to master or superiority over the victim that was established by his action. See Hampton, "Correcting Harms versus Righting Wrongs."

28. R. A. Duff, *Punishment, Communication, and Community* (Oxford: Oxford University Press, 2001), 79–80.

29. Duff, *Punishment, Communication, and Community*, 82, 96–106.

30. See von Hirsch, *Censure and Sanctions.*

31. American Law Institute, *Model Penal Code: Official Draft and Explanatory Notes* (1962), §2.01. Approximately two-thirds of all U.S. states have formally adopted criteria set out in Model Penal Code.

32. *Martin v. State,* 31 Ala. App. 334, 17 So. 2d 427 (1944). See also *Robinson v. California* 370 U.S. 660 (1962) on the unconstitutionality of a California statute that made the "status" of narcotic addiction a criminal offense.

33. Model Penal Code, §2.04.

34. *People v. Ireland,* 70 Cal.2d 522 (1969).

35. *County Court v. Allen,* 442 U.S. 140 (1979). The Court rejects the use of a "mandatory presumption," which a jury must accept, and permits a "purely permissive presumption," which "allows, but does not require, the trier of fact to infer the elemental fact from proof by the prosecutor of the basic one and which places no burden of any kind on the defendant."

36. See *Sandstrom v. Montana,* 442 U.S. 510 (1979); *Francis v. Frankin,* 105 U.S. 165 (1985).

37. Model Penal Code, §2.02.

38. For a criticism of the criminal negligence standard on retributivist grounds, see Larry Alexander and Kimberly Kessler Ferzan, *Crime and Culpability: A Theory of Criminal Law* (Cambridge: Cambridge University Press, 2009), chap. 3.

39. Model Penal Code, §2.02.

40. An exception is *State v. Everhart,* 291 N. C. 700, 231 S. E. 2d 604 (1977), in which the court reversed an involuntary homicide conviction of a girl with an IQ of 72. The girl had given birth in her bedroom and inadvertently smothered to death the baby she believed was already dead.

41. There are some controversial cases in which the courts have acknowledged the mitigating or excusing relevance of cultural factors. See *People v. Wu,* 286 Cal. Rptr. 869 (Cal. App. 1991); *People v. Rhines,* 182 Cal. Rptr. 478 (Cal. App. 1982). See also Elaine Chiu, "Culture as Justification, Not Excuse," *American Criminal Law Review* 43, no. 4 (2006): 1317–74.

42. *State v Patterson,* 131 Conn. App. 65 (2011).

43. *People v. Cassasa* 49 N.Y.2d 668, 404 N.E.2d 1310 (1980).

44. §2.09 of the Model Penal Code states: "It is an affirmative defense that the actor engaged in the conduct charged to constitute an offence because he was coerced to do so by the use of, or a threat to use, unlawful force against his person or the person of another, which a person of reasonable firmness in his situation would have been unable to resist."

45. *Dando v. Yukins,* 461 F.3d 791, 801 (6th Cir, 2006), supporting appellant's claim of the relevance of domestic abuse to the duress defense. Compare *United States v. Willis,* 38 F.3d 170 (5th Cir. 1994), and *Pickle v. State,* 635 S.E.2d 197, 206 (Ga. Appl. 2006). While courts are divided on the relevance of battered women's syndrome to duress as a defense to crimes other than homicide, they are now mostly in agreement that battered women's syndrome can support a defendant's self-defense argument that she reasonably perceived a threat of imminent danger from her abuser when she killed him. See *Rogers v. State,* 616 So.2d 1098, 1100 (Fla. Dist. Ct. Appl. 1993). See also relevant statutes: Cal. Evid. Code §1107(b) (2011) and Tex. Pen. Code §19.06 (2011).

46. *State v. Heinemann,* 920 A.2d 278 (Conn. 2007). See discussion in Sanford H. Kadish, Stephen J. Schulhofer, Carol S. Steiker, and Rachel E. Barkow, *Criminal Law and Its Processes: Cases and Materials,* 9th ed. (New York: Wolters Kluwer Law and Business, 2012), 929–32.

47. *Commonwealth v. DeMarco,* 570 Pa. 263, 273 (2002).

48. *United States v. Johnson,* 416 F.3d 464 (6th Cir. 2005).

49. *M'Naghten's Case,* House of Lords 10 Cl. & F. 200, 8 Eng. Rep. 718 (1843).

50. Model Penal Code, §4.01.

51. Model Penal Code, §4.01. For an argument in favor of the MPC position, see David O. Brink, "Responsibility, Incompetence, and Psychopathy," The Lindley Lecture, University of Kansas, April 30, 2013.

52. Kadish et al., *Criminal Law and Its Processes,* 982; see also 961.

53. *United States v. Lyons,* 731 F.2d 243 (5th Cir.), *cert. denied,* 469 U.S. 930 (1984). The court cites Richard J. Bonnie, "The Moral Basis of the Insanity Defense," *American Bar Association Journal* 69, no. 2 (February 1983): 194, 196. See also *United States v. Johnson,* 416 F.3d 464 (6th Cir. 2005).

54. While the law does not and need not suppose that any given subject is morally motivated, studies show that law does not reliably elicit compliance unless its subjects view it as unbiased and its officials as trustworthy. See Randolph Roth, *American Homicide* (Cambridge, MA: Harvard University Press, 2009); Paul H. Robinson, *Distributive Principles of Criminal Law: Who Should Be Punished How Much?* (New York: Oxford University Press, 2008), chap. 8; Paul H. Robinson and John M. Darley, "Intuitions of Justice: Implications for Criminal Law and Justice Policy," *Southern California Law Review* 81, no. 1 (November 2007): 1–68; Tom R. Tyler & John M. Darley, "Building a Law-Abiding Society: Taking Public Views about Morality and the Legitimacy of Legal Authorities into Account When Formulating Substantive Law," *Hofstra Law Review* 28, no. 3: 707–39; Joshua Kleinfeld, "Reconstructivism: The Place of Criminal Law in Ethical Life," *Harvard Law Review* 129, no. 6 (April 2016): 1485–1565.

55. See *Morissette v. United States,* 342 U. S. 246, 250 n.4 (1952), quoting Roscoe Pound, introduction to *A Selection of Cases on Criminal Law,* ed., Frances Bowes Sayre (Rochester, NY: Lawyers Co-operative Publishing Co., 1927).

56. I thank John Goldberg for discussion of these points.

57. See Jeremy Horder, *Excusing Crime* (Oxford: Oxford University Press, 2004), 144–45.

58. The trend is not entirely unidirectional. In *United States v. Booker,* 543 U.S. 220 (2005), the Court struck down mandatory sentencing guidelines, though it affirmed that judges may permissibly treat sentencing guidelines as "advisory."

59. The Court maintains that "their deficiencies do not warrant an exemption from criminal sanctions, but diminish their personal culpability"; *Atkins v. Virginia* 536 U.S. 304 (2002).

60. See also *Thompson v. Oklahoma* 487 U. S. 813, 835 (1988), where the Court affirms the diminished culpability of persons under the age of sixteen.

61. *Ford v. Wainwright,* 477 U.S. 399 (1986).

62. See Marie Gottschalk, *Caught: The Prison State and the Lockdown of American Politics* (Princeton, NJ: Princeton University Press, 2015), 172–76.

63. See Horder, *Excusing Crime,* 178–90.

64. *Miller v. Alabama,* 132 S. Ct. 2455 (2012).

65. *Jackson v. Hobbs,* 132 S. Ct. 548 (2011).

66. According to Bureau of Justice Statistics, over half of all prison and jail inmates suffer from an identifiable mental illness. Over 40 percent of state prisoners and more than half of jail inmates reported symptoms that met the criteria for mania; 23 percent of state prisoners and 30 percent of jail inmates reported symptoms of major depression; and approximately 15 percent of state prisoners and 24 percent of jail inmates reported symptoms that met the criteria for a psychotic disorder. See James and Glaze, "Mental Health Problems of Prison and Jail Inmates." Of course, from a moral perspective, a lot depends not only on what counts as a mental illness but also how severe it is.

67. See Human Rights Watch, "Branded for Life: Florida's Prosecution of Children as Adults under its 'Direct File' Statute," April 10, 2014, https://www.hrw.org/report /2014/04/10/branded-life/floridas-prosecution-children-adults-under-its-direct-file -statute.

68. Josh Rovner, "Juvenile Life without Parole: An Overview," *Sentencing Project* (October 2017), http://sentencingproject.org/doc/publications/jj_Juvenile_Life_Without _Parole.pdf. Pennsylvania currently has more than 480 people who are serving life sentences that they received when they were juveniles.

69. See Erica Eckholm, "Juveniles Face Lifelong Terms despite Rulings," *New York Times,* January 19, 2014, https://www.nytimes.com/2014/01/20/us/juveniles-facing -lifelong-terms-despite-rulings.html.

70. For a helpful review of the empirical literature on the "juvenile penalty," see Kareem L. Jordan, "Juvenile Status and Criminal Sentencing: Does It Matter in the Adult System?," *Youth Violence and Juvenile Justice* 12, no. 4 (2014): 315–31, http://yvj .sagepub.com/content/12/4/315.

71. *United States v. Lyons,* quoting "American Psychiatric Association Statement on the Insanity Defense," *American Journal of Psychiatry* 140, no. 6 (June 1983): 681–88.

72. *Penry v. Lynaugh,* 492 U.S. 302 (1989).

73. See Andrew Ashworth and Andrew von Hirsch, *Proportionate Sentencing: Exploring the Principles* (Oxford: Oxford University Press, 2005).

2. Skepticism about Moral Desert

1. William Barr, "The Case for More Incarceration," U.S. Department of Justice, Office of Policy and Communications, NCJ-139583, October 28, 1992, 10, https://www.ncjrs .gov/pdffiles1/Digitization/139583NCJRS.pdf.
2. "Reagan Seeks Judges with 'Traditional Approach': Interview with Edwin Meese, Attorney General of the United States," *U.S. News & World Report,* October 14, 1985, 67. For discussion of the impact of a criminal record on a person's public identity, including the consequences of criminal arrest, see James B. Jacobs, *The Eternal Criminal Record* (Cambridge, MA: Harvard University Press, 2015).
3. Michael S. Moore, "Choice, Character, and Excuse," *Social Philosophy and Policy* 7, no. 2 (Spring 1990): 29–58; reprinted in *Placing Blame: A General Theory of the Criminal Law* (Oxford: Oxford University Press, 1997).
4. Moore, "Choice, Character, and Excuse," 559.
5. David Schmidtz, *Elements of Justice* (New York: Cambridge University Press, 2006), 36–37. See also Robert Nozick, *Philosophical Explanations* (Cambridge, MA: Belknap Press, 1981), 394–5, and T. M. Scanlon, "Giving Desert Its Due," *Philosophical Explorations* 16, no. 2 (2013): 101–16.
6. Schmidtz, *Elements of Justice,* 60.
7. See Michael Sandel, *Liberalism and the Limits of Justice,* 2nd ed. (New York: Cambridge University Press, 1998), 82–95, and William Galston, *Justice and the Human Good* (Chicago: University of Chicago Press, 1980), 170–91. I note that Galston's view of the relevance of character to punishment might be different from what his broader view suggests. Although he holds a view like Schmidtz's with respect to rewards, he writes that "there may well be an asymmetry between 'positive desert' and punishment" (172–73).
8. Schmidtz might agree. In *Elements of Justice,* he does not endorse the ideal of retributive justice.
9. Here I am interested in the sense of "could" that signals the agent's competence, not the sense of could that indicates the agent's power to overcome Frankfurt-style interventions. For Frankfurt's challenge to the notion that freedom requires the possibility of doing otherwise, see Harry G. Frankfurt, "Alternate Possibilities and Moral Responsibility," in *The Importance of What We Care About: Philosophical Essays* (Cambridge: Cambridge University Press 1988), 1–10. I am in agreement with Michael Smith, Kadri Vihvelin, and Michael McKenna that an agent who is subject to Frankfurt-style interventions could do otherwise in a relevant sense that concerns the agent's own competence. In evaluating an agent's moral competence, we should abstract from masking and "finking" conditions. See Michael Smith, "Rational Capacities, or: How to Distinguish Recklessness, Weakness, and Compulsion" in *Ethics and the A Priori: Selected Essays on Moral Psychology and Meta-Ethics* (Cambridge: Cambridge University Press, 2004), 114–35, and Kadri Vihvelin, "Free Will Demystified: A Dispositional Account," *Philosophical Topics* 32, no. 1–2 (Spring and Fall 2004): 427–50. See also Michael Fara, "Dispositions and Habituals," *Noûs* 39, no. 1 (March 2005): 43–82, and his "Masked Abilities and Compatibilism," *Mind* 117, no. 468 (October 2008): 843–65, as well as Michael McKenna's "reasons-responsiveness"

version of this "new dispositionalism" in his "Reasons Responsiveness, Agents, and Mechanisms," in *Oxford Studies in Agency and Responsibility, Volume 1,* ed. David Shoemaker (Oxford: Oxford University Press, 2013). For a helpful summary of the literature, see Randolf Clarke, "Dispositions, Abilities to Act, and Free Will: The New Dispositionalism," *Mind* 118, no. 470 (April 2009): 323–51.

10. See Gary Watson, "Free Agency," *Journal of Philosophy* 72, no. 8 (April 1975): 205–20, and Christine M. Korsgaard, *The Sources of Normativity* (Cambridge: Cambridge University Press, 1996).

11. See Susan Wolf, *Freedom within Reason* (Cambridge: Cambridge University Press, 1990).

12. See Derk Pereboom, *Living without Free Will* (Cambridge: Cambridge University Press, 2001). See also Joel Feinberg, "Justice and Personal Desert," *Nomos VI: Justice,* ed. Carl J. Friedrich and John W. Chapman (New York: Atherton Press, 1963), re-printed in Joel Feinberg, *Doing and Deserving: Essays in the Theory of Responsibility* (Princeton: Princeton University Press, 1970), and T. M. Scanlon, *Why Does Inequality Matter?* (Oxford University Press, 2018), chap. 7.

13. For an illuminating discussion of vengeful anger, see Charles L. Griswold, "The Nature and Ethics of Vengeful Anger," in *Passions and Emotions,* ed. James E. Fleming (New York: New York University Press, 2013).

14. See Gary Watson, "Responsibility and the Limits of Evil: Variations on a Strawsonian Theme," in *Responsibility, Character, and the Emotions: New Essays in Moral Psychology,* ed. Ferdinand Schoeman (Cambridge: Cambridge University Press, 1987), 256–86, and David Shoemaker, *Responsibility from the Margins* (Oxford: Oxford University Press, 2015).

15. Stanley Milgram, "Behavioral Study of Obedience," *Journal of Abnormal and Social Psychology,* 67, no. 4 (October 1963): 371–78.

16. J. L. Austin, "Ifs and Cans," in *Philosophical Papers,* 3rd ed. (Oxford: Oxford University Press, 1979), 218n.

17. Daniel Dennett, *Freedom Evolves* (New York: Penguin Putnam, 2003), 75.

18. Dennett, *Freedom Evolves,* 76. (Emphasis in original.) See also, Daniel Dennett, *Elbow Room: The Varieties of Free Will Worth Wanting* (Cambridge, MA: MIT Press, 1984), chap. 6.

19. Michael Smith also uses counterfactual thinking to analyze attributions of moral competence. Smith describes comparing the behavior of agents in actual scenarios to their performance in nearby possible worlds, in which we have abstracted from irrel-evant factors and maintained "relevant properties of their brains." "Rational Capacities," 124. My analysis is less abstract than Smith's in characterizing factors relevant to counterfactual evaluation.

20. See, for example, John Martin Fischer and S. J. Mark Ravizza, *Responsibility and Control: A Theory of Moral Responsibility* (Cambridge: Cambridge University Press 1998).

21. Immanuel Kant, *Critique of Practical Reason* (1788), trans. Lewis White Beck (New York: MacMillan, 1956), 30.

22. Kant, *Critique of Practical Reason,* 30.

23. Kant does, however, acknowledge that there can be moral reasons to refrain from blaming. As I have suggested, Kant thinks that our inevitable and insurmountable ignorance of another's maxims provide us practical reasons to refrain from blame. In the *Lectures on Ethics*, he suggests further reasons. See Immanuel Kant, *Lectures on Ethics* (1930), trans. Lewis Infield, forward by Lewis White Beck (New York: Hackett Publishing, 1963). Kant writes that "if, for instance, a starving man steals something from the dining-room, the degree of his responsibility is diminished by the fact that it would have required great self-restraint for him not to do it" (63) and that "as a pragmatic lawgiver and judge man must give due consideration to the *infirmitas* and *fragilitas* of his fellows and remember that they are only human." (67). Also relevant is Christine Korsgaard's point that Kant rarely discusses blameworthiness. Christine M. Korsgaard, "Creating the Kingdom of Ends," in *Creating the Kingdom of Ends* (Cambridge: Cambridge University Press, 1996), 306. For a helpful compilation of Kant's arguments, see Jeffrie Murphy, "Does Kant have a Theory of Punishment?," *Columbia Law Review* 87, no. 3 (April 1987): 513–16.

24. *M'Naghten's Case,* House of Lords 10 Cl. & F. 200, 8 Eng. Rep. 718 (1843).

25. I borrow the idea of reverse-engineering from Daniel Dennett. See Dennett, *Freedom Evolves,* 203. See also Daniel C. Dennett, *Brainchildren: Essays on Designing Minds* (Cambridge, MA: MIT Press, 1998), chap. 16.

26. See Daniel C. Dennett, *The Intentional Stance* (Cambridge, MA: MIT Press, 1987).

27. Immanuel Kant, *Grounding for the Metaphysics of Morals* (1785), trans. James W. Ellington (Indianapolis: Hackett, 1981), 19.

28. Immanuel Kant, *Religion within the Boundaries of Mere Reason* (1793), trans. and ed. Alan Wood and George Di Giovanni, intro. Robert Merrihew Adams (Cambridge: Cambridge University Press, 1998).

29. See Erin Kelly and Lionel McPherson, "The Naturalist Gap in Ethics," in *Normativity and Nature,* ed. Mario De Caro and David Macarthur (New York: Columbia University Press, 2010).

30. *Smith v. United States,* 36 F.2d (D.C. Cir. 1929).

31. *Durham v. United States,* 214 F.2d (D.C. Cir. 1954).

32. David L. Bazelon, "The Morality of the Criminal Law," *Southern California Law Review* 49 (1975–76): 385–405. David Bazelon's reliance on the notion of proximate cause from tort law involves stretching that notion. The causation question in negligence concerns whether the defendant's careless act brought about the plaintiff's injury in an expected, nonhaphazard manner, not whether something about the defendant "proximately caused" him to take some action.

33. Bazelon, "The Morality of the Criminal Law," 391.

34. If the causal judgment were about possibility, then it would be warranted only when there is no scenario under which the agent would have complied with the dictates of law, including scenarios in which the agent was sure to be apprehended by law enforcement. But the norms of mental health permit ascriptions of mental illness even when rational and moral behavior is not, in that sense, precluded by the disease.

35. Behavior might not be dysfunctional when it is culturally normal. See Dominic Murphy, "Philosophy of Psychiatry," in *The Stanford Encyclopedia of Philosophy,* spring 2015 ed., Edward N. Zalta, http://plato.stanford.edu/archives/spr2015/entries/psychiatry/.

36. Ruth Benedict, "Anthropology and the Abnormal," *Journal of General Psychology* 10, no. 1 (1934): 59–82. See also Allan V. Horwitz and Jerome C. Wakefield, *The Loss of Sadness* (Oxford: Oxford University Press, 2007), 195.

37. See also study of the nonpathological nature of hopelessness, meaninglessness, and extreme sadness in the philosophical worldview of Sri Lankan Buddhists, discussed by Horwitz and Wakefield, *The Loss of Sadness,* 197.

38. See Horwitz and Wakefield, *The Loss of Sadness,* chap. 10. Many psychiatrists would, of course, recognize the relevance of cultural factors to a psychiatric diagnosis. Determining whether a criminal act was the product of mental disease or defect might require more contextual investigation than is required or allowed in most criminal proceedings.

39. Horwitz and Wakefield write, "Normal and disordered responses to stress can manifest similar symptoms, and some responses to severe stresses can be proportional and related to the ongoing presence of the stressor, while others may be disproportionate or continue despite changing circumstances" (*The Loss of Sadness,* 209).

40. When distress in response to ongoing circumstantial stressors is severe, it is not clear why only distress that is psychologically dysfunctional should mitigate blame. I will return to this theme in Chapter 6.

41. Centers for Disease Control and Prevention (CDC), "Suicide: Facts at a Glance 2015," National Center for Injury Prevention and Control, Division of Violence Prevention, http://www.cdc.gov/violenceprevention/pdf/suicide-datasheet-a.pdf. See also Centers for Disease Control and Prevention (CDC), Web-based Injury Statistics Query and Reporting System (WISQARS), National Center for Injury Prevention and Control, CDC (producer), https://webappa.cdc.gov/sasweb/ncipc/mortrate.html.

3. Blame and Excuses

1. On the idea that holding people morally responsible involves the cultivation of agency, see Manuel Vargas, *Building Better Beings: A Theory of Moral Responsibility* (Oxford: Oxford University Press, 2013), especially chap. 6. On the idea that an agent's capacities are partly the function of circumstances, see chap. 4.

2. I am not suggesting that, in being related to certain emotions and attitudes, excuses are purely emotive and unconnected to reasons. For example, pity involves feelings that are aptly or inaptly expressed, depending on whether the situation is one that warrants pity.

3. Mitchell Berman, "Justification and Excuse, Law and Morality," *Duke Law Journal* 53, no. 1 (October 2003): 1–77.

4. See John C. P. Goldberg, "Inexcusable Wrongs," *California Law Review* 103, no. 3 (June 2015): 467–512.

5. On whether illegality per se constitutes a moral reason, see Chapter 6.
6. Exceptions include Nicola Lacey and Hannah Pickard, "From the Consulting Room to the Court Room? Taking the Clinical Model of Responsibility without Blame into the Legal Realm," *Oxford Journal of Legal Studies* 33, no. 1 (Spring 2013): 1–29, and James Q. Whitman, "A Plea against Retributivism," *Buffalo Criminal Law Review* 7, no. 1 (April 2003): 85–107.
7. See Angela M. Smith, "Moral Blame and Moral Protest," in *Blame: Its Nature and Norms,* ed. D. Justin Coates and Neal A. Tognazzini (Oxford: Oxford University Press, 2013).
8. T. M. Scanlon groups together as blaming responses all responses that signify the meaning of a wrongdoer's morally criticizable attitudes and judgments for relationships in which she is involved. Questions about relational meaning, however, seem to me to be broader than questions about the responses a culpable wrongdoer deserves. See T. M. Scanlon, *Moral Dimensions: Permissibility, Meaning, Blame* (Cambridge, MA: Harvard University Press, 2008), chap. 4, especially 128–29. See also T. M. Scanlon, "Forms and Conditions of Responsibility," in *The Nature of Moral Responsibility,* ed. Randolf Clarke, Michael McKenna, and Angela M. Smith (New York: Oxford University Press, 2015), especially 90–105.
9. I thank Amelie Rorty for pressing me on this point.
10. Compare Allan Gibbard, *Wise Choices, Apt Feelings: A Theory of Normative Judgment* (Cambridge, MA: Harvard University Press, 1992).
11. Scanlon, *Moral Dimensions,* 175–79, 206–10. See also G. A. Cohen, "Casting the First Stone: Who Can, and Who Can't, Condemn the Terrorists?," in *Political Philosophy: Royal Institute of Philosophy Supplement: 58,* ed. Anthony Hear (Cambridge: Cambridge University Press, 2006): 113–36, and Antony Duff, "Blame, Moral Standing, and the Legitimacy of the Criminal Trial," *Ratio* 23, no. 2 (June 2010): 123–40.
12. It might be objected that the coach has a responsibility for the welfare of the players, which fans do not have. Given popular demand for the entertainment of football, however, it is not obvious that the public bears no responsibility for the welfare of football players.
13. John Martin Fischer and Neal Tognazzini describe these sorts of cases as occupying a space between morally attributing an act to an agent and holding that agent morally accountable. See John Martin Fischer and Neal A. Tognazzini, "The Physiognomy of Responsibility," *Philosophy and Phenomenological Research* 82, no. 2 (March 2011): 381–417.
14. Peter Strawson, "Freedom and Resentment," *Proceedings of the British Academy,* 48 (1962). Reprinted in *Free Will,* ed. Gary Watson (Oxford: Oxford University Press, 1982), 64–66.
15. R. Jay Wallace, *Responsibility and the Moral Sentiments* (Cambridge, MA: Harvard University Press, 1994), 135, and chaps. 5 and 6. See also Michael Zimmerman, *An Essay on Moral Responsibility* (Totowa, NJ: Rowman and Littlefield, 1988), chap. 3; and John Martin Fisher and S. J. Mark Ravizza, *Responsibility and Control: A Theory of Moral Responsibility* (Cambridge: Cambridge University Press 1998), chap. 3.

16. Moreover, although less relevant to the matters under discussion, some types of actions prohibited by criminal laws are not morally wrong.

17. As I indicated in Chapter 2, a person's capacity for morality has both cognitive and motivational dimensions. A morally capable person is capable of understanding morality's requirements and of so regulating her behavior. Not only can she recognize that other persons are sentient, concerned about their future, have meaningful relationships, and so on, but she also has a sensibility that moves her to care about these facts. In asserting that some people lack moral capacity, I am supposing that psychological factors influence our receptivity to moral reasons, in both cognitive and emotional respects. Cognitive and emotional factors influence the reach of moral considerations as reasons for particular persons. See Erin I. Kelly and Lionel K. McPherson, "The Naturalist Gap in Ethics," in *Naturalism and Normativity,* ed. Mario De Caro and David Macarthur (New York: Columbia University Press, 2010).

18. On the difference between judgments of moral permissibility and assessments of blameworthiness, see Scanlon, *Moral Dimensions.*

19. Thomas Nagel, *The View from Nowhere* (New York: Oxford University Press, 1986), 176.

20. We might suppose that a person of ordinary prudence would not have engaged in the type of behavior undertaken by the defendant without recognizing (1) the risk of its causing harm to others and (2) that harm so caused would constitute grounds for appropriate compensation to the victim. For this point, I am indebted to George E. Smith.

21. John C. P. Goldberg and Benjamin C. Zipursky, "Tort Law and Moral Luck," *Cornell Law Review* 92, no. 6 (2007): 1123–75. On debates about the philosophical foundations of tort law, see Jules Coleman, "Torts and Tort Theory: Preliminary Reflections," in *Philosophy and the Law of Torts,* ed. Gerald J. Postema (Cambridge: Cambridge University Press, 2001), 183–213.

22. Matthew Talbert takes a similar position and from it concludes that it is appropriate to direct blaming responses to all minimally rational wrongdoers. I resist Talbert's conclusion. See Matthew Talbert, "Blame and Responsiveness to Moral Reasons: Are Psychopaths Blameworthy?" *Pacific Philosophical Quarterly* 89, no. 4 (December 2008): 516–35.

23. This view fits with a familiar notion of desert: namely, that those who could not have done otherwise cannot be said to deserve blame for their wrongdoing. Those who lack excuse for their wrongdoing, by contrast, and hence could have acted well, deserve blame. The operative notion of blame, here, tends to be retributive in nature.

24. Wallace, *Responsibility and the Moral Sentiments,* 156.

25. Wallace, *Responsibility and the Moral Sentiments,* 157.

26. In Wallace's view, such agents are exempted not only from blame for their morally impermissible behavior, but also from the moral obligation to act as morality prescribes, since "it does not seem fair to demand that people comply with such obligations unless they have the general ability to grasp those reasons and to regulate their behavior accordingly" (*Responsibility and the Moral Sentiment,* 161). I have argued that all minimally rational persons are subject to moral directives and are obligated

to act morally. Contra Wallace's suggestion, this would include persons who lack the general capacity to recognize moral reasons and to regulate their behavior accordingly.

27. Gary Watson makes a similar suggestion, although he does not elaborate it. See his "Skepticism about Weakness of Will," in *Agency and Answerability: Selected Essays* (Oxford: Oxford University Press, 2004), 72.

28. Stephen Morse has proposed a "hard choice theory," along these lines. However, unlike my proposal, Morse's is designed for application in criminal law. It belongs to an attempt to ensure that criminal law tracks moral blameworthiness. See Stephen Morse, "Excusing and the New Excuse Defenses: A Legal and Conceptual Review," *Crime and Justice* 23 (1998): 341, 395–96. The typology popular among legal theorists does not line up with Strawson's distinction between excusing and exempting conditions. See Strawson, "Freedom and Resentment." Legal excuses include examples of what Strawson refers to as exempting conditions, and some of what Strawson classifies as excuses would be counted by legal theorists as justifications.

29. "After Michael Vick, the Battle to Stop Dogfighting," *Fresh Air,* September 24, 2009, https://www.npr.org/templates/story/story.php?storyId=113158123.

30. A notable exception to this includes Gary Watson, "A Moral Predicament in the Criminal Law," *Inquiry* 58, no. 2 (2015): 168–88.

31. Stephen Morse considers whether to view psychiatric problems, such as impulsive disorders and compulsions, as "unjustifiable internal threats," analogous to two-party coercion. Morse argues that while it is tempting to view these cases as "hard choices," they should instead be viewed as cases of irrationality. Stephen Morse, "Culpability and Control," *University of Pennsylvania Law Review* 142, no. 5 (May 1994): 1619–34. But even granting that irrationality is involved, these forms of irrationality seem to be experienced as internal threats or hard choices.

32. Compare John Gardner, "The Gist of Excuses," *Buffalo Criminal Law Review* 1, no. 2 (January 1998): 575–98. Gardner argues that a person is blameworthy if she fails to meet role-specific standards of character called for in her situation (as in the bravery required of a soldier, the attentiveness required of a driver). Outside of specific roles, Gardner treats reasonable expectations as uniform across persons—a position I am questioning.

33. On the notion of moral luck, see Thomas Nagel, "Moral Luck," in *Mortal Questions* (New York: Cambridge University Press, 1979). See also Neil Levy, *Hard Luck: How Luck Undermines Free Will and Moral Responsibility* (Oxford: Oxford University Press, 2011).

34. See Gary Watson, "Responsibility and the Limits of Evil," in *Agency and Answerability: Selected Essays* (Oxford: Oxford University Press, 2004), 244–45.

35. Hector Black, "We'd Known Death But Not Like This," Story Corps, *Morning Edition,* National Public Radio, February 8, 2008, http://storycorps.org/listen/hector-black/.

36. Hector Black, "Forgiveness," *The Moth: True Stories Told Live,* April 16, 2013, at 7:20. http://themoth.org/posts/storytellers/hector-black.

37. Black, "Forgiveness," at 7:30.
38. Black, "Forgiveness," at 10:25.
39. A moral judgment about which response would be most appropriate itself calls out for moral evaluation. See Avner Baz, "Being Right and Being in the Right," *Inquiry* 51, no. 6 (December 2008): 627–44.
40. I am grateful to Emily Robertson for pressing this objection.
41. Psychological difficulties might involve irrationalities, though these irrationalities do not always imply that the agent's self-control is diminished. See Morse, "Culpability and Control."
42. On agent-regret, see Bernard Williams, "Persons, Character, and Morality," in *Moral Luck: Philosophical Papers 1973–1980* (Cambridge: Cambridge University Press, 1981).
43. In this sense, the normative criteria for excuses are "objective," not "subjective." See Jeremy Horder, *Excusing Crime* (Oxford: Oxford University Press, 2004), 125–28, 130–31.

4. Criminal Justice without Blame

1. Associated Press, "U.S. to Seek Death Penalty in Charlestown Church Shooting," *Los Angeles Times,* May 24, 2016, http://www.latimes.com/nation/nationnow/la-na -charleston-church-shooting-death-penalty-20160524-snap-story.html.
2. *United States v. Dzhokhar A. Tsarnaev,* Crim. No. 13-10200-GAO, Document 167, Filed 01/30//2014, https://deathpenaltyinfo.org/documents/NoticeOfIntentBoston .pdf.
3. Barbara Greenberg, "Dylann Roof: Evil or Ill? Why Aren't We All Mass Murders?," *Psychology Today,* June 23, 2015, https://www.psychologytoday.com/blog/the-teen -doctor/201506/dylann-roof-evil-or-ill; Daniel R. Berger, "Dylann Roof: Morally Evil or Mentally Ill?," Daniel R. Berger: Alethia International Ministries. February 14, 2017, https://www.drdanielberger.com/single-post/2017/02/14/Dylann-Roof-Morally -Evil-or-Mentally-Ill.
4. Nancy Reagan, Address to the Nation on the Campaign against Drug Abuse, September 14, 1986, http://www.presidency.ucsb.edu/ws/?pid=36414.
5. On the notion of public reason, see John Rawls, "The Idea of Public Reason Revisited," *University of Chicago Law Review* 64, no. 3 (Summer 1997): 765–807, reprinted in John Rawls, *Collected Papers,* ed. Samuel Freeman (Cambridge, MA: Harvard University Press, 1999).
6. These *mens rea* criteria for criminal guilt are set out in the American Law Institute's "Model Penal Code" and formally adopted by approximately two-thirds of all U.S. states.
7. See Carissa Byrna Hessick, "Motive's Role in Criminal Punishment," *Southern California Law Review* 80, no. 1 (December 2006): 89–150.
8. An exception is Gary Watson, "Responsibility and the Limits of Evil," in *Responsibility, Character, and the Emotions: New Essays in Moral Psychology,* ed. Ferdinand David Schoeman (Cambridge: Cambridge University Press, 1987), 256–86.

9. P. F. Strawson, "Freedom and Resentment," *Proceedings of the British Academy,* 48 (1962), 1–25. Reprinted in Gary Watson, ed., *Free Will,* 2nd ed. (Oxford: Oxford University Press, 2003).

10. Strawson, "Freedom and Resentment," section 4.

11. Strawson, "Freedom and Resentment," section 3.

12. T. M. Scanlon, *Moral Dimensions: Permissibility, Meaning, Blame* (Cambridge, MA: Harvard University Press, 2010), 128–29.

13. See also Susan Wolf, "Blame, Italian Style," in *Reasons and Recognition: Essays on the Philosophy of T. M. Scanlon,* ed. R. Jay Wallace, Rahul Kumar, and Samuel Freeman (Oxford: Oxford University Press, 2011).

14. Scanlon, *Moral Dimensions,* 128–29. Scanlon writes, "A person is *blameworthy* . . . if he does something that indicates intentions or attitudes that are faulty by the standards of a relationship"; T. M. Scanlon, "Interpreting Blame," in *Blame: Its Nature and Norms,* ed. Neal Tognazzini and Justin Coates (New York: Oxford University Press 2012), 88. See also T. M. Scanlon, "Forms and Conditions of Responsibility," in *The Nature of Moral Responsibility,* ed. Randolf Clarke, Michael McKenna, and Angela M. Smith (New York: Oxford University Press, 2015), especially 90–105.

15. T.M. Scanlon, "Giving Desert its Due," *Philosophical Explorations* 16, no. 2 (2013): 104.

16. Scanlon explicitly describes his account of blame as a "desert-based" view; see *Moral Dimensions,* 188. See also Scanlon, "Giving Desert Its Due," 101–16.

17. Scanlon, *Moral Dimensions,* 146.

18. Nathanial Hawthorne, *The Scarlet Letter,* 3rd ed., ed. Seymour Gross, Sculley Bradley, Richmond Croom Beatty, and E. Hudson Long (New York: W. W. Norton, 1988), 40.

19. Stephen Morse suggests a similar criterion of fairness to characterize legal excuses. See his "Excusing and the New Excuse Defenses: A Legal and Conceptual Review," *Crime and Justice* 23 (1998): 341.

20. For an illuminating discussion of this idea, see Christopher Lewis, "Inequality, Incentives, Blameworthiness, and Crime," unpublished manuscript.

21. See Neil Levy, *Hard Luck: How Luck Undermines Free Will and Moral Responsibility* (Oxford: Oxford University Press, 2011), chap. 8.

22. T. M. Scanlon takes this position; see *Moral Dimensions,* 188, "Giving Desert Its Due," 105, 108, and "Forms and Conditions of Responsibility," 98–105.

23. Compare Pamela Hieronymi, who argues that compassion is compatible with anger and blame, in "Articulating an Uncompromising Forgiveness," *Philosophy and Phenomenological Research* 62, no. 3 (May 2001): 529–55.

24. It is true that privilege and receiving unjust benefits can also distort moral motivation and judgments. But "obstacles" such as these tend not to be counted as excusing conditions. They do not represent hardships and do not seem particularly difficult to overcome. Of course, the ease with which privilege and unjust benefits might be resisted could be an illusion, but I will set this challenge aside and focus instead on the clearer cases of commonly recognized hardships. I note, however,

one recent attempt to present affluence as a mitigating consideration: a controversial "affluenza" defense influenced the sentencing of sixteen-year-old drunk driver Ethan Couch, who was convicted on charges of vehicular manslaughter. Couch received ten years' probation instead of jail time of up to twenty years. See Madison Gray, "The Affluenza Defense: Judge Rules Rich Kid's Rich Kidness Makes Him Not Liable for Deadly Drunk Driving Accident," *Time Magazine,* December 12, 2013, http://newsfeed.time.com/2013/12/12/the-affluenza-defense-judge-rules-rich-kids-rich-kid-ness-makes-him-not-liable-for-deadly-drunk-driving-accident/.

25. While we cannot morally afford to occupy this perspective for long, its validity as an angle on reality cannot plausibly be denied. Through modesty about blame we can and should be sensitive to the limits of morality. See John Dewey, *Human Nature and Conduct* (New York: Modern Library, 1922), chap. 24. See also Barbara H. Fried, "Beyond Blame," *Boston Review* 38 (July / August 2013): 12–18.

26. Some philosophers who write about forgiveness agree that forgiveness cannot be morally required. See Cheshire Calhoun, "Changing One's Heart," *Ethics* 103, no. 1 (October 1992): 76–96. Compare Hieronymi, "Articulating an Uncompromising Forgiveness." The view that forgiveness should not be demanded of victims has generated criticism of the South African Truth and Reconciliation Commission, which included the aim that victims forgive perpetrators.

27. See Saira Mohamed, "Of Monsters and Men: Perpetrator Trauma and Mass Atrocity," *Columbia Law Review* 115, no. 5 (2015): 1157–1216.

28. This description is contentious. Tort theorists debate whether tort liability requires a harm that is simply a setback to the victim, or whether it requires the harm to be a *wrongfully inflicted* setback.

29. In some cases, a tortfeasor is an agent who is responsible for violating a legal duty to protect another from injury; for example, when an employer is responsible (and hence a tortfeasor) for injuries wrongfully caused by an employee. In all cases, the relevant wrongs are those defined so by law. My thanks to John Goldberg for help with these definitions.

30. See John C. P. Goldberg and Benjamin C. Zipursky, "Rights and Responsibility in the Law of Torts," in *Rights and Private Law,* ed. Donald Nolan and Andrew Robertson (Oxford: Hart Publishing, 2012).

31. Recourse is normally represented by compensatory payments, although punitive damages can be awarded in the case of intentional torts.

32. See Jules Coleman, "A Mixed Conception of Corrective Justice," *Iowa Law Review* 77, no. 2 (January 1992): 427–44, and Stephen R. Perry, "The Moral Foundations of Tort Law," *Iowa Law Review* 77, no. 2 (January 1992): 449–514.

33. John C. P. Goldberg and Benjamin C. Zipursky, "Tort Law and Responsibility," in *Philosophical Foundations of the Law of Torts,* ed. John Oberdiek (Oxford: Oxford University Press, 2014), 26.

34. Similarly, tortfeasors are not bound by justice to offer compensation.

35. It would be possible, on the account of the conditions of moral responsibility I am proposing, to argue for a "subjective" interpretation of some legally recognized excuses. I leave this interesting question for another time.

36. Victor Tadros also relies on a notion of redress in developing a nonretributivist account of punishment. However, he conceives of the duty of redress as falling on individual offenders, while I am suggesting that the duty is collective. See his *The Ends of Harm: The Moral Foundations of Criminal Law* (Oxford: Oxford University Press, 2011), especially chap. 12.

37. Arthur Ripstein takes a similar position. See Arthur Ripstein, *Equality, Responsibility, and the Law* (Cambridge: Cambridge University Press, 1999). I agree with Ripstein's emphasis on the distinction between punishment and blame (146). Where I differ is in the idea that a response to criminal wrongdoing must involve hard treatment. If it does not, Ripstein argues, the public response to the criminal wrong will function as a mere price tag. I doubt that moral condemnation of criminal acts can be expressed only via hard treatment. On the public nature of criminal law and its relation to democratic equality, see also Vincent Chiao, *Criminal Law in the Age of the Administrative State* (New York: Oxford University Press, 2018).

38. For a powerful historical overview and analysis, see Alison Edwards, "Rape, Racism, and the White Women's Movement: An Answer to Susan Brownmiller," 2nd ed., Sojourner Truth Organization, 1979, http://www.sojournertruth.net/main.html.

39. In 2010, the Fair Sentencing Act reduced a 100:1 federal sentencing differential for crack versus powder cocaine to an 18:1 disparity.

40. See Anjana Malhotra, "Witness to Abuse: Human Rights Abuses under the Material Witness Law since September 11," ed. Jamie Fellner, Lee Gelernt, Jim Ross, Joseph Saunders, Robin Goldfaden, *Human Rights Watch* 17, no. 2 (June 2005), https://www.hrw.org/report/2005/06/26/witness-abuse/human-rights-abuses-under-material-witness-law-september-11.

41. For example, international criminal tribunals have demonstrated a cautious approach. The International Criminal Court rejects the death penalty and aims for reconciliation. It is moderated by international standards and is less easily confounded with a particular society's mechanisms of social exclusion, hierarchical structure, or systems of oppression. See Alex Whiting, "In International Criminal Prosecutions, Justice Delayed Can Be Justice Delivered," *Harvard International Law Journal* 50, no. 2 (June 2009): 323–64; *Prosecutor v. Plavšić*, Case No. IT-00-39&40/1-S, Sentencing Judgment, 73–81 (February 27, 2003); Michael P. Scharf and William A. Schabas, *Slobodan Milosevic on Trial: A Companion* (New York: Continuum, 2002).

5. Rethinking Punishment

1. I thank Seana Shiffrin for helping me to settle on the expression "reasonable opportunity."

2. Diversionary programs do not count as punishment when they do not depend on a defendant's conviction.

3. See Allegra M. McLeod, "Prison Abolition and Grounded Justice," *UCLA Law Review* 62, no. 5 (June 2015): 1156–1239.

4. On some theories of justified self-defense, necessity is not always required. It is not required when a person has no duty to retreat (as when confronting a burglar in one's own home).

5. See Daniel M. Farrell, "The Justification of General Deterrence," *Philosophical Review* 93, no. 3 (1985): 367–94. See also Warren Quinn, "The Right to Threaten and the Right to Punish," *Philosophy and Public Affairs* 14, no. 4 (Autumn 1985): 327–73. On the distinction between rights and privileges, see Wesley Newcomb Hohfeld. "Some Fundamental Legal Conceptions as Applied in Legal Reasoning," *Yale Law Journal* 23, no. 1 (November 1913): 16–59, reprinted in Wesley Newcomb Hohfeld, *Fundamental Legal Conceptions as Applied in Judicial Reasoning and Other Legal Essays*, ed. Walter Wheeler Cook (New Haven: Yale University Press: 1919).

6. Farrell, "The Justification of General Deterrence," 372.

7. It seems plausible to hold that a right to self-defense does not depend on the moral fault of the aggressor who poses the threat. Judith Jarvis Thomson has emphasized this point. She claims that "the aggressor's fault or lack of fault has no bearing on when you may kill the aggressor to defend [yourself]." See Judith Jarvis Thomson, "Self-Defense," *Philosophy and Public Affairs* 20, no. 4 (Autumn 1991): 285. Compare Jeff McMahan, *The Ethics of Killing: Problems at the Margins of Life* (New York: Oxford University Press, 2002), 398–411. McMahan argues that the case for a right to defend ourselves against innocent threats is weaker. Still, he allows for self-defense in such cases.

8. Quinn emphasizes this in "The Right to Threaten and the Right to Punish." See also H. L. A. Hart, "Legal Responsibility and Excuses," in *Punishment and Responsibility: Essays in the Philosophy of Law* (Oxford: Oxford University Press, 1968), especially 44.

9. On the notion that retaliatory harm stabilizes social cooperation, see Gerald Gaus, "Retributive Justice and Social Cooperation," in *Retributivism: Essays on Theory and Practice*, ed. Mark D. White (Oxford: Oxford University Press, 2011), 73–90.

10. Farrell, "The Justification of General Deterrence," 369.

11. Many thanks to David Luban for this point and for suggestions about ideas in the next paragraph.

12. Farrell, "The Justification of General Deterrence," 368.

13. Victor Tadros, *The Ends of Harm* (Oxford: Oxford University Press, 2011), chap. 12. On the notion of remedial responsibility, see also David Miller, "Two Concepts of Responsibility," *National Responsibility and Global Justice* (Oxford: Oxford University Press, 2007), chap. 2.

14. See Norval Morris and Michael Tonry, *Between Prison and Probation: Intermediate Punishments in a Rational System* (Oxford: Oxford University Press, 1990), and Nigel Walker, *Sentencing in a Rational Society* (London: Allen Lane, 1969).

15. See Lode Walgrave, ed. *Restorative Justice and the Law* (Collumpton, U.K: Willan Publishing, 2002), and also Lode Walgrave, *Restorative Justice, Self-Interest, and Responsible Citizenship* (Collumpton, U.K.: Willan Publishing, 2008).

16. Hart emphasizes the importance of law as a choosing system in "Legal Responsibility and Excuses" (44–48), and "Punishment and the Elimination of Responsibility" (181–82), in *Punishment and Responsibility*.

17. Chapter 6 takes up the requirement of basic distributive justice.

18. On justification of criminal law by hypothetical agreement, see Sharon Dolovich, "Legitimate Punishment in Liberal Democracy," *Buffalo Criminal Law Review* 7, no. 2 (January 2004): 307–442.

19. Issues in the next two sections of this chapter are also discussed in Erin I. Kelly, "Criminal Justice without Retribution," *Journal of Philosophy* 106, no. 8 (August 2009): 440–62.

20. There are arguably exceptions to this requirement in the case of extremely wrongful acts, such as crimes against humanity. See Kevin John Heller, *The Nuremberg Military Tribunals and the Origins of International Criminal Law* (Oxford: Oxford University Press, 2011), especially chap. 5.

21. See H. L. A. Hart, "Punishment and the Elimination of Responsibility," especially 181–82.

22. See Quinn, "The Right to Threaten and the Right to Punish," 356–59. What I say here suggests an understanding of the insanity defense that is broader than the defense currently recognized by U.S. law.

23. See Alice Goffman, *On the Run: Fugitive Life in an American City* (Chicago: University of Chicago Press, 2014), and Victor Rios, *Punished: Policing the Lives of Black and Latino Boys* (New York: New York University Press, 2011).

24. Strict application of this principle to sentencing conflicts with a reasonable principle of parsimony in the imposition of punishment. See Norval Morris, *Madness and the Criminal Law* (Chicago: University of Chicago Press, 1982), chap. 5.

25. H. L. A. Hart, *The Concept of Law* (Oxford: Oxford University Press, 1961), 157–67, and Ronald Dworkin, *Law's Empire* (Cambridge, MA: Harvard University Press, 1986), especially chap. 6.

26. See T. M. Scanlon, "Punishment and the Rule of Law," in *The Difficulty of Tolerance: Essays in Political Philosophy* (Cambridge: Cambridge University Press, 2003).

27. This may not be equivalent to an insanity defense, and the differences would be interesting to explore.

28. Social conditions under which a system of criminal justice loses political legitimacy raise a different kind of challenge, which I will discuss in Chapter 6.

29. This reasoning favors a "subjective" interpretation of legally recognized excuses. A subjective interpretation of excusing conditions, however, brings with it skeptical doubts about our ability to distinguish between a defendant's inability, compromised ability, or unwillingness to comply with the demands of the law, a problem discussed in Chapter 2.

30. In New York, fare evasion is a misdemeanor punishable by up to a year in jail. See Maura Ewing, "Will New York Stop Arresting People for Evading Subway Fares?," *Atlantic,* August 4, 2017, https://www.theatlantic.com/politics/archive/2017/08/new -york-subway-fares/535866/. In Texas, truancy is a misdemeanor that is frequently prosecuted in adult criminal court. See report by Claudio Sanchez on *Morning Edition,* National Public Radio, April 27, 2015, https://www.npr.org/sections/ed/2015/04 /27/400099544/in-texas-questions-about-prosecuting-truancy.

31. Andrew von Hirsch and Andrew Ashworth, *Proportionate Sentencing: Exploring the Principles* (New York: Oxford University Press, 2005), 144.

32. I am not referring to felony murder.

33. In many U.S. states, "excessive speeding" (fifteen to twenty or more miles per hour over the speed limit) is a misdemeanor criminal offense.

34. Researchers have found that members of the public in several countries, including but not limited to the United States, are generally surprised to learn how severe existing criminal penalties are. See Julian V. Roberts, Loretta J. Stalans, David Indermaur, and Mike Hough, *Penal Populism and Public Opinion: Lessons from Five Countries* (Oxford: Oxford University Press, 2003), chap. 2. See also Paul Robinson, *Intuitions of Justice and the Utility of Desert* (Oxford: Oxford University Press, 2013), chap. 7.

35. I am grateful to Paul Guyer for discussion of ideas in this paragraph.

36. See David Brink's analysis of what constitutes fair opportunity to avoid criminal sanctions, which resembles my notion of reasonable opportunity to avoid. Brink understands duress to involve an unfair deprivation of situational control. David O. Brink, "Responsibility, Incompetence, and Psychopathy," The Lindley Lecture, University of Kansas, April 30, 2013.

37. See Marc Mauer and Meda Chesney-Lind, eds., *Invisible Punishment: The Collateral Consequences of Mass Imprisonment* (New York: The New Press, 2002).

38. This sets a natural limit to how cost-effective it is to punish certain crimes with high rates of commission. Bentham stresses that we should include in these costs the anxiety that innocent persons may experience at the prospect that their actions could be misconstrued as illicit (for example, "fornication"). See Jeremy Bentham, *The Principles of Morals and Legislation,* intro. Laurence J. LaFleur (New York: Hafner Press, 1948), chaps. 13 and 17.

39. For instance, in the state of Massachusetts, the average cost to house an inmate in the 2006 fiscal year was $43,026. See Massachusetts Department of Correction website, http://www.mass.gov/?pageID=eopsagencylanding&L=3&L0=Home&L1 =Public+Safety+Agencies&L2=Massachusetts+Department+of+Correction&sid =Eeops.

40. Jeremy Travis, Bruce Western, and Steve Redburn, eds., *The Growth of Incarceration in the United States: Exploring Causes and Consequence* (Washington, DC: National Academies Press, 2014), chaps. 3 and 5.

41. See Andrew von Hirsch, Anthony E. Bottoms, Elizabeth Burney, and P-O. Wikstrom, *Criminal Deterrence and Sentence Severity: An Analysis of Recent Research* (Oxford: Hart, 1999), and Daniel S. Nagin, "Deterrence: A Review of Evidence by a Criminologist for Economists," *Annual Review of Economics* 5, no. 1 (May 2013): 83–105, and Steven N. Durlauf and Daniel S. Nagin, "Imprisonment and Crime: Can Both be Reduced?," *Criminology and Public Policy* 10, no. 1 (January 2011): 13–54.

42. See Chapters 3 and 4.

43. See Michael S. Moore, "Choice, Character, and Excuse," in *Placing Blame: A General Theory of the Criminal Law* (New York: Oxford University Press, 1997), 557. For discussion, see Chapter 2.

44. See Samuel H. Pillsbury's discussion of the difference between act- and character-based assessments of criminal conduct, *Judging Evil: Rethinking the Law of Murder and Manslaughter* (New York: New York University Press, 1998), 72–74, 83–86. Pillsbury stresses that *mens rea* considerations should focus on particular features of choice or conduct, rather than broader judgments of character (as in "depraved" or "malicious"). See, for example, his chap. 7.

45. See Joel Feinberg, "The Expressive Function of Punishment," in *Doing and Deserving: Essays in the Theory of Responsibility* (Princeton, NJ: Princeton University Press, 1974). Feinberg himself explicitly disavows a retributivist theory of punishment (116–18).

46. For criticism of these policies and prescriptions for reform, see Michael Tonry, "Making American Sentencing Just, Humane, and Effective," *Crime and Justice: A Review of Research,* 45 (July 9, 2016), Minnesota Legal Studies Research Paper, section 3, https://ssrn.com/abstract=2853579.

47. See James Q. Whitman, "A Plea against Retributivism," *Buffalo Criminal Law Review* 7, no. 1 (April 2003): 85–107. For an interesting comparison between harsh punishment practices in the United States and more merciful and dignified treatment of offenders in Europe, see James Q. Whitman, *Harsh Justice: Criminal Punishment and the Widening Divide between America and Europe* (Oxford: Oxford University Press, 2003). See also Joshua Kleinfeld, "Two Cultures of Punishment," *Stanford Law Review* 68, no. 5 (June 2016): 933–1036, and Michael Tonry, "Equality and Human Dignity: Missing Ingredients in American Sentencing," in *Sentencing Policies and Practices in Western Countries: Comparative and Cross-National Perspectives,* ed. Michael Tonry (Chicago: University of Chicago Press, 2016), 459–96.

48. See Pillsbury, *Judging Evil,* chap. 5.

49. A "broken windows" law enforcement strategy is no remedy for this loss of legitimacy. See Bernard Harcourt, *Illusion of Order: The False Promise of Broken Windows Policing* (Cambridge, MA: Harvard University Press, 2005).

50. See Tommie Shelby, "Justice, Deviance, and the Dark Ghetto," *Philosophy and Public Affairs* 35, no. 2 (Spring 2007): 126–60.

6. Law Enforcement in an Unjust Society

1. For a critical review of the literature on whether social disadvantages interfere with the justification of criminal punishment, see Benjamin Ewing, "Recent Work on Punishment and Criminogenic Disadvantage," *Law and Philosophy* 37, no. 1 (February 2018): 29–68.

2. Bernadette Rabuy and Daniel Kopf, "Prisons of Poverty: Uncovering the Pre-Incarceration Incomes of the Imprisoned," Prison Policy Initiative, July 9, 2015, 1, https://www.prisonpolicy.org/reports/income.html. See also Bureau of Justice Statistics, "Survey of Inmates in State Correctional Facilities," 2004, https://www.bjs.gov/index.cfm?ty=dcdetail&iid=275.

3. William Julius Wilson, *The Truly Disadvantaged: The Inner City, the Underclass, and Public Policy* (Chicago: University of Chicago Press, 1987).

4. William Julius Wilson, *More than Just Race: Being Black and Poor in the Inner City* (New York: W. W. Norton, 2009), 27.

5. Wilson, *More than Just Race,* 64. See also William Julius Wilson, "The New Urban Poverty and the Problem of Race," The Tanner Lectures on Human Values, University of Michigan, October 22–23, 1993.

6. Wilson *More than Just Race,* 64.

7. Wilson *More than Just Race,* 65.

8. Paul Guerino, Paige M. Harrison, and William J. Sabol, "Prisoners in 2010," Bureau of Justice Statistics, U.S. Department of Justice, appendix table 15, http://bjs.gov /content/pub/pdf/p10.pdf. See also James Austin, Todd Clear, Troy Duster, David F. Greenberg, John Irwin, Candace McCoy, Alan Mobley, Barbara Owen, Joshua Page, *Unlocking America: Why and How to Reduce America's Prison Population* (Washington, DC: JFA Institute, November 2007), http://www.jfa-associates.com/publications/srs /UnlockingAmerica.pdf.

9. The Economic Mobility Project and The Public Safety Performance Project of the Pew Charitable Trusts, *Collateral Costs: Incarceration's Effect on Economic Mobility* (Washington DC: Pew Charitable Trusts, 2010), http://www.pewtrusts.org/~/media /legacy/uploadedfiles/pcs_assets/2010/collateralcosts1pdf.pdf. This report was based on research by Bruce Western and Becky Pettit.

10. The following statistics come from Bruce Western, *Punishment and Inequality in America* (New York: Russell Sage, 2006), 45.

11. For a helpful review of the empirical literature, see Jeremy Travis, Bruce Western, and Steve Redburn, eds., *The Growth of Incarceration in the United States* (Washington, D.C.: National Academies Press, 2014), chap. 5. The most consistent finding is that "the incremental deterrent effect of increases in lengthy prison sentences is modest at best" (155).

12. Marie Gottschalk, *Caught: The Prison State and the Lockdown of American Politics* (Princeton, NJ: Princeton University Press, 2015), 17.

13. Michelle Alexander, *The New Jim Crow: Mass Incarceration in the Age of Colorblindness* (New York: The New Press, 2010), 73.

14. Adam Andrzejwewski, "War Weapons for America's Police Departments: New Data Shows Feds Transfer 2.2B in Military Gear," *Forbes,* May 10, 2016, https://www .forbes.com/sites/adamandrzejewski/2016/05/10/war-weapons-for-americas-local -police-departments/#58fa04044af4. See also Adam Andrzejwewski and Thomas W. Smith, "The Militarization of Local Police Departments," Open the Books: Snapshot Report, May 2016, https://www.openthebooks.com/assets/1/7/OTB_SnapshotReport _MilitarizationPoliceDepts.pdf.

15. Western, *Punishment and Inequality in America,* 50.

16. Western, *Punishment and Inequality in America,* 50. See also Alexander, *The New Jim Crow.*

17. For example, in schools with a "school resource officer," possession of illegal drugs is almost twice as likely and robbery without a weapon is three and a half times more likely to be referred to local law enforcement. See Kyla Spencer, "Bullied by the Badge," data reporting by Adam Hooper, *Huffington Post,* August 10, 2016, http:// data.huffingtonpost.com/2016/school-police/mississippi.

18. For a devastating overview, see Stephen B. Bright and Sia M. Sanneh, "Fifty Years of Defiance and Resistance after *Gideon v. Wainwright*," *Yale Law Journal* 122, no. 8 (June 2013): 2150–74. http://library.law.yale.edu/sites/default/files/fifty_years_of _defiance.pdf.

19. Bright and Sanneh, "Fifty Years of Defiance and Resistance after *Gideon v. Wainwright*," 2150.

20. The National Center on Addiction and Substance Abuse at Columbia University, "Behind Bars II: Substance Abuse and America's Prison Population," Forward by Joseph Califano, February 2010. https://www.centeronaddiction.org/addiction-research /reports/behind-bars-ii-substance-abuse-and-america's-prison-population.

21. Doris J. James and Doris E. Glaze, "Mental Health Problems of Prison and Jail In-mates," Bureau of Justice Statistics Special Report, September 2006, https://www.bjs .gov/content/pub/pdf/mhppji.pdf. See also Kim KiDeuk, Miriam Becker-Cohen, and Maria Serakos, "The Processing and Treatment of Mentally Ill People in the Crim-inal Justice System: A Scan of Practice and Background Analysis," Research Report, The Urban Institute, March 2015, https://www.urban.org/research/publication /processing-and-treatment-mentally-ill-persons-criminal-justice-system/view/full _report.

22. For example, this recent review of the literature does not mention incarceration: Cyn-thia L. Lancaster, Jenni B. Teeters, Daniel F. Gros, and Sudie E. Back, "Posttraumatic Stress Disorder: Overview of Evidence-Based Assessment and Treatment," *Journal of Clinical Medicine* 5, no. 11 (November 2016): 105. https://www.ncbi.nlm.nih.gov /pmc/articles/PMC5126802/.

23. Jennifer Gonnerman, "Before the Law," *New Yorker,* October 6, 2014, https://www .newyorker.com/magazine/2014/10/06/before-the-law.

24. Jim Dwyer, "A Life that Frayed as Bail Reform Withered," *New York Times,* June 9, 2015, https://www.nytimes.com/2015/06/10/nyregion/after-a-shocking-death-a-renewed -plea-for-bail-reform-in-new-york-state.html.

25. See Erving Goffman, "On the Characteristics of Total Institutions," in *Asylums: Es-says on the Social Situation of Mental Patients and Other Inmates* (New York: Anchor, 1961), 1–124.

26. Human Rights Watch, "US: Look Critically at Widespread Use of Solitary Confine-ment," written statement submitted to a U.S. Senate committee, June 18, 2012, https://www.hrw.org/news/2012/06/18/us-look-critically-widespread-use-solitary -confinement.

27. See Marie Gottschalk, "Staying Alive: Reforming Solitary Confinement in U.S. Prisons and Jails," *Yale Law Journal Forum* 125 (January 2016): 253–66, http://www .yalelawjournal.org/forum/reforming-solitary-confinement-in-us-prisons-and-jail. See also Association of State Correctional Administrators, "Aiming to Reduce Time-in-Cell," The Arthur Liman Public Interest Program, Yale Law School, November 2016, https://law.yale.edu/system/files/area/center/liman/document/aimingtoreducetic .pdf; and Allen J. Beck, *Use of Restrictive Housing in U.S. Prisons and Jails, 2011–12,* U.S. Department of Justice, October 2015, http://www.bjs.gov/content/pub/pdf

/urhuspj1112.pdf. See also data collected by Solitary Watch, http://solitarywatch.com/facts/faq/.

28. Justice Center, Council of State Governments, "National Inventory of the Collateral Consequences of Conviction," https://niccc.csgjusticecenter.org/search/?jurisdiction =10.

29. See Erin I. Kelly, "Desert and Fairness in Criminal Justice," *Philosophical Topics* 40, no. 1 (Spring 2012): 63–77.

30. Jeffrie Murphy, "Marxism and Retribution," in *Philosophy and Public Affairs* 2, no. 3 (Spring 1973): 217–43. See also Herbert Morris, "Persons and Punishment," *Monist* 52, no. 4 (October 1968): 475–501.

31. Murphy, "Marxism and Retribution," 55.

32. Murphy, "Marxism and Retribution," 64.

33. For a disturbing example, see Joanna Walters, "An 11-Year-Old Reported Raped Twice, Wound Up with a Conviction," *Washington Post,* March 12, 2015, http://www.washingtonpost.com/lifestyle/magazine/a-seven-year-search-for-justice/2015/03/12/b1cccb30-abe9-11e4-abe8-e1ef60ca26de_story.html.

34. U.S. Department of Justice, Civil Rights Division, "Investigation of the Baltimore City Police Department," August 10, 2016, https://assets.documentcloud.org/documents/3009376/BPD-Findings-Report-FINAL.pdf.

35. Michael S. Moore, "The Moral Worth of Retribution," in *Responsibility, Character, and the Emotions,* ed. Ferdinand Schoeman (Cambridge: Cambridge University Press, 1987).

36. Morris Mason, whose I.Q. was 62–66, was executed in 1985 in Virginia after being convicted of rape and murder. Before his execution, Mason was so uncomprehending about what was about to happen to him, that he asked one of his legal advisors for advice on what to wear to his funeral. Robert Perske, *Unequal Justice? What Can Happen When Persons with Retardation or Other Developmental Disabilities Encounter the Criminal Justice System* (Nashville: Abingdon Press, 1991), 100–1. See also Rosa Ehrenreich and Jamie Fellner, "Beyond Reason: The Death Penalty and Offenders with Mental Retardation," ed. Malcolm Smart and Cynthia Brown, *Human Rights Watch* 13, no. 1 (March 2001): 1–50, https://www.hrw.org/report/2001/03/05/beyond-reason/death-penalty-and-offenders-mental-retardation.

37. Tommie Shelby, *Dark Ghettos: Injustice, Dissent, and Reform* (Cambridge, MA: Harvard University Press, 2016), 238–44.

38. Andrew von Hirsch, *Censure and Sanctions* (Oxford: Oxford University Press, 1996).

39. See T. M. Scanlon, *Moral Dimensions: Permissibility, Meaning, Blame* (Cambridge, MA: Harvard University Press, 2008), chap. 4. See also Angela M. Smith, "On Being Responsible and Holding Responsible," *Journal of Ethics* 11, no. 4 (January 2007): 465–84.

40. See Scanlon's discussion of circumstances that undermine a person's standing to blame in *Moral Dimensions,* 175–79. See also R. A. Duff, "Principle and Contradiction in the Criminal Law: Motives and Criminal Liability," in *Philosophy and the Criminal Law: Principle and Critique* (Cambridge: Cambridge University Press,

1998); R. A. Duff "'I Might Be Guilty, But You Can't Try Me': Estoppel and Other Bars to Trial," *Ohio State Journal of Criminal Law* 1 (2003); G. A. Cohen, "Casting the First Stone: Who Can, and Who Can't, Condemn the Terrorists?," *Political Philosophy: Royal Institute of Philosophy Supplement 58,* ed. Anthony O'Hear (Cambridge: Cambridge University Press, 2006): 113–36.

41. Political commentator Ta-Nehisi Coates observes that for most Americans, the police and the criminal-justice system are figures of authority who rule with legitimacy ("The Myth of Police Reform," *Atlantic,* April 15, 2015, http://www.theatlantic.com /politics/archive/2015/04/the-myth-of-police-reform/390057/). Coates writes:

> This is why whenever a liberal politician offers even the mildest criticism of the police, they must add that "the majority of officers are good, noble people." Taken at face value this is not much of a defense—like a restaurant claiming that on most nights, there really are no rats in the dining room. But interpreted less literally the line is not meant to defend police officers, but to communicate the message that the speaker is not questioning police authority, which is to say the authority of our justice system, which is to say—in a democracy—the authority of the people themselves.

42. For further discussion, see Kelly, "Desert and Fairness in Criminal Justice," especially 68–75.

43. I am grateful to Michael Mitchell for research assistance and numerous suggestions for this section.

44. See Cesare Beccaria, *On Crimes and Punishment* (1764), trans. H. Paolucci (New York: Macmillan, 1986), and Jeremy Bentham, *The Principles of Morals and Legislation* (London: T. Payne, 1789). See Gary S. Becker, "Crime and Punishment: An Economic Approach," *Journal of Political Economy* 76, no. 2 (March-April 1968): 169–217.

45. See Isaac Ehrlich, "Participation in Illegitimate Activities: A Theoretical and Empirical Investigation," *Journal of Political Economy* 81, no. 3 (May-June 1973): 521–65, especially 538–40, 544–53.

46. See Robert Merton, "Social Structure and Anomie," *American Sociological Review* 3, no. 5 (October 1938): 672–82. See also Judith R. Blau and Peter M. Blau. "The Cost of Inequality: Metropolitan Structure and Violent Crime," *American Sociological Review* 47, no. 1 (February 1982): 114–29, especially 118–20.

47. See Elijah Anderson, *Code of the Street: Decency, Violence, and the Moral Life of the Inner City* (New York: W. W. Norton, 1999); Philippe Bourgois, *In Search of Respect: Selling Crack in El Barrio,* 2nd ed. (Cambridge: Cambridge University Press, 2003); Martín Sanchez Jankowsky, *Islands in the Street: Gangs and American Urban Society* (Berkeley: University of California Press, 1991); Ruth Horowitz, *Honor and the American Dream: Culture and Identity in a Chicago Community* (New Brunswick, NJ: Rutgers University Press, 1983).

48. See Clifford Shaw and Henry McKay, *Juvenile Delinquency and Urban Areas* (Chicago: University of Chicago Press, 1942), and Robert J. Sampson and William Julius Wilson, "Toward a Theory of Race, Crime, and Urban Inequality," in *Crime and Inequality,* ed. John Hagan and Ruth D. Peterson (Stanford, CA: Stanford University Press, 1995), 37–56.

49. Sampson and Wilson, "Toward a Theory of Race, Crime, and Urban Inequality," 41–43.

50. Sampson and Wilson, "Toward a Theory of Race, Crime, and Urban Inequality," 44. See also Robert J. Sampson and Janet L. Lauritsen, "Violent Victimization and Offending: Individual-, Situational-, and Community-Level Risk Factors," in *Understanding and Preventing Violence 3: Social Influences,* ed. Albert J. Reiss Jr. and Jeffrey Roth (Washington, DC: National Academy Press, 1994), 1–114.

51. Robert J. Sampson, "The Place of Context: A Theory and Strategy for Criminology's Hard Problems," Presidential Address to the American Society of Criminology, *Criminology* 51, no. 1 (February 2013): 1–31. See also Robert J. Sampson, *Great American City: Chicago and the Enduring Neighborhood Effect* (Chicago: University of Chicago Press, 2012), and Loïc Wacquant, *Urban Outcasts: A Comparative Sociology of Advanced Marginality* (Cambridge, UK: Polity Press, 2008).

52. American Law Institute, *Model Penal Code: Official Draft and Explanatory Notes* (1962), §2.01.

53. H. L. A. Hart and Tony Honoré, *Causation in the Law,* 2nd ed. (Oxford: Oxford University Press, 1959), 32–41.

54. Sampson, "The Place of Context," 5.

55. Hart and Honoré, *Causation in the Law,* 37.

56. Here I disagree with Victor Tadros's argument that the state's loss of standing to blame depends on the state's *complicity* with the criminal act. See Victor Tadros, "Poverty and Criminal Responsibility," *Journal of Value Inquiry* 43, no. 3 (September 2009): 391–413.

57. See Sanford H. Kadish, Stephen J. Schulhofer, Carol S. Steiker, and Rachel E. Barkow, *Criminal Law and Its Processes: Cases and Materials,* 9th ed. (New York: Wolters Kluwer Law and Business, 2012), 659.

58. See Michael Bratman, *Shared Agency: A Planning Theory of Acting Together* (Oxford: Oxford University Press, 2014); Margaret Gilbert, *Joint Commitment: How We Make the Social World* (Oxford: Oxford University Press, 2014), part 1; and Christopher Kutz, *Complicity: Ethics and Law for a Collective Age* (Cambridge: Cambridge University Press, 2000). On the idea that the *mens rea* for complicity could involve being "reconciled to an unjustifiable risk," see discussion of the German notion of *dolus eventualis* by David Luban, Julie R. O'Sullivan, and David P. Stewart, *International and Transnational Criminal Law* (New York: Aspen Publishers, 2010), chap. 17. See also *Prosecutor v. Lubanga,* Case No. ICC-01/04–01/06, decision on the confirmation of charges, January 29, 2007.

59. See Tadros, "Poverty and Criminal Responsibility."

60. For a history and analysis of twentieth-century U.S. law and policies that racially segregated every metropolitan area in the country, see Richard Rothstein, *The Color of Law: A Forgotten History of How our Government Segregated America* (New York: Liveright Publishing, 2017).

61. See Allen Buchanan, *The Heart of Human Rights* (Oxford: Oxford University Press, 2013), chap. 5.

62. The rights of noncitizens who are legal subjects raises difficult issues that go beyond the scope of the present discussion.

63. See Tommie Shelby, *Dark Ghettos*, chap. 8; Allen Buchanan, "Legitimacy and Democracy," *Ethics* 112 (July 2002): 689–719; A. John Simmons, "Justification and Legitimacy," *Ethics* 109 (July 1999): 739–71; and David Copp, "The Idea of a Legitimate State," *Philosophy and Public Affairs* 28, no. 1 (Winter 1999): 3–45.

64. See Shelby, *Dark Ghettos,* chap. 8.

65. See R. A. Duff, *Punishment, Communication, and Community* (Oxford: Oxford University Press, 2001), 197–201.

66. See, for example, the Department of Justice's scathing report on policing in Ferguson, Missouri, United States Department of Justice Civil Rights Division, "Investigation of the Ferguson Police Department" (March 4, 2015), http://www.justice.gov/opa/pr /justice-department-announces-findings-two-civil-rights-investigations-ferguson -missouri.

Conclusion

1. Joanna Shepard, "Deterrence versus Brutalization: Capital Punishment's Differing Impact among States," *Michigan Law Review* 104, no. 2 (2005): 204–55. For a review of research and public debate on this question, as well as a discussion of challenges for research on this topic, see Evan J. Mandery, *A Wild Justice: The Death and Resurrection of the Death Penalty in America* (New York: W. W. Norton, 2013), n300, 474–82. See also Daniel S. Nagin, "Deterrence: A Review of Evidence by a Criminologist for Economists," *Annual Review of Economics* 5, no. 1 (May 2013), especially 92–93. On the history of the death penalty in the United States see Mandery's book and also Carol S. Steiker and Jordan M. Steiker, *Courting Death: The Supreme Court and Capital Punishment* (Cambridge, MA: Harvard University Press, 2016).

2. Joel Feinberg, "Evil," *Problems at the Roots of Law: Essays in Legal and Political Theory* (Oxford: Oxford University Press, 2003), 129.

3. Feinberg, "Evil," 141.

4. See *Hidalgo v. Arizona* 583 U.S.___ (2018), http://www.scotusblog.com/case-files/cases/ hidalgo-v-arizona/. See also David C. Baldus, George Woodworth, and Charles A. Pulaski, Jr., *Equal Justice and the Death Penalty: A Legal and Empirical Analysis* (Boston, MA: Northeastern University Press, 1990); Steiker and Steiker, *Courting Death*, chap. 5; Evan J. Mandery, "Gregg at 40," *Southwestern Law Review* 46, no. 2 (Spring 2017): 275–301; and Chelsea Creo Sharon, "The 'Most Deserving' of Death: The Narrowing Requirement and the Proliferation of Aggravating Factors in Capital Sentencing Statutes," *Harvard Civil Rights-Civil Liberties Law Review* 46, no. 1 (Winter 2011): 223–51.

5. Data indicates a recent drop in arrest rates for disorderly conduct. See Ryan J. Reilly, "Dubious 'Disorderly Conduct' Arrests Plummet as the Public Turns Cameras on Cops," *Huffington Post,* September 26, 2016, https://www.huffingtonpost.com/entry /contempt-of-cop-arrests-disorderly-conduct-charges_us_57e94d56e4b0e80b1ba32d57.

6. Baxter Oliphant, "Support for Death Penalty Lowest in More than Four Decades," Pew Research Center, September 29, 2016, http://www.pewresearch.org/fact-tank /2016/09/29/support-for-death-penalty-lowest-in-more-than-four-decades/.

7. Michael Meltsner, "The Dilemmas of Excessive Sentencing: Death May Be Different, but How Different?," *Northeastern University Law Journal* 7, no. 1 (Spring 2015): 5–19.

8. See Ashley Nellis, *"Life Goes On: The Historic Rise of Life Sentences in the United States"* (Washington, DC: The Sentencing Project, 2013), https://sentencingproject .org/wp-content/uploads/2015/12/Life-Goes-On.pdf.

9. Beverly Lowry, "Good Girl, Bad Girl," *New Yorker,* February 9, 1998, 62.

10. Debbie White, "Forgiving the Dead Man Walking," Christian Broadcasting Network, http://www.cbn.com/spirituallife/BibleStudyAndTheology/Discipleship/Forgiving _The_Dead_Man_Walking.aspx.

11. Sue Anne Pressley, "Pro-Death Penalty but Chivalrous Texans Debate the Fate of Karla Faye Tucker," *Washington Post,* January 25, 1998, https://www.washingtonpost .com/archive/politics/1998/01/25/pro-death-penalty-but-chivalrous-texans-debate -fate-of-karla-faye-tucker/a21c62bf-5c89-4df9-bbda-6ed714a5311b/?utm_term =.2e74e8322983.

12. Lowry, "Good Girl, Bad Girl," 69.

13. Werner Herzog, dir. *Into the Abyss: A Tale of Death, A Tale of Life,* U.S.A, U.K. and Germany: Produced by Creative Differences and Skellig Rock, in association with Spring Films and Werner Herzog Film Produktion, and in collaboration with Investigation Discovery, More4, and Revolver Entertainment, 2011, at 1:29.

14. "'Rage, Redemption' for Tookie Williams," Farai Chideya interviews Barbara Becnel, National Public Radio, November 26, 2007, https://www.npr.org/templates/story /story.php?storyId=16622404.

15. Stanley Tookie Williams, *Blue Rage, Black Redemption: A Memoir,* epilogue by Barbara Bencel, forward by Tavis Smiley (New York: Touchstone, 2007), 17–18.

16. Research on age-crime curves demonstrates that most criminal "careers" are short, peaking in the teenage years and declining sharply in the early twenties. Even the most determined offenders typically desist in their thirties. David P. Farrington, "Age and Crime," *Crime and Justice: A Review of Research* 7, ed. Michael Tonry and Norval Morris (Chicago: University of Chicago Press, 1986); Gary Sweeten, Alex R. Piquero, and Laurence Steinberg, "Age and the Explanation of Crime, Revisited," *Journal of Youth and Adolescence* 42, no. 6 (June 2013): 921–38; cited in Michael Tonry, "Making American Sentencing Just, Humane, and Effective" *Crime and Justice: Reinventing American Criminal Justice* 46, no. 1 (2017): 459.

17. Sigmund Freud, "On Transience" (1915), in *The Standard Edition of the Complete Psychological Works of Sigmund Freud, Vol. XIV (1914–1916): On the History of the Psycho-Analytic Movement, Papers on Metapsychology, and Other Works*, trans. James Strachey (London: Hogarth Press and the Institute of Psycho-Analysis: 1957), 305–7.

18. Psychoanalysts describe a dynamic called "displacement." It occurs when a person attempts to avoid thoughts that are painful or threatening by substituting for them aims or goals that seem more manageable or desirable.

19. Herzog, *Into the Abyss,* at 1:31.

20. See Bernard Williams, "Internal Reasons and the Obscurity of Blame," in *Making Sense of Humanity and Other Philosophical Papers* (Cambridge: Cambridge University Press, 1995). See also Bernard Williams, "Nietzsche's Minimalist Morality," in *Making Sense of Humanity and Other Philosophical Papers,* especially 72–74.

21. See Erin I. Kelly, "The Historical Injustice Problem for Political Liberalism," *Ethics* 128 (October 2017): 75–94.

ACKNOWLEDGMENTS

I have worked on this book for many years. Earlier versions of some chapters have appeared in print. Chapter 1 revises and extends "Free Will and Criminal Law," in *The Routledge Companion to Free Will*, edited by Kevin Timpe, Meghan Griffith, and Neil Levy (New York: Routledge, 2017), 577–89; © 2017 Taylor & Francis. Chapter 3 incorporates and further develops arguments in "What Is an Excuse?" in *Blame: Its Nature and Norms*, edited by D. Justin Coates and Neal A. Tognazzini (Oxford: Oxford University Press, 2013), 244–62; © 2013 Oxford University Press. Chapter 5 rebuilds and expands on "Criminal Justice without Retribution," in the *Journal of Philosophy* 106, no. 8 (August 2009), 440–62; © 2009 The Journal of Philosophy, Inc. I am grateful to the publishers for allowing me to revisit those essays in this volume. I thank Winfred Rembert for allowing me to use an image of one of his paintings as a frontispiece and for speaking with me about his experience with the criminal justice system.

This book was improved through opportunities I had to discuss it with colleagues in philosophy and law at a number of universities and conferences. Chapter 1 was presented to the UCLA Philosophy Department, a workshop at the University of Michigan Law School, and a conference at Cornell University. Chapter 2 was presented to the Philosophy Departments at the University of Pennsylvania and Tufts University, and a conference sponsored by the Center for the Philosophy of Freedom at the University of Arizona. Chapter 3 was presented to an ethics group at Boston University, the Philosophy Departments at Syracuse University and the University of Roma Tre, and a seminar at Yale Law School. Chapter 4 was presented to conferences at the John Jay College of Criminal Justice and the Chinese University of Hong Kong, the Philosophy Department at SUNY Binghamton, the University of Toronto Law School, and a philosophy seminar at the University of Sassari. Chapter 5 was presented to philosophy departments at Union College, Kansas State University, and the National Autonomous University of Mexico, the social ethics group at Stanford University, and (with Chapter 6) the NYU Colloquium in Legal, Political, and Social Philosophy. Chapter 6 was presented to the Dartmouth College Political Economy Project, the New York City Criminal Law Colloquium, the Law and Philosophy Colloquium at the Harvard Law School, an annual meeting of the European Council for Political Research, a seminar at the Georgetown Law School, and the Stanford University Political Theory Workshop. I also gave papers related to this book at Ohio State University, Vanderbilt University, and the University of Ottawa.

I thank the Edmond J. Safra Foundation Center for Ethics at Harvard University and the School of Arts and Sciences at Tufts University for their generous faculty fellowships and the Harvard Law School for hosting me as a visiting scholar.

I am grateful to my students at Tufts who helped me work through my ideas during courses I taught, and to my colleagues at Tufts who provided an intellectually supportive and friendly environment in which to write this book. I would also like to acknowledge the people who commented on central ideas or parts of the manuscript. I am grateful to Fabio Bacchini, Avner Baz, Micah Bluming, William Bülow, Faviola Rivera Castro, Joshua Cohen, Helen Coverdale, Adam Cureton, Mario De Caro, Daniel Dennett, Daniel Farrell, Samuel Freeman, Barbara Fried, Laura Gillespie, Shmuel Gomes, Pamela Hieronymi, Abigail Jacques, Adriaan Lanni, Annabelle Lever, Neil Levy, Christopher Lewis, Judith Lichtenberg, Runeko Lovell, Evan Mandery, Michael McKenna, Liam Murphy, Orlando Patterson, Andre Poama, Travis Quigley, Samuel Scheffler, Tommie Shelby, Carol Steiker, Sigrun Svavarsdottir, William Tadros, Jeremy Waldron, Stephen White, Alex Whiting, and Molly Wilder. Their suggestions and engagement with my work were very helpful. I owe a special debt to David Luban for pressing my argument in Chapter 5; to George E. Smith for providing important advice on Chapters 2 and 6; and to T. M. Scanlon, who commented in detail on several parts of the manuscript and has, together with John Rawls, in so many ways shaped my philosophical thinking.

I thank Michael Mitchell for excellent research assistance and philosophical challenges; Constance Hale and Tatiana Holway for astute editing; JodieAnne Sclafani for managing the production process; Lindsay Waters for shepherding the book through the approval channels at Harvard University Press; Amolina Bhat and Erna Cooper for proofreading; and Samuel Weitzman and Asa Zabarsky for preparing the index. Vincent Chiao, Göran Duus-Otterström, and Victor Tadros provided detailed, perceptive comments on the entire manuscript; the book is much better for their contributions. I am also indebted to John Goldberg, who generously helped me to improve the final version of the book and encouraged me as I struggled with it.

My deep appreciation to Lionel McPherson for many conversations on these topics over the years. Though he may disagree with aspects of my approach and arguments, this book reflects his thinking as well as my own.

Finally, I am grateful for the patience of my daughters, Iman and Rayha, who have been supportive despite the many times the book crowded my thoughts. Girls, I hope you will take your wise political sensibilities out into the world.

INDEX

Mackie, John, and paradox of retribution, 21–23

Mala in se crimes, 6, 174

Mala prohibita crimes, 174

Mandatory minimum sentencing, 2–3, 39, 41, 146, 176; and juveniles, 42

Mandela, Nelson, 112

Martin v. State, 26

Mass incarceration. *See* Incarceration

Material Witness Law, 120

Meese, Edwin, 45

Mens rea, 4, 25–27, 31, 79; and complicity, 168; and criminal negligence, 28–30, 79; not required for strict liability, 8, 29–30; and physical and psychological limitations, 28–29; subjective character of, 26–28

Mental illness: and blameworthiness, 38, 74, 179–180; and criminal liability, 26–27, 30, 34–38, 60–64, 133; and criminal negligence, 29; and explanations of human behavior, 64–68; and felons as a social group, 11; and fighting crime, 185; as a hardship, 110; and mitigation of blame, 4, 8, 41–42, 105, 159, 179–180; and moral choices, 99; and prison population, 16, 153–154; and reasonable opportunity to avoid criminal action, 30, 52; treatment of, 17, 122, 128, 133, 173. *See also* Insanity defense; Moral competence

Milgram experiment. *See* Yale University experiment

Miller v. Alabama, 41

Minimal rationality: and blame, 114, 117, 119; and criminal liability, 133; and fairness, 136; and Kant's analysis of, 55–60; and legally recognized excuses, 74; and moral competence, 53–60; and moral evaluation of actions, 83–87

Mitigation. *See* Excuses

M'Naghten formulation of insanity defense. *See* Insanity defense

Model Penal Code (MPC), 25–26; and criminal negligence, 28; and duress, 32–33; and insanity, 34–36; versus *M'Naghten* formulation, 34–35; and provocation, 31–32; and recklessness, 28

Moore, Michael S., 19–20, 158–160; and role of emotions in choice, 47

Moore, Sean, 88–91

Moral accountability, 102, 106, 112–113; of juveniles, 40–41

Moral authority of state. *See* Democratic authority of state

Moral capacity. *See* Moral competence

Moral competence: and causal determinism, 54; cognitive and volitional dimensions of, 46; defined, 31, 36; and desert, 159; disconnect with criminal liability, 43; doubts about rational person's possession of, 58; and excuses, 87–88, 98; and hardship, 104, 110; and intellectual disability, 40–41; judgments about, 59; and just harm reduction, 123; and juveniles, 40–42; and the law, 31, 33; and mental illness, 64–68, 86, 88, 159; and minimal rationality, 55–58, 83–84; minimum level of, 46; and moral blameworthiness, 31, 43, 46, 48–51; and moral reasons, 36–37; not required for liability to punishment, 137, 144–145; and reasonableness of moral demands, 68; and retributive accounts of criminal justice, 46; and sentencing, 38–42; skepticism about, 38, 42, 67–69, 83, 87, 92, 97; testing of, 54–55

Moral criticism: and blame or blameworthiness, 75, 77–79; compatible with compassion, 92; and moral competence, 83; and moral responsibility, 91; within personal relations, 49; as a way for victims to affirm their moral worth, 50–51

Moral culpability. *See* Blameworthiness

Moral incompetence, 31, 108, 113

Moral judgments. *See* Evaluations

Moral justification, tension with causal explanation, 52

Moral responses to wrongdoing. *See* Blame; Evaluations; Excuses

Moral responsibility, 68, 70; defined, 36; does not fit criminal law, 60; hard to reconcile with psychological abnormalities, 53; Kant's notion of, 57–58, 60